A Bioethicist's Dictionary

A Bioethicist's Dictionary

WILLIAM EISENHOWER

CASCADE *Books* · Eugene, Oregon

A BIOETHICIST'S DICTIONARY

Cascade Books
An Imprint of Wipf and Stock Publishers
199 W. 8th Ave., Suite 3
Eugene, OR 97401

www.wipfandstock.com

PAPERBACK ISBN: 978-1-6667-0511-9
HARDCOVER ISBN: 978-1-6667-0512-6
EBOOK ISBN: 978-1-6667-0513-3

Cataloguing-in-Publication data:

Names: Eisenhower, William author.

Title: A bioethicist's dictionary / William Eisenhower.

Description: Eugene, OR : Cascade Books, 2022 | Includes bibliographical references.

Identifiers: ISBN 978-1-6667-0511-9 (paperback) | ISBN 978-1-6667-0512-6 (hardcover) | ISBN 978-1-6667-0513-3 (ebook)

Subjects: LCSH: Bioethics—Dictionaries. | Bioethics. | Bioethics—Dictionary—English.

Classification: R725.5 .E375 2022 (paperback) | R725.5 .E375 (ebook)

VERSION NUMBER 12272021

This resource is dedicated to my teachers:

Douglas Ottati,
Paul Meyer,
Rendell Mabey Jr.,
and to Gaylen Lewis,
who said to a young student,
"When you do your Tillich-thing,
send me a copy."

(Gaylen, this isn't the Tillich-thing.
Maybe that will be next.)

Contents

Preface

The drawing together of this dictionary's 854 definitions and brief biographies has been influenced by many people, but no one more than Mandy. That's not her real name, but she's a real person, someone I met while studying bioethics at a world-famous medical university. Uncommonly bright and articulate, she had a background in molecular biology, and now—at the same time that she was preparing for one of healthcare's more demanding professions—she was also working toward an MA in bioethics.

Here's how she is significant. During a discussion in one of our classes, I asked our professor if he thought that Martin Luther's emphasis on individual conscience had paved the way for the present-day emphasis on the principle of autonomy. He ran with the question, jotting down points on the classroom whiteboard. Then when the break came and he had stepped out of the room, Mandy turned and asked, "Who is Martin Luther?" Surprised, I replied, "Um, there's the Reformation, right?" Her face was blank, so I followed up with, "The Protestant Reformation . . . in European history." She shook her head. I tried again with, "Well, you remember the Renaissance, right?" She replied meekly, "Yeah . . . from high school." To sum up: she was one of the stellar students in class, on her way toward mastering a challenging healthcare field; and she was interested in ethics. But she didn't know who Martin Luther was.

A reader might ask, "Yes, but how important is Luther in this context, anyway?" One possible answer is that the Reformer's name shows up nine times in the index for *Bioethics*, 4th edition (which in previous iterations had been the *Encyclopedia of Bioethics*), and that's just as many times as Galen.[1] That being the case, without debating the point, we can stipulate: there's obviously some kind of significance here. But Luther isn't really the issue. Not recognizing one particular man is a symptom. The underlying condition is the divide between the sciences and the humanities, a divide which if

1 Jennings, "Index," 6:3450, 6:3413.

left unbridged makes bioethics impossible. Bioethics was originally created to avoid (or correct) the medical and research professions being given over to well-trained, lab-coated, applied scientists who, lacking an exposure to the classic portrayals of human values, also lack the ability to appreciate and engage with the human needs of their patients and/or research subjects.

The Mandy anecdote illustrates the need for resources designed to provide information for those coming to bioethics with education gaps. One kind of gap could be characterized as science-heavy/values-light. But that isn't the only kind, surely, for the reverse is also possible. Which was your author's situation. I came to bioethics with foundations in Christian ethics and philosophical theology, having written a PhD dissertation in the latter area (Union Presbyterian Seminary) and having taught courses in the former area (Fuller Theological Seminary). But of science in general and of medicine in particular, I knew very little.

So it was that I enrolled in Loma Linda University's MA in Bioethics program; that introduced me to the lay of the land. Upon graduation, I was invited to serve on the university's Hospital Ethics Committee. Weekly and monthly consideration of cases, along with case-specific hospital consultations, meant being regularly exposed to medical terms, many of which I had to write down and look up later. Trisomy 13 was one of the early ones, and I remember it because I was pleasantly surprised that it is spelled exactly like it sounds. Initially I had definitions of terms on a yellow notepad so that I could flip back and review them later. But before long, everything was transferred to my computer. And once I realized that they needed to be alphabetized, it was clear that I had a dictionary underway. All of which is to say that this effort began as a personal research exercise; only later was it repurposed into a for-publication project so that others could benefit from what I was learning. Others like me and others like Mandy.

To succeed in such an enterprise requires relying on "a great cloud of witnesses," and I wish to thank many of them now. First and foremost, I acknowledge the debt of gratitude I owe to Karl Wallenkampf. He read the entire manuscript and made invaluable suggestions, providing corrections, clarifications, and enrichment for the definitions and identifications that I had come up with. I doubt that better medical/editorial advice is to be found anywhere. Then there are the faculty members, administrators, and clinicians of Loma Linda University: Roy Branson (of hallowed memory), Whitny Braun, David Chooljian, Dawn Gordon, Marquelle Klooster, Andy Lampkin, Jon Paulien, Zack Plantak, Leo Ranzolin, Janet Sonne, Siroj Sora-jjakool, Sigve Tonstad, Jim Walters, and Gerald Winslow. Held back and singled out for special mention are: (a) David Larson, for the many helpful and informative conversations we had in his office; and (b) Carissa Cianci,

Gina Mohr, Jukes Namm, and Grace Oei, for their outstanding leadership in the every-Wednesday Clinical Ethics Case Conference meetings that I have profited from greatly. Each and all of these individuals I wish to thank deeply. A special note of appreciation goes to Raelene Brower, who helped me find my way into the bioethics program in the first place. And I must add that I am continuingly grateful that, postgraduation, I have had access to university programs and continuing education events—and that the members of LLU's Sanctuary Brass Band were willing to make room for an E-flat alto horn player.

Most of all, I express my gratitude to the lovely and charming Mrs. Eisenhower, without whose constant encouragement nothing I do would be possible, neither this project nor any other.

Introduction

Thinking bioethically involves taking account of technical details, ethical concepts, and ultimate questions. The details can be those of a healthcare field, or they can be those of other applied sciences. Either way, for many who take up the study of bioethics, because of years of pre-professional and professional training, the relevant technical particulars are quite familiar and provide no stumbling blocks. But it turns out that there can be a downside. In our current setup, an education leading to a high level of scientific proficiency in a field such as medicine—in many cases—allows precious little time for discussions of moral values: what makes something right or wrong, together with how we know, how such knowledge has been viewed in various times and places, and how it can provide situational guidance, here and now. This corresponds to the divide identified by C. P. Snow, a divide between the sciences on the one hand, and the humanities on the other.

There is a second group, those for whom ethics discussions are more or less familiar. For many of us in this second category, it is the science terminology that can be strange and difficult. And then of course, there may well be a third camp comprised of those who have not had an exposure to either side of the divide.

Be that as it may, to move forward in bioethics means finding one's bearings; and that in turn requires that the unfamiliar become familiar. Scientific details, ethical categories, and ultimate concerns are each important in their own way. But the ultimacy of the latter is imbedded in the particulars of the former—and these are mediated by, structured by, and informed by the considerations that a long history of moral philosophy and/or religious reflection has positioned between them.

This dictionary was designed for the three audiences just mentioned: the science-minded, the humanities-minded, and, shall we say, the open-minded. It has been divided into two parts: *Part 1—Important Terms,* and *Part 2—Historical Figures.*

Part 1—Important Terms offers definitions of 759 words drawn from a wide variety of contexts: medicine, nursing, behavioral health, forensic science, research ethics, public safety, social work, child protective services, and epidemiology and public health, on the one hand—and bioethics, ethics, law, history, philosophy, and theology, on the other. As one would expect, essential medical terms are covered—together with a number of common hospital-slang expressions (for example, "Onk" and "Bronk," pronounced as such but written as "Onc" and "Bronch"). Bioethical approaches (Principlism) and ethical categories (Fallibilism) are given their due, as are major theoretical orientations (Feminist Bioethics).

But there is more. There are a number of ethically significant terms from the fields of psychiatry and psychology; examples include multiple entries having to do with civil commitment (*Parens Patriae*). Out of the long history of not-guilty-by-reason-of-insanity cases, the major standards are explained (the American Law Institute Model, the Durham Rule; and the M'Naghten Rule). From the field of public safety, concise explanations of all the major laws named after victims are provided, seventeen in all (Laura's Law). Noteworthy shop terms from research ethics are defined (Painting the Mice), as are technical expressions from pharmacy (Prescribing Cascade), biotechnology (Phytoremediation), and environmental ethics (Sustainable Development). And since bioethics is a global phenomenon, *A Bioethicist's Dictionary* includes many English-language expressions from outside the USA (Sectioning).

In keeping with the author's background, there are Christian ethics concepts salted throughout (Agape; Athens and Jerusalem; Middle Axioms Theory; and Spirit of the Law and Letter of the Law). There are also terms defined in relation to major Christian theologians such as Thomas Aquinas and Reinhold Niebuhr.

In terms of organization, from time to time contrasting emphases are paired up (A Priori vs. A Posteriori). With each duo, the concepts are defined in relation to each other in a single location for the busy reader's convenience. Moreover, epidemiological and public health concepts are covered here more than one might expect.

Another feature: for some entries, the original Greek is supplied. For example: **Epidemic vs. Pandemic** (ἐπί + δῆμος = upon the people; πάν + δῆμος = all the people). This will be when the etymology is historically significant, or linguistically noteworthy, or otherwise interesting. (It is presumed that seminarians and students of the history of medicine—together with others who have been introduced to Ancient Greek—will take note.) In fewer cases, the Latin is given (First, Do No Harm: *primum non nocere* or *primum nil nocere*). That said, for most entries no linguistic background is provided. The same is true with pronunciation: where a word is daunting enough, a pronunciation guide is offered (Zooanthroponosis: ZŌ-ō-AN-thrō-pō-NŌ-sis); but otherwise, which is the majority of cases, it is not.

Part 2—Historical Figures is shorter but equally important. It is comprised of single-paragraph introductions, ninety-five in all, to noteworthy thought leaders who represent a number of fields. There are the doctors that one might expect (Hippocrates) and the nurses (Florence Nightingale), along with key dentists (Francis Brodie Imlach), and pharmacists (Ibn al-Baitar). However, there are also important philosophers (Aristotle); scientists (Marie Curie); inventors (Forrest Bird); geneticists (Francis Crick); mental health reformers (Philippe Pinel); public health pioneers (John Snow); celebrated environmentalists (Rachel Carson); and groundbreaking psychologists and psychiatrists (Jean Piaget and Emil Kraepelin).

There are a number of ethically significant Christian theologians (Augustine) together with nine scholar/clinicians from the Islamic Golden Age (Averroes/Ibn Rushd). Also worth mentioning are the historically important "firsts," such as: the first African-American to earn a medical degree (James McCune Smith); the first Native American to receive such a degree (Susan La Flesche Picotte); and the first American woman to win the Nobel Peace Prize (Jane Addams, "the mother of social work"). These entries are intended to be brief-but-accurate portraits of people every bioethicist should know.

As should be clear, in its selection of important terms and historical figures, this resource aligns itself with those who see bioethics as a "big tent" discipline. Quoting just a part of this dictionary's definition of **Bioethics**:

> (W)hat has emerged since the 1970s is an applied ethics programme with a relevance that, so some bioethicists believe, extends far beyond the initial applications provided by science and medicine. If medicine and biotechnology, then why not social services, marriage and family therapy, public safety, criminology, social/cultural analysis, political philosophy, global/environmental concerns—and many other arenas as well? The view here is that bioethics is "the ethics of life," and that its questions, together with its answers, deserve to be at the heart of most if not all present-day moral reflection.

Bioethics is often described as multidisciplinary; and it isn't limited to contemporary medical ethical dilemmas alone, important as those are. Which is why concepts and thought-leaders from so many diverse fields have been included herein. If they are not currently a part of everyone's understanding of bioethics, they should be.

Turning to matters of stance and style, attention is called to the post-modern and retro-modern features of what follows. This work is formally postmodern in that both "highbrow" and "lowbrow" sources have been utilized side-by-side. Certainly great care has been taken in researching every entry, and multiple scholarly sources have been consulted for each one whenever possible. But when write-up time came, if a quotation from a pop source on the internet was accurate and appropriate, and if it stated the point the most succinctly, then that's the reference that was used.

And secondly, this work takes a measure of pride in being materially retro-modern, not the least in regards to some of what has been selected for inclusion. That is, while the descriptions of, for example, scientific terms are as up-to-date as possible, and of ethics entries as well, the latter also include a number of echoes from an earlier era. The simple reason is that these echoes deserve to continue to resound. Eric Hoffer's description of a "true believer" is a good example; Hoffer's observation rings as true today as it did in the 1960s when he first advanced it. So, too, with Henri Nouwen's take on the "wounded healer." The early-to-mid twentieth century produced a generation of thinkers and a supply of profoundly useful insights that—so it is believed—deserve to continue to be pondered. In the 1960s, "kaleido-scopic" was a much-applied adjective of approval. If, because of all of the above, that adjective fits what has been assembled here, the author will be very pleased.

Which brings us to the title. This gathering of terms and figures is not intended to approximate what a committee might come up with, which would be a generic resource written from a neutral point of view. To the contrary, it is one person's deliberately personal statement of what bioethicists need, dictionary-wise. It is *A Bioethicist's Dictionary*.

PART 1

Important Terms

Letter A

Abandonment, Patient: discontinuation of care and/or termination of the treatment relationship when effected by the provider, on the conditions: that the patient did not consent; and that he or she was not given sufficient notice, a satisfactory rationale, or a viable chance to find a new provider. Regarded as unprofessional conduct, it can also qualify as medical malpractice. Among social workers, abandonment can also go by "premature termination"; among marriage and family therapists, "abandon or neglect" are treated as a matched set. ▪ **Constructive Abandonment:** not exactly what it sounds like. In one form, it means that necessary medical attention was not provided in a timely manner even though the patient was not officially discharged from the practice. In another, said patient was left functionally abandoned because, for example, the physician failed to provide suitable coverage for an anticipated period of unavailability. ▪ **Inadvertent Abandonment:** similar to the just stated instance but resulting from an intermediating snafu. As in: a covering doctor or office staff member or chronically slipshod answering service failed to follow through. The patient was left functionally abandoned because the physician responsible failed to take reasonable steps to ensure that **continuity of care** would be maintained. See also **Malpractice, Medical; Negligence, Medical;** and **Patient Dumping**

Abortifacient: anything, though commonly a pharmaceutical drug, that induces an abortion.

Abortion: the removal of an embryo or fetus from its mother's uterus, ending the pregnancy. Descriptions of **A** can be hotly contested. For some, it is the interruption of a physical process; and for others, it is the ending of a nascent human life. These two views partake of two separate moral universes. In one, a woman's choice is primary; in the other, the baby's life is primary. ▪ **Elective Abortion:** the removal undertaken for nonmedical reasons and at the request of the mother. ▪ **Spontaneous Abortion:** an unplanned, naturally occurring miscarriage. ▪ **Therapeutic Abortion:** terminating a pregnancy for medical reasons. The two most frequently mentioned reasons are: to protect the life or health of the mother; and when the fetus has severe abnormalities that are incompatible with life.

Abscess: an enclosed collection of liquified tissue, pus, often caused by bacteria.

Absolutism, Moral: ethical theories which hold, in opposition to **consequentialism**, that particular acts can be right or wrong independent of intentions, contexts, or consequences. For example: holding that "the police should never fabricate evidence, even if a perpetrator is known to be guilty" is an absolutist stance. Compare with **Emotivism; Fallibilism, Moral; Relativism, Moral; Subjectivism;** and **Universalism, Moral**

ACE (Aid to Capacity Evaluation): a short, **hospitalist**-friendly tool for judging patient decisional capacity. Developed by the Joint Centre for Bioethics at University of Toronto, it focuses on seven key areas. 1–4: the ability to understand the medical condition, the proposed treatment, the alternatives, and the option of refusing treatment. 5–6: the ability to appreciate living with the consequences of accepting or rejecting the proposed treatment. 7: the ability to make a rational choice, that is, one not produced by depression or psychosis. This instrument, like the **MacCAT-T (MacArthur Competence Assessment Tool for Treatment)**, focuses on the actual medical condition-and-choice being considered. See **Decision-Making Capacity**

ACE Inhibitors: These are "angiotensin-converting enzyme inhibitors," a class of drugs used to treat high blood pressure and heart failure. Common examples are Lisinopril and Ramipril.

Active Shortening of the Dying Process: the seemingly-preferred phrase in some European discussions for what is elsewhere referred to as "physician-assisted hastening of death."[1] See **Physician-Assisted Suicide**

Active vs. Passive Euthanasia: the former (AKA mercy killing) involves taking deliberate steps to end a person's life so as to bring about a "good death." The latter is allowing a person to die because steps which would have prevented the death are not taken. Though it is not the position taken here, some bioethicists argue that in actual practice, this duality constitutes a **moral distinction without a moral difference**. See **Acts and Omissions**

1. Beauchamp and Childress, *Principles*, 406–7.

Doctrine and **Euthanasia;** compare with **Omission vs. Commission, Sins of**

Acts and Omissions Doctrine: a time-honored principle in philosophical ethics that there can be a moral difference between taking steps to achieve a result and refraining from steps that would have prevented it. When it is applied to the question of causing harm vs. allowing harm, everyone's favorite example is the distinction between killing and letting die. When cited in support of a moral distinction between **withholding and withdrawing life-prolonging treatment**—and elsewhere as well—the doctrine is often faulted for being hard to uphold in practice. See **Active vs. Passive Euthanasia;** compare with **Omission vs. Commission, Sins of**

Act-Utilitarianism: this is a form of **consequentialism,** the ethical theory that right and wrong are determined by the outcome. The difference with A-U is that: (a) what matters is the greatest amount of good for the greatest number of people (thus "utilitarianism"); but also (b) the greatest amounts and greatest numbers are always tallied up on a case-by-case basis (thus "act"). So the focus is on consequences of actions, with each situation considered separately. See **Rule-Utilitarianism;** and **Bentham, Jeremy** and **Mill, John Stuart** (in **Part 2**)

Acute (Condition): one characterized by rapid onset, severe symptoms, short course, and in need of urgent care.

Acute Rehab: an inpatient facility (and its program) which offers advanced, intense medical help (possibly three to five hours of therapy a day, five days a week) for patients after a stroke, serious injury, or other debilitating event. Offerings can include physical, occupational, and speech therapy. Stays at an acute rehab center tend to be shorter, and at a subacute facility, longer. See **SNF, "Sniff" (Skilled Nursing Facility)**

Acute Respiratory Distress Syndrome (ARDS): a potentially life-threatening complication of some severe disease states characterized by shortness of breath, low blood oxygen, and fluid accumulation in the tiny air sacs (alveoli) of the lungs. The fluid accumulation leaves less room for air, and patients with **ARDS** often require intubation. It can be rated mild, moderate, or severe.

Addiction: compulsivity—either in a behavior (process addiction) or in the use of a chemical (substance addiction)—in the face of negative consequences. **A** is characterized by: uncontrollable and unnatural cravings; an inability to stop; a failure to meet life's obligations; and sometimes, physiological tolerance and withdrawal. With these latter two, **A** overlaps with **physical dependence**, that is, the body's adaptation to a chemical agent. But this latter condition is not the same as addiction because: (1) an addiction to a behavior, such as gambling, sexual activity, etc., is possible without **PD**; and (2) dependence on a substance like caffeine or nicotine is possible without addiction. Nevertheless, physical dependence often accompanies addiction. Finally, there is a growing literature on the social aspects of addiction indicating that socially isolated individuals are significantly more likely to be affected by addiction.

Ad Hominem Argument: *ad hominem argumentum* is Latin for "an argument to (or against) the person." Listed as one of the logical fallacies, it usually refers to an attempt to undermine an opponent's position by attacking him or her personally—this rather than addressing and refuting the substantive issues at hand. However, an **AHA** can be positive as well as negative. "Subjects will not be harmed by Dr. A's research because Dr. A is kind to his patients."[2] Connections between **AHA** and patient care are explored by Maurice Bernstein in "Medical Slang Leading to Logical Fallacy: A Practice to Be Avoided."[3]

ADL (Activities of Daily Living): important in hospital discharge planning, but also widely cited in many behavioral health and social services settings, these are the six basic self-care tasks determined to be necessary for a person to live independently: bathing, dressing, toileting, transferring (mobility), continence, and feeding. They were first identified in the 1950s by Dr. Sidney Katz and his team at the Benjamin Rose Hospital in Cleveland, Ohio. Katz made them the focus of a functional-status assessment tool called the Index of Independence in Activities of Daily Living. Nursing homes, assisted-living facilities, and in-home care services exist to provide assistance to residents who are unable to perform their **ADLs**. See **Custodial Care vs. Skilled Care**

Adult Respiratory Distress Syndrome: see **Acute Respiratory Distress Syndrome**

Advance Directive: a document stipulating a person's choices about medical treatment at the end of life. Many states recognize an approach called **The Five Wishes**. Another example is the "Advance Health Care Directive,"

2. Boyd, "Ad Hominem or Ad Personam," 5.
3. Bernstein, "Medical Slang," para. 3.

the official form in the state of California. In common usage, **AD** is the inclusive category covering at least two things: a durable power of attorney for health care (AKA a medical power of attorney) or a health care proxy (Part 1 of the California form); and a living will (Part 2). Two caveats are in order: first, most states will accept a valid **AD** from another state. California, for example, does—but not every state follows suit; and some states are silent on the matter. Part of the appeal of The Five Wishes is that it is recognized in forty-two states. And second, do not expect Emergency Medical Technicians to honor an **AD**. Their job is to do everything necessary to stabilize an individual and then transport him or her to a hospital. (By contrast, a **DNR** or a **POLST** form, posted or maintained near a patient, is to be honored.)

Adverse Event: in human subjects research, this is an unintended and unexpected downturn, one that is relevant to the clinical trial but that is not necessarily related to the investigational product; and typically there are reporting requirements, such as to the institutional review board. In a healthcare context, this is any occurrence that is not produced by the underlying disease but that negatively impacts a patient's health. A medication error is one example; a fall is another.

A-fib or AF (Atrial Fibrillation): the most common kind of abnormal heartbeat: irregular or quivering, and often rapid. It results in poor blood flow and, by contributing to multiple diseases, is associated with increased **morbidity** and **mortality**. Notably, it predisposes people to clot formation (think strokes) and may require placement on long-term anticoagulation.

Agape (ἀγάπη) (Ah-GAW-pay): one of the words for love in the Greek language. **A** is highly significant for **Christian ethics.** Under the influence of writers such as Anders Nygren and C. S. Lewis, Christians have viewed agape as distinctively biblical and as wholly selfless and **altruistic.** However, the presence of the term in Greek culture dates as far back as Homer, which means that it isn't a uniquely Christian term. Moreover, its use in the Septuagint, the ancient Greek translation of the Hebrew Scriptures, shows that its biblical meaning isn't always self-sacrificial or even other-centered. That said, its significance for Christian ethicists is directed by two New Testament considerations: the teaching that God himself is agape-love; and the twin commands to return agape to God and to share it with one's neighbors. Thus, the common meaning of **A** is: engaged devotion to the well-being of others; and reconciliation with and/or rescue of them—specifically without any concern about it being deserved. See also: **Love**

AIDS (Acquired Immune Deficiency Syndrome): the final stage of infection with **HIV**, that is, the human immunodeficiency virus, it is characterized by low immune cell count and the presence of opportunistic infections. **HIV** weakens the body's immune system by destroying cells that are necessary for normal protection against disease. This weakness leaves the body susceptible, more liable to get infections or infection-related cancers. Left untreated, in eight to ten years' time these accumulating conditions can rise to the level of what is commonly called "full-blown AIDS," in which case, death will come within two to three years. However, while there is still no cure, aggressive treatment can mean that persons with HIV can live well, with longer and healthier lives than was true in the past. But patient noncompliance is a serious concern, reducing treatment effectiveness for the individual and risking the spread of drug-resistant HIV within the community.

À La Carte Medicine: this can refer to a micromanagement problem, that is, to patients or surrogates picking and choosing from among various medical procedures which standard practice bundles together into a single package. Alternately, in pay-as-you-go healthcare, the meaning is different: a physician forswears the healthcare insurance payment system, and patients pay for services, à la carte.

ALS (Amyotrophic Lateral Sclerosis): (AKA Lou Gehrig's Disease) a progressive and fatal neurological disease that destroys the motor neurons (the nerve cells in the brain and spinal cord that control voluntary muscles). It is characterized by stiff muscles, muscle twitching, and gradually worsening weakness. Speech, swallowing, and eventually breathing become impossible, requiring that a **PEG tube** be placed for feeding and mechanical ventilation. Motor Neuron Disease (MND) is used to designate a group of conditions, **ALS** being the most common.

Altered: short for altered level of consciousness (AKA altered sensorium). Thus "patient came in altered" means that he or she arrived at the hospital thinking and behaving abnormally, lacking the ability to focus or process rationally. The level of functioning can be either lessened (hypoactive) or heightened (hyperactive)—or more specifically, the patient can be: (a) hyped up; (b) nodding off; (c) somnolent but rousable; or (d) unconscious. See **CAM Positive**

Altruism/Altruistic: selflessness; the opposite of selfishness. Coined by Auguste Comte to contrast with egoism, the term indicates a concern for the welfare of others. The distinctive characteristic is that steps are taken to benefit another, in the words of medical ethicist David Steinberg, "in the absence of any quid pro quo external rewards."[4] In the field of zoology, the emphasis is slightly different: an altruistic action is one that advantages others in the species, while potentially disadvantaging the animal performing it. A typical example is the self-endangering cry to warn the rest of the herd of a predator. See **Agape**

AMA: the release of a patient Against Medical Advice, which is also known as Discharge Against Medical Advice (DAMA). (One occasionally hears, "The patient AMA'd," which means that a patient left a medical facility without having been cleared to do so.) To amplify, there are some patients who *cannot* leave AMA, e.g., someone on a 5150 hold, but most can as long as they have decision-making capacity. And note: AMA can also refer to the American Medical Association, or to "Ask Me Anything," which indicates that the presenter will respond to questions from the audience.

Amber Alert: (AKA Child Abduction Emergency Alert) is a communiqué sent via an urgent messaging system. The original namesake was Amber Hagerman, a nine-year-old girl who was abducted and murdered in Arlington, Texas, in 1996. The first AA efforts involved simple messages sent manually to radio stations for public broadcast. In 1998, a way to automate them was found. Today, announcements are made on TV, radio, and various other media, including cellphones and electronic freeway signs. Overseen by the National Center for Missing and Exploited Children, the system operates in all fifty states, as well as twenty-seven other countries. See **Laws Named after Victims**

American Law Institute Model: (AKA the Brawner Rule) from *United States v. Brawner* (1972), this is the more recent standard in the long history of not-guilty-by-reason-of-insanity cases. The **ALIM** holds that an individual is not to be held responsible for a criminal act if at the time it was committed he or she lacked either: (1) the *substantial* capacity to appreciate the criminality of the action; or (2) the *substantial* ability to control his or her behavior enough to refrain from breaking the law. (This is sometimes called the "substantial capacity test"—"substantial" understood as a looser, easier-to-satisfy requirement than "total"). The **Durham Rule** had been the immediately previous standard; concern was that Durham gave too much prominence to dueling psychiatrists. Roughly half of the United States use the **ALIM**, the other half use the earlier **M'Naghten Rule**, with New Hampshire still standing by the Durham standard. See **Insanity Defense**

4. Steinberg, "Altruism," 249.

American Medical Association (AMA): founded in 1847, the oldest, largest, and most influential of the professional associations for physicians and med students. Its stated mission is "to promote the art and science of medicine and the betterment of public health." It fulfills this mission "by representing physicians with a unified voice in courts and legislative bodies across the nation, removing obstacles that interfere with patient care, leading the charge to prevent chronic disease and confront public health crises, and driving the future of medicine to tackle the biggest challenges in health care and training the leaders of tomorrow."[5] There are critics who describe the group differently, however; for example: as a self-protective guild which speaks for only a small minority of the nation's practicing physicians.

American Society for Bioethics and the Humanities (ASBH): the preeminent learned society for bioethicists in the United States. Formed in 1998, it resulted from the merger of three similar organizations: Society for Health and Human Values, the Society for Bioethics Consultation, and the American Association of Bioethics. It sponsors a Healthcare Ethics Consultant-Certified program, which is based on nationwide standards for healthcare ethics consultations. Members include physicians, nurses, and other healthcare professionals—together with chaplains, pastors, social workers, therapists, educators, researchers, analysts, administrators, and humanities' artists and scholars.

Amniocentesis: the invasive introduction of a needle into the uterus and amniotic sac for the removal of **amniotic fluid** to diagnose various disease states in the fetus, notably genetic abnormalities. The procedure yields definitive results. Yet it is not without risk and may result in the loss of the fetus. Moreover, it may be in decline as cell-free DNA testing (a noninvasive blood test of the mother that can diagnose fetal illnesses) is becoming more reliable.

Amniotic Fluid: the watery liquid that surrounds and cushions an embryo or fetus while it grows in the uterus. See **Amniocentesis**

Amyotrophic Lateral Sclerosis: see **ALS (Amyotrophic Lateral Sclerosis)**

Anaphylaxis / Anaphylactic Reaction: a sudden, potentially fatal allergic reaction to an **antigen,** such as a bee sting, to which the person had previously developed a hypersensitivity. Other triggers can include food, insect bites, and certain medications. A shot of epinephrine should be

---

5. American Medical Association, "About," paras. 1–2.

administered ASAP and a trip made to the Emergency Room where intubation may be necessary.

Anencephaly (ανεγκέφαλος) (an-en-SEF-a-lee): a fatal birth defect. Not having developed in the womb, major portions of the brain and skull are missing; this includes those parts which make thought, sight, hearing, and movement possible. Diagnostic tests for the condition can be undertaken during pregnancy, and they are highly reliable. If not stillborn, anencephalic babies die shortly after birth. See **Neural Tube Defects**

Aneuploidy (AN-yoo-ployd-ee): although chromosomes normally come as twenty-three pairs, forty-six total, **A** involves a deviation. Cells have a nonstandard number of chromosomes, either less or more. There are monosomy conditions, for example, where with one particular chromosome, instead of the usual two there is just one. In the case of monosomy X (Turner's syndrome), for instance, a female will be born with only one X chromosome. And pivoting to the more side, with **Trisomy** conditions, instead of the usual two chromosomes there are three. Examples include **Trisomy 21** (Down syndrome), **Trisomy 18** (Edward's syndrome), **Trisomy 13** (Patau's syndrome)—the list goes on. Tetrasomy and pentasomy are quite rare.

Animation: see **Ensoulment**

Anosognosia (ἀ + νόσος + γνῶσις = no knowledge of a disease) (uh-NŌ-sog-NŌ-ze-uh): the loss, complete or partial, of the ability to recognize one's mental illness. "Impaired awareness of illness (anosognosia) is a major problem because it is the single largest reason why individuals with schizophrenia and bipolar disorder do not take their medications. It is caused by damage to specific parts of the brain, especially the right hemisphere. It affects approximately 50 percent of individuals with schizophrenia and 40 percent of individuals with bipolar disorder."[6] While **A** is routinely described in terms of a patient denying his or her condition, it is to be distinguished from **denial**, understood as a psychological defense mechanism.

Anoxic Brain Damage: brain injury caused by lack of oxygen. **Hypoxia** is the term to describe low oxygen. Without enough oxygen, the cells of the brain begin to die after about four minutes. This can be a possible complication of: (a) a successful, yet prolonged **cardiopulmonary resuscitation (CPR)**; or (b) survived drownings or suicides.

---

6. Torrey, "Impaired Awareness of Illness," para. 1.

Anthropology, Medical: application of the tools of the discipline of anthropology to the study of health and illness, human flourishing and languishing, and healthcare system functionality all within and in relation to their social-cultural and global-environmental contexts.

Anticoagulation: using blood-thinning drugs to delay or prevent blood clots so as to eliminate or reduce the risk of blockages in arteries, veins, and the heart. The downside is that they carry the important side effect of increased bleeding risk.

Antigen: a substance that can provoke an immune response. More specifically, it's a molecule or molecular structure, originating outside or inside the body, which the body's immune system will recognize as a threat, and will counter with the production of specific antibodies. The antibodies' binding capability works to eliminate the antigen problem, tagging it or neutralizing it directly.

Antinomianism (ἀντί = over against, in substitution for; νόμος = law): the position that rejects all moral, ethical constraints. It is primarily a Protestant ethics term, and as such it is the polar opposite of legalism. For the Christian, authentic moral existence is not to be found in either of two extremes; it is neither a slavish obedience to the letter of the law (legalism); nor an irresponsible indifference to the spirit of the law (antinomianism). See **Situation Ethics** and **Spirit of the Law and Letter of the Law**

Anuria or Anuresis (Anuric): nonpassage of urine. It is often caused by the kidneys not functioning, but it can also occur because of an obstruction such as kidney stones or tumors.

Aortic Stenosis: a constriction or tightening which reduces the flow of blood from the left ventricle to the aorta. In the United States, it is one of the most common cardiac valve dysfunctions.

APACHE II (Acute Physiology and Chronic Health Evaluation II): a classification system for rating the severity of disease in patients admitted to ICU. Scores run from 0 to 71, with a higher score corresponding to a greater risk of death. It is one of several such rating systems; newer ones include **SAPS II** and **MODS**.

Apgar Score System: an assessment tool for quickly gauging the health-needs of a baby at one minute and again at five minutes after birth. Mnemonic-wise, the letters of Dr. Virginia Apgar's last name can be used for the five signs to be checked: Appearance (skin color), Pulse (heart rate),

Grimace (reflexes), Activity (muscle tone), and Respiration (breathing). Utilized by doctors, midwifes, and nurses around the world, this simple routine can be seen as the mother of the field of clinical neonatology. For after the **ASS** was presented at a national meeting in 1952, and shared in print in 1953, the first neonatal intensive care units began to appear. See **Apgar, Virginia** (in **Part 2**) and **NICU (Neonatal Intensive Care Unit)**

Apnea: temporary cessation of breathing.

A Priori vs. A Posteriori (ā-prē-OR-ē vs. ā-po-stē-rē-OR-ē): a contrast posed in Latin phrases meaning "from what is before" and "from what is after," and referring to knowledge which is not derived from experience versus knowledge which is. "Traditionally, a priori arguments work from cause to effect (the fact that the patient has liver disease explains the yellow discoloration of her skin), while a posteriori arguments work from effect to cause (from the patient's yellow skin, dark urine and pale stools, the doctor diagnosed obstructive jaundice)."[7] Note: multiple pronunciations are possible for each term.

Armamentarium (pl. armamentaria): a complete collection of the implements necessary to carry out a field of activities, especially the equipment used by a clinician in the practice of medicine.

Arrhythmia (ἀρρυθμία): an abnormal heartbeat, either in pace—quick or slow—or in regularity. There are many kinds of **As**, varying as to point of origin and as to degree of seriousness, with a spectrum of asymptomatic to fatal.

Asepsis (α = not; σῆψις = decay): freedom from disease-causing microorganisms and thus from infection as well as steps taken to that end. Medical (clean asepsis) refers to those practices designed to reduce the number and transfer of pathogens, avoiding the spread of infection from one person to another. Surgical (sterile asepsis) refers to those practices that render and keep objects and areas free of contamination: sterilization, etc. See **Sepsis**

Aspiration: in medical contexts, there are two usual meanings. (1) Aspiration as a procedure is the suctioning out of a fluid or air, either because it's unwelcome or because a sample is needed for a diagnostic test. (2) Aspiration as a problem is the well-known "something going down the wrong pipe" (AKA "pulmonary aspiration"). The "something" can be food or fumes or liquid. And since it can be a person's own vomit while he or she is

---

7. Boyd, "A priori / a posteriori," 15.

under anesthesia, as a precaution, surgeons ask their patients to fast before surgery. This is often expressed as "NPO after midnight." (*Nil per os* in Latin = nothing by mouth). ▪ **Aspiration Pneumonia:** an important complication of aspiration, it results from contents from the stomach or mouth being inhaled into the lungs or windpipe. It is the most common cause of healthcare-associated pneumonia (HAP).

Assay (ASS-ay): an analysis undertaken to gauge the presence, amount, and/or potency of a substance. ("With the introduction of these and other forthcoming Zika virus assays, public health can anticipate seeing increased testing in the private sector.")[8]

Assent: the category of personal permission which parallels informed consent, but which is called for when the patient or research subject is a minor (who is mature enough to understand) or an adult not having **decision-making capacity** (but who is lucid enough to communicate). It indicates agreement to a medical procedure or willingness to participate in a research project. See **Autonomy, Respect for** and **Informed Consent,** under **Consent**

Assisted Suicide: see **Physician Aid in Dying,** under **Physician-Assisted Suicide**

Asymmetry Argument: in population ethics, this usually refers to the "Procreation Asymmetry Argument," which is: given that on the one hand, there is a compelling ethical rationale for not bringing into the world a life that would not be worth living, the simple fact that a life might indeed be worth living is not a compelling enough reason for creating it. See **Beneficence**; **Nonmaleficence**; and **Symmetry Arguments**

Asystole: medical name for the "flatline" condition often seen on TV hospital shows. The heart stops beating; nothing is registering on the EKG. Note, however, that a pause in the heartbeat, obviously less serious, is commonly covered by the same term.

Athens and Jerusalem: a contrast posed by Tertullian (CE 155–240), an early Christian theologian. His rhetorical question, "What has Athens to do with Jerusalem?" memorably sums up an argument that has been made by many since. To wit, worldly culture and Christian faith are unbridgeably divided; and those on the sacred side have nothing to learn from those on the other. Biblical revelation is all the believer needs. Such a simple view has

---

8. APHL, "Commercially Available Zika Virus," para. 1.

not been shared by most Christian theologians down through the centuries, nor is it the stance adopted here. It is, however, a conviction bioethicists sometimes encounter. See **Fideism**

Atonic, Atony, and Atonia (ἄτονος = slack, powerless): lacking in normal tone and strength; weakness. Atony of bladder is the inability to urinate due to low muscle tone, commonly seen after traumatic deliveries or after the use of an epidural anesthesia. Gastric atonia is the stomach's inability to contract normally, causing a delay in food passing out of the stomach.

Atraumatic (α = not; τραῦμα = wound): in Forensic Science discussions, as well as elsewhere, it means "not causing an injury."

Attachment Disorders: these are psychological diagnoses thought to result from negative care-reception experiences in early childhood. The core characteristic is having difficulty forming and sustaining healthy relationships with others, at a young age certainly, but also on into adulthood. ▪ **Reactive Attachment Disorder:** a condition in young children in which the child is emotionally distant, incapable of receiving care and reassurance from an appropriate adult, and unable to respond with trust. ▪ **Disinhibited Social Engagement Disorder:** a condition with the opposite set of symptoms. The child is insufficiently cautious, too trusting of strangers, and shows little age-appropriate hesitance in unfamiliar situations.

Attending Physician: in a hospital or clinic, this is the medical doctor in charge of a patient's medical care overall. Attendings can also educate, train, and oversee residents, interns, and med students. "This term is typically used at teaching facilities to differentiate fully credentialed senior-level physicians from junior physicians who are still completing their higher education. In the hierarchy of physicians, the attending is at the top under only the physicians who run the hospital itself, while the medical student is at the bottom."[9] See **Physician vs. Doctor**

Authenticity: being real, as in: being the same person on the inside as on the outside, and from one political or social environment to the next. In existentialism, **A** is a matter of self-determination, of choosing to be true to one's unique self despite the threat of life's absurdities, on the one hand, and its herd-pressures to conform, on the other. See **Bad Faith**

Authority, Moral: the capacity to influence others by symbolizing and/ or appealing to the goodness of life in its ultimate context, a context from

9. Whitlock, "Doctors, Residents, and Attendings," paras. 13–14.

which contemporary phenomena are existentially estranged but to which they essentially belong. ▪ **Moral Authority Figure:** individuals such as **Dorothea Dix**, **Albert Schweitzer**, and **Mother Teresa,** who stand within the vagaries and moral contradictions of present experience while yet pointing beyond them to life's ultimate goodness.

Autogenic Training (AKA self-hypnosis): a desensitization and relaxation procedure developed in 1932 by Johannes Heinrich Schultz, a German psychiatrist. According to the American College of Cardiology, "Autogenic training (AT) is a technique that teaches your body to respond to your verbal commands. These commands 'tell' your body to relax and control breathing, blood pressure, heartbeat, and body temperature. The goal of AT is to achieve deep relaxation and reduce stress."[10]

Autonomy, Respect for (αὐτο = self; νομία = law): one of the four key principles highlighted in **principlism**. In that context, it is shorthand for the obligation to honor the **A** of recipients of care and subjects of research. And as such, some regard this particular principle, either for good or for ill, as the first among equals in the four principles approach. Two points can be made. The first is that this is not primarily a norm that a moral agent aims for or claims for him- or herself (like courage or civil rights would be). It is inherently other-focused, involving respecting a quality in another. More specifically, it means honoring the self-legislating personhood of vulnerable patients and subjects who cannot protect their own interests as they normally would. And, precisely because they cannot, their choices and preferences are to be adhered to as fully as possible. Yet despite all that, the second point is that **A** generally has more to do with the right to refuse and less to do with a license to demand. It does not give a patient the right to demand an inappropriate medical procedure, for example. See **Negative vs. Positive Autonomy**

10. Healthwise Staff, "Autogenic Training," para. 1.

Letter B

Baby Doe Rules: a set of federal regulations addressing medical care of infants born with a serious illness or with severe congenital defects. The original "Baby Doe" was born in Bloomington, Indiana, in 1982, with Down syndrome and tracheoesophageal fistula. The latter condition was correctable; but the delivering obstetrician encouraged the parents not to authorize it because of the former. That is, he persuaded them to allow their newborn to die. The hospital nurses objected, however, and the family's primary care physician did as well; and as a consequence, rapid-fire efforts were undertaken to find another way. But the court upheld the right of the parents to make the call. So "Baby Doe" died six days after he was born. In response, the Reagan administration issued guidelines, and Congress passed the "Child Abuse Prevention and Treatment Act" in 1984. The resultant rules require that babies be given nutrition, hydration, and medications; and that life-sustaining care should only be withheld in cases of irreversible coma or cases in which procedures would be futile or inhumane.

Bad Apples Theory: taking a side in the contrast between crediting a few bad apples and a system-wide bad barrel, this theory has wide applicability. In research ethics, **BAT** attributes most research misconduct to a small number of irresponsible individuals (as opposed to departmental, corporate, financial, and governmental factors). And in hospital safety investigations, it supports arguments such as the following: "This study of formal patient complaints filed with health service ombudsmen in Australia found that a small number of doctors account for a very large number of complaints from patients: 3% of doctors generated 49% of complaints, and 1% of doctors accounted for 25% of all complaints." The lesson to be drawn, according to **BAT**, is that "we need to take seriously the performance and behaviours of individual clinicians if we are to make healthcare safer for patients."[1]

1. Shojania and Dixon-Woods, "'Bad Apples,'" paras. 3, 2.

Bad Barrels Theory: the opposite of **Bad Apples Theory**. One simple definition is, "People cause harm to others when the social context allows for such behavior."[2] Frequently discussed along with Bad Barrel Makers.

Bad Faith: in the existentialism of John-Paul Sartre, this means caving in to the expectations of others, forfeiting individual freedom, and losing one's personal **authenticity**. Yes, and one more thing: it means claiming, "It wasn't my choice. I couldn't have done otherwise."

Baseline: a starting point that subsequent measurements (e.g., temperature, blood pressure, or even behavior) can be contrasted with. It is an initial or typical (in the sense of customary for this patient with this condition) level of functioning.

Battery, Medical: the performance of a nonemergency medical or surgical procedure without the necessary consent.

Bayesian: in forensic science, this is a method of inference for evaluating laboratory results. An application of **Bayes's Theorem**, it has to do with assigning a role to the investigator's prior knowledge in estimating the strength of a new piece of evidence. See **Bayes, Rev. Thomas** (in **Part 2**)

Bayes's Theorem: an approach to probability with wide applicability. It was initially advanced by **Rev. Thomas Bayes** and subsequently popularized by Pierre-Simon Laplace. In clinical contexts, it is understood to involve the twin propositions: if a disease is extremely rare, a patient testing positive is nevertheless unlikely to have it; and if having it would normally be highly likely, a negative test result does not prove otherwise. See **Bayesian**

Bedside Rationing: the common way of referring to limiting medically beneficial treatments—specifically when an individual patient is in view rather than all patients system-wide. Usually cost-containment is the reason, although other rationales are possible. The practice has its critics and its defenders, the latter arguing that it is unavoidable.

Begging the Question: this is one of the classical fallacies in reasoning and debate, but be warned: it is not what it sounds like. All it means is that an argument has gone in a circle, failing to actually prove anything. The speaker ends up concluding with a point which he or she assumed at the beginning, as in the following: "The fact that our country has the best healthcare in the world means that our citizens are the healthiest; and since we have all these

---

2. Filabi, "Bad Apples, Bad Barrels," para. 3.

healthy people, that proves that our country has the best healthcare in the world." See **Circular Reasoning**

Belmont Report: findings published in 1979 by the National Commission for the Protection of Human Subjects of Biomedical and Behavioral Research. The report had a powerful influence on all things bioethical, inspiring protections covering the use of human beings in scientific experiments, and laying down the groundwork for **The Common Rule**. Beyond all this, it remains noteworthy for pulling together three principles: respect for persons, beneficence, and justice. Compare with **Principlism**

Beneficence: as one of the four principles celebrated in **principlism**, this is the obligation to actively do good, to perform deeds which will positively affect the well-being and the interests of others. In some ethical systems, when this norm is compared with **nonmaleficence**, the point is made that the obligation of the latter (to refrain from acting harmfully) can be applied more extensively than the requirement of the former (to do good, to proactively benefit others). That is, it is said that nonmaleficence is more fully incumbent upon all, and that beneficence in its broader applications rests primarily with a specialized few—and medical professionals would be among them. Perhaps so. But Christian ethics, as understood here, does not support such a view—at least not Protestant Christian ethics. For starters, the teachings of Jesus leave no room for treating avoidance of the negative as a more widely relevant norm than pursuit of the positive.

And note: it has been appropriately observed that the Golden Rule in its various forms, expressing the idea of reciprocity, can be located in all the world's religions. Still, it seems that the distinction referred to above does actually correspond to the two best-known formulations of that rule. The one, associated with Confucius, limits itself to nonmaleficence. "Do *not* do to others what you do *not* want done to yourself." The other, issued by Jesus, emphasizes beneficence. "*Do* unto others as you would have them *do* unto you." There's a difference.

Benefit vs. Burden: see **Burden vs. Benefit**

Benign Neglect: a term coined by Daniel Patrick Moynihan to suggest that withholding assistance or support in certain circumstances can be more beneficial than becoming directly involved. See **First, Do No Harm**; **Nonmaleficence**; and **Precautionary Principle**

Best Interest Standard: see **Substituted Judgment vs. Best Interest Standard**

Biblical Counseling: in ultraconservative Christian circles, the term can refer to a strict form of pastoral counseling which holds that the Bible is a Christian pastoral caregiver's all-sufficient resource. The idea is that secular psychologies have nothing to add, for one thing; and they rest on anti-Christian assumptions, for another. Jay E. Adams was an early proponent. Billed as "nouthetic counseling" for a while, Adams's methodology was rebranded as BC. But note: this approach is quite different from what can be called "mainstream Christian counseling," that is, talk therapy as practiced in both evangelical and liberal denominational circles. Mainstream Christian counseling typically aims for a both/and approach, integrating psychological insights and techniques, on the one hand, with Christian beliefs and values, on the other.

Bioconservatism vs. Techno-Progressivism: contrasting stances toward technological change. The former, while not completely obstructionist, is nevertheless guarded and suspicious about new developments in applied science, not the least when it comes to human enhancement à la **transhumanism**. Much in pop culture reflects a dystopian bioconservativism, as the *Terminator* movies illustrate: unstoppable killer robots threatening to take over the world, with clueless scientists helping to make it happen. The opposite posture welcomes technological advances, trusting that positive politicocultural developments can best be supported by scientific progress—and vice versa. And oddly enough, one can find techno-progressive positions espoused by activists who are mostly on the right, politically, and bioconservative views espoused by activists who are otherwise on the left. We see this in the climate change debate, for example.

Bioethics (βίος = life; ἦθος = custom): normally thought of as the ethical assessment of case, issue, and policy alternatives in medicine and scientific research. The term "Bio-ethics" was coined in 1927 by German pastor/philosopher Fritz Jahr. However, as a movement, present-day bioethics arose in the United States in the 1970s, indelibly shaped by the cultural milieu of the times. Technological advances and societal changes had already prompted questions about the duties of physicians and researchers, and the rights of patients and research subjects—and old customs and simple answers were increasingly being regarded as insufficient. (See for example **God Committee, The**.) Then in 1972, the revelation of the **Tuskegee Syphilis Study**, viewed against the backdrop of: (a) memories of the **Nazi medical war**

crimes; and (b) fears that unaccountable scientists were fast creating a world of ecological degradation and possible nuclear annihilation—such factors prompted many to reckon with modern medical science's potential for evil, as well as for good. Better safeguards and more searching reflections were called for, reflections in which others besides the doctors and the scientists themselves needed to be involved. Thus bioethics was born. That said, what has emerged since the 1970s is an applied ethics program with a relevance that, so some bioethicists believe, extends far beyond the initial applications provided by science and medicine. If medicine and biotechnology, then why not social services, marriage and family therapy, public safety, criminology, social/cultural analysis, political philosophy, global/environmental concerns—and many other arenas as well? The view here is that bioethics is "the ethics of life," and that its questions, together with its answers, deserve to be at the heart of most if not all present-day moral reflection.

Biological Determinism: see **Determinism**

Biopsy: the removal of cells or tissue for diagnostic study in order to check for cancer or other irregularities. This may occur before the surgical excision of an entity, or a biopsy may be sent during an operation to confirm a tumor or cancer, with subsequent removal.

Biopsychosocial Model: this paradigm looks to the mutual interaction of biological, psychological, and social/environmental factors for understanding health, disease, and its treatment. It was proposed in 1977 by George L. Engel, a psychiatrist and internist at the University of Rochester School of Medicine—Engel intending it as a holistic, humanistic alternative to the biomedical model (set in stone by the Flexner Report of 1910). He argued that the older biomedical approach was reductionistic and materialistic, overlooking the health impact of the patient's subjective experience, the doctor-patient relationship, and much else. In creating his new model, Engel drew on systems theory and on the developmental psychology of Urie Bronfenbrenner. See **Biopsychosocial-Spiritual Model** and **Reductionism**

Biopsychosocial-Spiritual Model: as advanced by many, including Daniel P. Sulmasy, this variant "expands on the **biopsychosocial model** to include the spiritual concerns of patients . . . [because] the healing professions should serve the needs of patients as whole persons. Persons can be considered beings-in-relationship, and illness can be considered a disruption in biological relationships that in turn affects all the other relational aspects of a person. Spirituality concerns a person's relationship with transcendence. Therefore, genuinely holistic health care must address the totality of the patient's relational existence—physical, psychological, social, and spiritual."[3] Perceived as going against the grain of a predominantly secular medical culture, this model has nevertheless been embraced from a variety of angles, and this includes practitioners and institutions with traditional religious commitments. See **Spirituality**

Bioremediation: a biotech term, it means applying living organisms to the task of cleaning up polluted air, soil, groundwater, or oceans. Microorganisms (bacteria, fungi, yeasts, or algae) are used to decontaminate areas affected by unhealthy pollutants or chemicals. See **Phytoremediation**

Black Alert: in the UK's National Health Service (NHS), this is an informal term for the notice sent out to the healthcare community that a particular hospital is maxed out. That is, crowding has now reached the point where any new patients trying to be admitted to A&E (the Accident and Emergency unit) will have to be directed to other hospitals. Officially known as "Operational Pressures Escalation Level (OPEL) Four," this is the highest level of alert; and—even under normal, nonpandemic circumstances—it is fairly common during the winter months. (The American TV program *Code Black* drew its name from a similar usage. But in the United States that is not the standard definition; "Code Black" more typically signals a bomb threat.) See **Corridor Nursing**

Black Swan: a term popularized by Nassim Nicholas Taleb.[4] One meaning, prominent in public health discussions, is: a rare, unforeseeable, and unpredictable event with a large-scale impact. Typically, this event will catch public health systems off guard, and emergency funding will be required. For an example, consider the headline "The Coronavirus Could Be the Black Swan of 2020."[5] However, in other contexts, a black swan need not be so catastrophic. And note: Karl Popper, a philosopher of science, famously argued that, since proving the proposition "All swans are white" is impossible, science should concentrate on disconfirmation, on seeking the black swan that will disprove the claim. Only theories that are falsifiable in such a way qualify as scientific, says Popper. See **Falsification, Popper's Principle of**

Black Wednesday: in Great Britain, the first Wednesday in August is the day that new med school graduates report for duty at National Health Service (NHS) hospitals to begin their "foundation year." A 2009 study found

---

3. Sulmasy, "Biopsychosocial-Spiritual Model," para. 1.
4. Taleb, *Black Swan.*
5. Abramsky, "Coronavirus Could Be the Black Swan of 2020."

that on that particular day, death rates were 6 percent higher than on the Wednesday one week earlier. Although corrective measures were undertaken, the appellation persists; and "the killing season," which refers to the same general time frame, does as well. For the closest American equivalent, consult the **July Effect.**

Blamestorming: in British medical contexts, this means attempting to find a scapegoat for a particularly significant medical error. See **Collusion of Anonymity**

Blood Pressure: the pressing power of the blood against the vessel walls during circulation. According to the American Heart Association, the five blood pressure ranges are: Normal, which is less-than-120 over less-than-80; Elevated, which is 120–29 over less-than-80; Hypertension Stage 1, which is 130–39 over 80–89; Hypertension Stage 2, which is 140-or-higher over 90-or-higher; and Hypertensive Crisis, which is higher-than-180 over higher-than-120.[6] The explanations of these sets of numbers are as follows. ▪ **Systolic Blood Pressure** (συστολή = contraction): this is the first/higher number in each set, and it measures the pressure of the blood during the exertion phase of the heartbeat cycle, when the heart contracts and sends blood out. ▪ **Diastolic Blood Pressure** (διαστολή = dilation): this is the second/lower number; it measures the pressure of the blood during the resting phase of the heartbeat cycle, when the ventricles refill. ▪ **Mean Arterial Pressure:** different from the systolic/diastolic measures, and for some purposes more useful, this is the blood pressure average in a person's arteries during one full pulse sequence.

Bounceback: English hospital slang for a patient who all-too-quickly reappears at the A&E (Accident and Emergency unit) with the same medical issue. See **Failed Discharge**

Brain Death: the full and nonrestartable stop of all the operations of the brain, including the brain stem. This is different from "cerebral" or "upper brain death," in which the involuntary functions of the brain stem (such as heartbeat and respiration) can continue. In the United States, there are two ways to legally determine when a person has died: according to circulatory-respiratory criteria, which is the older method, and according to neurological criteria, which is the relatively newer procedure. **BD** is established by the latter. Yet doubts about it persist; the rules in the various states are not all in

---

6. American Heart Association, "Understanding Blood Pressure Readings," para. 2.

sync, and questions about it, including ethical ones, continue to be raised.[7] See **Circulatory-Respiratory Death**; **Dead Donor Rule**; and **Uniform Determination of Death Act**

Brain Infection: infection-caused inflammation of the brain and sometimes other parts of the central nervous system as well. Common ones are: **meningitis; encephalitis;** and ▪ **Brain Abscess:** a bacterial or fungal infection creating a collection of pus, immune cells, and other material in the brain.

Brawner Rule: with regards to the **insanity defense**, see **American Law Institute Model**

Break Scrub: hospital slang for any action that compromises sterility—that is, that fails to maintain the sterile field of an operating room—and that requires a clinician to scrub again. Usually associated with interrupting surgery to take a call, or with exiting the operating room for any reason.

Brief Therapy: a counseling approach committed to wrapping up after a limited number of appointments, possibly from six to ten, though some versions stretch it out longer. The therapist is typically proactive and directive; and the sessions tend to be devoted to building on client strengths, solving specific problems, and achieving short-term goals.

"Bronk," usually written as "Bronch": perform a bronchoscopy, using a bronchoscope, to examine a patient's lower airways. A fiberoptic instrument with a camera at the tip is sent through the patient's nose or mouth, down the throat, and into the lungs. The purpose is to look for problems in the respiratory system. Moreover a bronchoscopy may be a curative intervention, and may also serve to withdraw a biopsy, e.g., a bronchoalveolar lavage, to diagnose pneumonia.

Burden of Disease, Global (GBD): a public health tool which measures the planet-wide impact of health-related conditions: diseases, injuries, and risk factors. "Burden of disease is a concept that was developed in the 1990s by the Harvard School of Public Health, the World Bank, and the World Health Organization (WHO) to describe death and loss of health due to diseases, injuries, and risk factors for all regions of the world."[8] (Using the GDB as a pattern, the U.S. Armed Forces Health Surveillance Branch developed a

---

7. Singer, "Challenge of Brain Death," 3–4, 153–65.
8. World Health Organization, "Burden of Disease," para. 1.

burden of disease report of its own, specifically for members of the US Military, the *Medical Surveillance Monthly Report*.)[9]

Burden vs. Benefit: a commonly cited contrast in hospital ethics consultations. It refers to the weighing and balancing of the potential negatives of an intervention (degree of intrusiveness, discomfort, etc.) in relation to the potential positives. It has affinities with the **principlism** of Beauchamp and Childress in this way. Burdens, impingements on a patient's well-being, are what the principle of **nonmaleficence** aims to minimize; and benefits, contributions to his or her health, are what **beneficence** seeks to maximize. Difficult cases usually involve the search for the optimum solution, the greatest benefit to the patient with the smallest amount of burden. Everything else being appropriately considered, the principle of **autonomy** assigns the final say-so to the patient.

Burnout: hitting bottom physically and/or emotionally because of work or institutional requirements and expectations. When bureaucratic tasks and administrative hassles mean extra hours so that work-life balance is out of whack; when the effort to maintain one's involvement in a not-entirely-meaningful enterprise becomes too great; when the workplace starts to feel like a giant hamster wheel—when those things are true, if something doesn't change, burnout is the predictable result. One might call it physical, mental, and/or emotional **decompensation**. The ability to care evaporates and is replaced by exhaustion, alienation, and/or cynicism. Closely related to, and sometimes used interchangeably with, either **compassion fatigue** or **provider fatigue**.

Buster's Law: a New York law named after a cat. In 1997, Chester Williamson doused Buster, his neighbor's cat, with kerosene and lit it on fire with his cigarette. This law makes aggravated cruelty against a "companion animal" a felony with a penalty of up to two years in prison. See **Laws Named after Victims**

---

9. Military Health System, "Medical Surveillance."

Letter C

Cabulance: a slang term for a taxi used as an emergency transport vehicle for taking someone to the hospital. A taxicab-as-ambulance.

Calvinism, Pharmacological: see **Pharmacological Calvinism**

CAM Positive: is in reference to the Confusion Assessment Method which is a delirium identification instrument designed so that clinicians who do not have psychiatric training can diagnose mental functioning using a standardized format. It assesses the four signature features of delirium: (a) sudden onset plus variability; (b) lack of focus; (c) jumbled thought-processing; and (d) off-**baseline** level of conscious awareness. See **Altered**

Cancer (καρκίνος = crab): a variety of diseases that involve the abnormal and unregulated proliferation of cells. This proliferation can produce a malignant mass or **tumor**; and it has the potential to advance to other parts of the body. Some cancers do not produce tumors, however, leukemia being a prime example. Use of the term traces back to **Hippocrates**.

Capitated: in Latin *per capita* means "for each head" and indicates "for each patient." Our term refers to a reimbursement system in which regular, uniform payments are made irrespective of services rendered. A patient can be said to be capitated; this means that his or her provider is to receive a set amount, periodically (from an HMO for example). The payments themselves can also be referred to as capitated, as can contracts and healthcare systems.

Cardiac Arrest (καρδία = heart): the abrupt loss of heart function, breathing, and consciousness. The heart's pumping action. having stopped, the flow of blood to the rest of the body ceases as well. This is not to be confused with a heart attack (acute **myocardial infarction** [MI]) which involves a blockage of the flow of blood to a portion of the heart and which therefore may precipitate a **CA**, though not necessarily. See **ROSC: Return of Spontaneous Circulation**

Cardiac Catheterization: insertion of a catheter (a long, thin tube) through an artery or vein in the groin, neck, or arm, channeling it through a large blood vessel to the heart.

Cardiopulmonary Resuscitation: see **CPR (Cardiopulmonary Resuscitation)**

Care, Ethics of: an understanding of morality as located in interpersonal relationships, that is, in experiences of caring and being cared for. Milton Mayerhoff's *On Caring* (1971) was a pioneering work. But credit for a distinct theory is usually awarded to feminists Carol Gilligan and Nel Noddings, who maintain that traditional ethical approaches represent male bias. As an alternative, each argues for "care" in immediate relations as constituting an authentic alternative to the universalized and principled orientation of (male) human rights theorists.

Carrier: the epidemiological definition is an individual who, although infected with a disease and able to transmit it to others, shows no signs of being sick him- or herself. That is, "carrier" generally means "asymptomatic carrier." For a transient carrier, the carrier state is short-lived; for a chronic carrier, it is long-term.

CASA (Court-Appointed Special Advocate): (AKA guardian ad litem) in the field of Child Protective Services, these are "specially trained community volunteers appointed by Juvenile and Domestic Relations Court Judges to speak in the best interest of children who are brought before the court for reasons of abuse or neglect."[1] The role involves gathering information, making recommendations, monitoring services, and keeping the child safe.

Case Fatality Rate (CFR) vs. Infection Fatality Rate (IFR): for epidemiologists, the former correlates the number of people who die from a specific disease with the number of those clinically diagnosed with it. The disease's severity is then couched as a percentage. (Case Fatality *Ratio* and Case Fatality *Risk* can each be a synonym—or the three terms can be technically distinguished.) It must be borne in mind, however, that during an **outbreak**, a certain number of infected individuals will remain undiagnosed. So the **IFR** aims to include everyone with the disease: both the detected and the

---

1. CASA, "Job Description," para. 1.

undetected (a number for whom will always have to be an estimate). A great deal of confusion results when these two rates are not clearly distinguished, as, for example, when **CFR** is treated as if it were **IFR**. See **Mortality Rate**

Casey's Law: provides for court-ordered, involuntary treatment of victims of addiction. Kentucky's Matthew Casey Wethington Act for Substance Abuse Intervention (2004) was sparked by twenty-three-year-old Casey's death. Prior to his fatal heroin overdose in 2002, his parents had made every effort to get him into a chemical dependency treatment program. Impaired, he would not cooperate; and because he was of age, they could not commit him against his will. When someone is impaired by an addiction, this law allows parents, relatives, and/or friends to petition the court for an involuntary commitment. The treatment can be either inpatient or outpatient, type and length varying from case to case. Ohio passed a version of Casey's Law in 2012. See **Laws Named after Victims**

Casuistry: among medical ethicists, this is evaluating a current case in light of previous ones thought of as paradigmatic, with careful attention going to how the new one and the old ones are similar and different. This, as opposed to appealing to abstract principles or anticipated consequences. It's a method that originated in Roman Catholicism, arising out of the sacrament of confession. For a time it was thought of, certainly among Protestants, as synonymous with protracted legalistic nitpicking. Yet in the Anglo-American court systems, this very method is foundational, cases being decided according to the legal precedent established by previous cases. See **Situation Ethics**

Categorical Imperative: in the Kantian system, there are hypothetical imperatives ("To achieve outcome X, perform deed Y") and there are categorical imperatives ("Perform deed Z, no matter what!") The former are conditional, in that they are relative to the particular goals which a person might adopt. The latter, however, are unconditional; their moral absoluteness is not (and could not be) based on any particular person's intentions or preferences, nor do they (nor could they) change from one situation to another. Instead they involve acting according to the autonomous determination of universal reason—that's Kant's argument. Can such actions be put as simply doing one's duty for the sake of doing one's duty (as is sometimes suggested)? Only if we recall that for Kant, duty does not consist in obedience to dictates imposed from without, for duty is reason governing itself. See **Universalizability; Kant, Immanuel** (in **Part 2**)

Caylee's Law: addresses the failure to report a missing child. Legislation proposed or passed at state and federal levels makes it a felony for a parent or legal guardian to neglect to notify law enforcement about a child who is missing and potentially in danger. Named after two-year-old Caylee Anthony. Her mother, Casey Anthony, was tried for Caylee's murder in Orange County, Florida, in a trial that ended on July 5, 2011. Ms. Anthony was found guilty of misdemeanors, but not guilty of the more serious charges. An angry public outcry ensued; a number of **CL** efforts, in the form of bills and petitions, were initiated as a result. See **Laws Named after Victims**

Cerebrovascular Accident: see **Stroke**

Chain of Custody (or Chain of Evidence): in forensic science, both of these terms refer to the written and witnessed history of everything to be submitted in a legal case to prove or disprove an issue. Relevant are: who obtained the evidence, when and where, who secured it, and who has had responsibility for it. For anything evidentiary to be legally admissible, there must be an unbroken chain that has been carefully documented.

Character (χαρακτήρ = impression): the moral personality of an individual, that is, the unique combination of his or her enduring moral attributes, both positive and negative. Traditionally, and in the contemporary ethics of **virtue**, this dimension of personhood has been thought of as the accumulation of a person's virtues (good habits) and vices (bad habits), especially as they are liable to be demonstrated in times of ethical choice-making—when push comes to shove, as it were.

Chart Wars: see **Dueling in the Chart**

Chelsea's Law: legislation originating in California under the official title of the Chelsea King Child Predator Prevention Act of 2010. Passed in response to the murder of seventeen-year-old Chelsea by an already-registered sex offender, the law beefed up penalties, increased oversight of parolees, lengthened parole periods, and made sex offender treatment mandatory. It also adopted the **Containment Model** for the supervision of offenders. See **Laws Named after Victims**

Chemo Brain or **Chemo Fog:** informal terms for "Post-Chemotherapy Cognitive Impairment," PCCI, the mental fuzziness reported by some people after cancer treatment.

Chronic (χρόνος = time): lasting a long time. That's in contrast with diseases that are **acute** (abrupt, sharp, and brief) and **subacute** (between acute and chronic). According to the U.S. National Center for Health Statistics, a chronic disease or condition lasts three months or more. But that's generally speaking, for chronic, acute, and subacute differ in duration based on the injury or disease.

Circular Reasoning: sometimes regarded as a logical fallacy, either a formal or an informal one, this is the kind of argument that loops around and ends up right where it started. One view, espoused by the nineteenth-century Scottish philosopher Edward Caird and kept alive by Alvin Plantinga, is that "there is no harm in arguing in a circle if the circle is large enough."[2] See **Begging the Question**

Circulatory-Respiratory Death: (AKA cardiopulmonary death) the full and nonrestartable stop of the operations of the heart and lungs. In the United States, there are two ways to legally determine when a person has died: this is the older, long-trusted method. However, changes in medicine, starting with the invention of machines that can keep breath flowing and blood pumping after the brain has ceased to function, have meant that there can be times when the traditional standard of death has nothing to contribute. For this and other reasons, death according to neurological criteria has been embraced as a second definition. See **Brain Death; Dead Donor Rule; and Uniform Determination of Death Act**

Civil Wrong vs. Criminal Wrong: a fundamental legal distinction. The former involves one person injuring another and calls for compensation or restitution; the latter is an offense against society and warrants punishment in the form of a fine or jail time—some would add execution—and traditionally it has elicited society's condemnation as well. "Importantly, because a single wrongful act may constitute both a public offense and a private injury, it may give rise to both criminal and civil charges. A widely cited example is that of the former American football player O. J. Simpson: in 1995 he was acquitted of having murdered his wife and her friend, but two years later he was found liable for their killings in a civil suit for wrongful death."[3]

Clery Act: a federal student-safety statute, it mandates that colleges and universities keep track of, and make available information about, crime on and near campus. It was named after Jeanne Clery, whose murder in a Lehigh University residence hall in 1986 touched off national outrage over the unreporting of crime on campus. See **Laws Named after Victims**

---

2. Edward Caird, quoted in Plantinga, *Warrant*, 69.
3. Duignan, "What Is the Difference?," para. 5.

Clinical Equipoise: a medical research term. In randomized clinical trials, it is important—at the beginning—for those in charge to be open-minded (equally poised) regarding which of the care options being studied is going to provide the best results for their research subjects. This state of initial evenhandedness goes by the name **CE.** Benjamin Freedman fixed its classic definition as: "a state of genuine uncertainty on the part of the clinical investigator regarding the comparative therapeutic merits of each arm in a trial. Should the investigator discover that one treatment is of superior therapeutic merit, he or she is ethically obliged to offer that treatment" to all of the participants. But Freedman added an important qualification. The equipoise requirement "is satisfied if there is genuine uncertainty within the expert medical community—not necessarily on the part of the individual investigator—about the preferred treatment."[4] Discussions of, and debates about, these points are ongoing.

Clinical (or Care) Pathway: a methodology recommending evidence-based best practice approaches for sets of patients with the same condition. It emphasizes standardization for the purpose of improving outcomes, boosting efficiency, and reducing **Variation in Care / Practice Variability.** At the least formal, a **CP** can be a set of guidelines, arrayed as a simple flow chart for example, depicting a treatment sequence. However the approach can also be much more formalized, taking shape as a sophisticated information system, which maps patients' therapeutic ventures, and offers guidance to their medical teams. Ideally this is not "cookie-cutter" medicine, for treatment deviations are recorded and analyzed so that improvements can be incorporated into future pathways. (See **Pragmatic Bioethics.**) All that said, the same term can also be used for a plan for a particular patient, the contributions of each discipline involved being integrated into it. In this latter case, another designation would be "Case Management Plan."

Clinician (κλίνη = bed): any healthcare practitioner working with patients and providing healthcare services as distinct from administration, research, or academia. Doctors, nurses, pharmacists, dentists, speech pathologists, and physician assistants are all clinicians. Clinical psychiatrists are as well. Social workers divide their field into macro, direct, and clinical.

Cloning (κλών = twig or branch): the word was coined in 1903 by American horticulturalist Herbert J. Webber to refer to the propagation of a new plant using a cutting from a previous one; so in various contexts, it can have various meanings. But even so, the most familiar definition is: the artificial

---

4. Freedman, "Equipoise," para. 2.

creation of a biological copy, a "clone," which has a genetic makeup that is identical to the original.

Closure, Moral: Martin Luther King warned about "the paralysis of analysis." (Actually, King borrowed the catchy phrase from the American Baptist pastor Josephus Pius Barbour.)[5] While there is always a real danger that a decision might be made too hastily, King's point is that in every ethical deliberation, there comes a time when some kind of choice has to be made. "Ethics likes to ask questions, whereas medicine needs answers. This is one of the tensions in any form of applied ethics; at some stage, consideration of different options and arguments will have to stop, and a decision be taken about what should be done."[6]

Cluster: see **Outbreak vs. Cluster**

Code: a shortened version of "Code Blue." This widely used term alerts a designated "code team" that a patient's heart or breathing has stopped. It summons them to rush to the patient's location and to immediately begin using emergency measures, such as **CPR**, or to provide other medical attention. See **Slow Code**

Code Adam: a missing child protocol. This set of procedures was developed in 1994 by Walmart in cooperation with the National Center for Missing and Exploited Children. It was named in honor of Adam Walsh. Many years earlier, six-year-old Adam was abducted from a Sears department store in Hollywood, Florida, and murdered. In the **CA** program, employees are trained to respond quickly to a report of a missing child and to follow a series of six steps. Currently, all federal office buildings follow the protocol, along with many department stores, hospitals, museums, amusement parks, and other facilities. See **Laws Named after Victims**

Code Black: see **Black Alert**

Codependency: a pop psychology term given wide exposure by Melody Beattie, it refers to a relationship in which one partner accommodates and reinforces the unhealthy behaviors of another. The **irony** is that codependents need those others' problems to remain uncorrected, even as they, the codependents, seem committed to fixing them. Psychologist Shawn Meghan Burn characterizes the dynamic as "a dysfunctional helping relationship where one person supports or enables the other person's addiction, poor

5. Lischer, *Preacher King*, 58.
6. Higgs, "Closure, moral," 44.

mental health, immaturity, irresponsibility, or under-achievement."[7] Note: some point out that **C** is not an officially diagnosable behavioral health problem, and they advise mental health professionals against regarding it as if it were.

CODIS: the forensic science acronym for "Combined DNA Index System." This is the FBI operation that supports all participating criminal-justice-system DNA databases. It makes it possible for crime labs to share DNA profiles electronically at the federal, state, and local levels, which in turn means that violent crimes, and offenders already in the system, can potentially be connected. The acronym refers to both the entire program, and the computer software involved.

Cognitive Dissonance: in the field of psychology, this means mental phenomena (thoughts, ideas, attitudes, etc.) that are discordant or self-contradictory. Becoming aware of such incompatibilities tends to be anxiety-producing; yet it can provide therapeutic opportunities. The basic concept is associated with Leon Festinger who held that human beings need internal consistency to operate in the external world.

Cognitive Function: the intellectual processes involved in gathering and assimilating information: awareness and perception, thinking and imaging, judging and reasoning, and deciding and remembering. ("It is necessary to establish whether the patient's cognitive function is improving.")

Cold Hit: in forensic science, a fortuitous match-up between evidence taken from a crime scene, a scene for which there had been no investigative leads, and an offender profile in a criminal justice DNA database. Important for connecting a particular individual to the location of a crime.

Collusion of Anonymity: a phrase of Michael Balint's, long familiar in British medical circles, denotes the impersonality of a healthcare system in which a patient is being seen by multiple physicians—none of whom can be identified as responsible for the case. That is, there is no "ringmaster" at the center of the course of treatment, and worse, no one showing any interest in the patient as a person. Think of it as Kafka-esque medicine. See **Blamestorming**

Commodification: as explained by Erich Fromm, someone or something objectified and turned into a meaningless "thing" for commerce or trade. "Modern man has transformed himself into a commodity; he experiences

---

7. Johnson, "Codependency and Codependent Relationships," para. 2.

his life energy as an investment with which he should make the highest profit, considering his position and the situation on the personality market. He is alienated from himself, from his fellow men and from nature."[8]

Common Good: the shared, positive inheritance-and-prospects of a broadly inclusive community. These can involve physical structures, like a schoolhouse; institutional operations, like a department of education; or cultural values, like a commitment to learning. The **CG** is the sum total of all those public benefits which are advantageous for each only because, and only for as long as, they are available to all. At least, that's the traditional view. More recently critics have countered that cultural pluralism, together with other destabilizing factors, have eroded the foundation that makes any sort of cooperation toward a "common good" possible. John Rawls holds this view and argues that the basic concept "is no longer a political possibility for those who accept the constraints of liberty and toleration of democratic institutions."[9]

Common Rule, The: as the moral and legal standard to which all government-funded research in the United States is held, it aims to protect the rights and welfare of the persons involved. Officially known as "The Federal Policy for the Protection of Human Subjects," it was originally formulated in 1981, published in 1991, and has been codified in separate regulations by a number of federal departments and agencies. Nearly all American academic institutions involved in biomedical and behavioral studies with human subjects hold their researchers to it. Complicating the picture: work on updating the policy's definitions and requirements has been underway for some time and has resulted in important, substantial changes. As a result, reference is often made to "The Revised Common Rule" and "The New Common Rule," sometimes with a particular year specified.

Common Source Outbreak: see **Propagated Outbreak vs. Common Source Outbreak**

Communitarianism: this view starts with the rejection of a specific kind of liberalism: the minimalist, skeletal kind that reduces the moral life to universal rights of individuals needing nanny-state protections. In truth, so the communitarians counter, fleshed-out ethics, being history-borne and community-specific, involve far more than that. Fleshed-out ethics are animated by the muscular rituals and customs of culture—and they are kept

8. Fromm, *Art of Loving*, 97.
9. Rawls, quoted in Hollenbach, *Common Good*, 9.

alive by the lifeblood of religious symbols and values. So in a nutshell: ethics without traditions are dead; and the hope that big government life-support can turn things around is delusive. A reader may object, "Since different cultures disagree with one another, doesn't that mean that morality becomes completely relative?" To such a question, communitarians have two answers. First, the place where one finds relativists in the greatest number is in the camp of the liberals—so if that's really a problem, liberals should solve it among themselves first. Otherwise the pot is criticizing the kettle. And second, it is by bearing witness to the moral standards of one's group, and by demonstrating their fruitfulness in illumining contemporary quandaries, that one does right by them. Why ask for anything more? See **Common Good** and **Universalizability**

Community Spread: the proliferation of a disease within a geographic area when the actual transmission and timing of the expansion cannot be ascertained. So, people are being infected but no one can pin down the how, where, when, or by whom.

Comorbidity: the problem of more than one medical condition affecting or exacerbating a patient's health difficulties. Often used of a patient with two or more behavioral health diagnoses. See **Dual Diagnosis**

Compassionate Use / Expanded Access Program: the informal and formal names for the Food and Drug Administration's long-standing pathway for patients with life-threatening illnesses to request experimental therapies. It has many similarities to more recent **Right to Try** laws. Differences include: medical devices are covered along with medications; liability protections are not a part of the deal; and there is much more bureaucratic supervision. In fact, a major reason for **RtT** is that the FDA **EAP** program's requirements were found to be confusing, forbidding, and user-unfriendly. **RtT** was specifically designed to provide a less-labyrinthine alternative. Aware of the difficulties, the FDA has streamlined **EAP** procedures in recent years. Note: in Europe, similar pathways go by the name "Early Access Programs." But what is involved varies widely from country to country.

Compassion Fatigue: exhaustion from connecting with and caring for those who suffer. It is described as "the cost of caring," and as "secondary traumatic stress." Close and empathetic relationships with people in pain or with difficulties means sharing their struggles. Over time, such empathy takes its toll, physically and emotionally. Closely related to, and sometimes used interchangeably with, either **burnout** or **provider fatigue**.

Complicity, Moral: coming from the same root as "accomplice," this refers to a kind of secondary or indirect guilt. An individual who is not the primary or direct agent is nevertheless associated with an action; and it is possible that the association is less than fully voluntary. ("The nurse believed that she had had no choice, but still felt that she was morally complicit in the hospital's treatment of the patient's family.") See **Moral Distress vs. Moral Injury**

Concurrent Care: (1) in discussions of billing, **CC** refers to a particular patient on a particular day being treated for a particular diagnosis by more than one medical professional, each practitioner taking (this is crucial) an active and essential part in said treatment (lest the insurance company deny the claim as duplicative). (2) In discussions of end-of-life medical alternatives, **CC** means that a patient is not required to choose between staying with curative-care efforts or entering hospice; a transition is in view instead. So in both senses, **CC** means a both/and where one might expect to find an either/or.

Confidentiality vs. Privacy: the first is a duty; the second is a right. Patients and research volunteers have a right to having their health information kept private; physicians and researchers have the duty to see that it is kept confidential. See **Deidentification**

Confounding vs. Effect (Measure) Modification: epidemiologists use "confounding" to mean confusing or distorting of a result. Specifically, in a study focused on a particular factor and an outcome, a confounding factor is an additional, extraneous factor—a "nuisance variable"—that can seem to be relevant to the study but really isn't. With "effect modification," however, the additional factor is not extraneous, but an important variable in its own right.

Confusion Assessment Method: see **CAM Positive**

Congenital Disorder: present at birth, a **CD** is a medical abnormality, such as clubfoot or congenital heart disease, of whatever source. It can be inherited or acquired during fetal development. Such disorders are also called birth defects or congenital anomalies.

Congestive Heart Failure (CHF): or simply "heart failure," the two terms sometimes being used interchangeably. Both designations indicate that the heart is not functioning efficiently. It has become stiff or weak to the point that it "fails" to pump as much blood as the body requires. This general condition of heart failure is more specifically "congestive" when the slowdown out of the heart causes the blood en route to the heart to back up. The result is the congestion, or the buildup of fluids, in the body's tissues. The liver, abdomen, lower limbs, and the lungs can all be affected; swelling (**edema**) can result. (Note, "failure" should not be taken as indicating that the heart has completely stopped. That would be **cardiac arrest**.)

Conscience: the nearly universal inner sense of what is good, right, just, and fair versus what is evil, wrong, unjust, unfair, and therefore guilt- or blame-worthy. In Christian ethics, much is made of Rom 2:15, which associates **C** with God's law written on the hearts of all, believers and unbelievers alike.

Conscientious Objection: in healthcare contexts, the grounds for medical professionals to abstain from providing a medical service that is within their scope of practice, but for which they have moral or religious objections. Abortion is the commonly cited example.

Consent: an individual's voluntarily given go-ahead. ▪ **Informed Consent:** permission granted to a procedure or experiment—specifically by a person who has **decision-making capacity** and who has been given full knowledge of the alternatives and possible consequences. Adequate prior disclosure of relevant information is important, as is a demonstration that the patient's understanding of it forms the basis of his or her uncoerced authorization. (Commonly used: "The nurse *consented* the patient.") ▪ **Implied Consent:** permission inferred even though it wasn't stated. For example, making an appointment to see a doctor implies consent. In a medical emergency, when a person is unable to indicate authorization, the **reasonable person standard** conveys **IC** on the grounds that a reasonable person would agree to being treated. ▪ **Emergent Consent** (AKA "The Emergency Exception Rule"): as just stated, **IC** specifically in a situation in which death or irreparable harm could result if treatment were to be put off. ▪ **Parental/Guardian Consent:** informed consent granted by a parent or legally authorized decision-maker on behalf of a minor or an adult lacking in **decision-making capacity**. See also **Two-Doctor or Two-Physician Rule, The**

Consequentialism: a catch-all category for various theories that tie moral justification to results. For these theories, the right course of action is the one that produces the good outcome, and the wrong one is the one that produces the bad outcome. Utilitarianism, for example, holds that ethical acts or norms are those that produce the greatest amount of good for the greatest number of people. Often contrasted with **Deontology**. See **Act-Utilitarianism**; **Rule-Utilitarianism**; and **Virtue; and Bentham, Jeremy** and **Mill, John Stuart** (in **Part 2**)

Conservatorship: the appointment by court order of a guardian (conservator) to make legal decisions for an individual unable to decide for him- or herself. These decisions can be in various areas, including healthcare arrangements. When the latter is included, the guardian is assigned legal authority to make medical treatment determinations for the conservatee.

Consumer-Driven Healthcare: any of a wide variety of notions, such as: (1) a set-up in which people who are anxious about their health, misinformed by the media, frustrate the medical community by demanding care that isn't feasible, necessary, or cost-effective; or by contrast, (2) a situation in which self-confident, knowledgeable patients direct healthcare professionals to provide them with optimal medical services; or again, (3) one in which technological marvels free up patients and providers, enabling them to work together as never before—the end result being the medical counterpart to a workers' paradise: healthcare flowing through wireless, internet channels from each according to his ability, to each according to his needs. Thus, **CDH** is one of those buzz phrases, the meanings of which have little to do with each other.

Contact Tracing: a public health term referring to measures taken to identify infected individuals and others whom they could possibly have endangered. "In case investigation, public health staff work with a patient to help them recall everyone with whom they have had close contact during the timeframe while they may have been infectious. Public health staff then begin contact tracing by warning these exposed individuals (contacts) of their potential exposure as rapidly and sensitively as possible."[10]

Containment Model: an influential approach to the case management and treatment of sex offenders. Relying on a team of professionals, the aim is to maximize victim protection and public safety through stepped-up monitoring and interagency cooperation. **CM** presumes that most sex crimes are planned and that the unfolding of the plan follows a pattern. If specific to the individual offender, this pattern is nevertheless discernible. "Working together, criminal justice and forensic mental health professionals can effectively identify, monitor, interrupt, and modify this pattern in many cases."[11]
See **Chelsea's Law**

Continuity of Care: once a person comes under the care of a physician, the physician assumes responsibility for the patient's continuing medical needs.

---

10. CDC, "Case Investigation and Contact Tracing," para. 3.
11. Pimentel and Muller, "Containment Approach," para. 3.

Certainly the patient has the right to terminate the relationship; and of course the doctor does as well, once the patient has been given time to look for another provider. That said, one way to understand **CoC** is as the opposite of patient abandonment. Doctors are obligated to follow through with their patients over as long a period of time as is necessary. Traditionally, this has been connected to the fact that many patients have had a personal doctor—idealized as "the trusted family physician." And even today, for many that traditional arrangement remains the crucial factor in **CoC**. (See the concluding sentence below.) However, fewer and fewer Americans get all their medical needs met by a solo clinician; a multidisciplinary team and/or an integrated healthcare system is likely to be involved. The advantage is that this way, the very best of modern medicine can be targeted to each patient at reasonable cost—or so it is said. Those who welcome this new state of affairs speak about a different, specialist-friendly understanding of continuity, the "**warm handoff**" approach being one way to achieve it. Others, however, maintain that **CoC** remains a reason for choosing primary care over specialized care, whenever possible, because instead of brief, limited interactions, the patient gets an ongoing therapeutic relationship. See **Abandonment, Patient; Collusion of Anonymity;** and **Negligence, Medical**

Contraindicated: shown by the evidence that a study, test, or intervention in question should be withheld because of its potential for harm. For example, if a CT scan with contrast (a special dye used to enhance the scan) in a patient with kidney disease is contraindicated, that indicates that the contrast material could further injure the kidney. ▪ **Relative Contraindication:** a consideration that provides a reason for proceeding with caution in the administration of a therapy—or often in the use of two meds together—and requiring that a case-specific assessment of potential benefits in light of evident burdens be undertaken. If the former outweigh the latter, the treatment can go forward, heedfully. ▪ **Absolute Contraindication:** a condition that overwhelmingly puts a particular treatment or procedure "off limits" without exception. See **Indicated, Medically**

Controlled Substances: see **Scheduled Drugs**

Conundrum: a broad and imprecise term for any convoluted and perplexing (and oftentimes apparently unsolvable) problematic situation or moral dilemma.

Coronary Thrombosis: see **Myocardial Infarction or Acute Myocardial Infarction**

Corridor Nursing: in the UK's National Health Service (NHS), this refers to patients—under normal, pre-COVID-19 pandemic circumstances—receiving medical care in the crowded hallway of a hospital A&E (Accident and Emergency) unit. Typically, a nurse who would normally work in a specialist ward is reassigned to a corridor. There the patients can be lying on trolleys or sitting in chairs or on the floor; procedures can include drawing blood and administering intravenous antibiotics. One downside is that the nurse's own ward will typically be left understaffed. "A poll of A&E nurses found almost three quarters (73 percent) provide care to patients in a non-designated area—such as a corridor—on a daily basis."[12] See **Black Alert**

Cosmesis: (κόσμησις = an adorning or decorating; κόσμος = order) medical attention directed to a patient's appearance: its recovery, its perpetuation, or its enhancement. Specifically, the repair of a malformation can be in view, or the elimination or minimization of scars from an operation, or again cosmetic surgery for beautification or improvement requested by the patient. It also refers to the fabrication of prosthetic limbs and to the limbs themselves.

Cosmetic Psychopharmacology: a term coined by Peter Kramer in *Listening to Prozac* to mean writing prescriptions for patients who are not clinically diagnosable for meds which will provide them with a boost that leaves them "better than well" and "more socially attractive."[13] See **Cosmesis** and **Pharmacological Calvinism**

Cost-Benefit Analysis (CBA): examination of expenditures correlated with benefits to be received. When either particular medical interventions (the micro) or healthcare policies (the macro) are being discussed—as long as resource constraints are a potential concern, the focus will naturally turn to setting priorities and making choices. Critics maintain that worrying about the financial angle is just plain wrong, and moreover that doing so will place medical practice on a slippery slope where economic pressures will soon enough determine clinical and ethical questions (think: **Death Panels**). Supporters answer that it would be irresponsible not to seek to make efficient use of the resources at hand. They might also add: let the doctor who charges no fee level the first objection. Note: though **CBA** is sometimes used to mean **risk-benefit analysis,** the two are best distinguished. However, for

---

12. Pickover, "Treating A&E Patients," para. 2.

13. Kramer, *Listening to Prozac*, xvi.

a take which places them together, see Baruch Fischhoff, "The Realities of Risk-Cost-Benefit Analysis."[14] See **Cost-Effectiveness Analysis**

Cost-Effectiveness Analysis (CEA): a wonky healthcare policy methodology which grew out of **CBA**, and which aims to be an objective means for identifying healthcare interventions that are good values. Typically interventions are compared in terms of price and end product to determine a cost-effectiveness ratio. Another variation starts with an economic reality ("Our budget is X") and then asks what is the most effective way to spend X. Some oppose all considerations of this sort. They maintain that there is an inherently intersubjective, possibly even sacred, quality to all medical practice for which economic quantifying is inappropriate. Proponents counter that the alternatives (relying on the whim of providers; holding a lottery) are morally inferior. And they add that just as recognizing good and poor physical health requires objective information, so does recognizing good and poor healthcare expenditures; and neither is inherently dehumanizing. Critics disagree, observing that objectifying human beings is what the word "dehumanizing" means.

Court-Appointed Special Advocate: see **CASA (Court-Appointed Special Advocate)**

CPR (Cardiopulmonary Resuscitation): a familiar staple of TV hospital shows, this life-saving technique pairs chest compressions with artificial ventilation. It is an emergency, short-term measure; the basic idea is to maintain efforts until the return of spontaneous circulation (**ROSC**) or until the person is declared dead. Or if out of hospital, then generally to continue **CPR** until the EMTs arrive.

Crepe Hanging: when a doctor, expecting a treatment to be successful, misdirects patient expectations by overemphasizing the possible negatives. The thought is that this will provide cover in the off-event that things go poorly, and if they don't go poorly, it will make him or her look like a miracle worker. **CH** has long been regarded as unethical.

CRISPR: short for "clustered regularly interspaced short palindromic repeats," this acronym describes certain DNA sequences in bacteria and other microorganisms. More importantly, it also refers to a technique, based on those sequences and the operations related to them, for altering the DNA of

---

14. Fischhoff, "Realities of Risk-Cost-Benefit Analysis."

human beings, other animals, and plants. "CRISPR is a technology that can be used to edit genes and, as such, will likely change the world."[15]

Critical (condition) (κριτικός = able to judge): vital signs are unstable and not within normal limits; indicators for recovery are unfavorable. (Critical is worse than **serious**.)

CT (or CAT) Scan: computed tomography (or computerized axial tomography, the earlier term). A diagnostic technique which uses many X-rays synthesized by a computer to create images of cross sections of tissues, blood vessels, and bones. The technology was developed, contemporaneously but independently, by Godfrey Hounsfield, an English electrical engineer, and Allan Cormack, a South African-born American physicist. The two were jointly awarded a Nobel Prize in 1979 for their invention. (The Greek word τόμος, meaning "slice" or "section," gave rise to the English words "tome" and "atom.")

Curative Intent: with the thought and for the purpose of supplying a remedy and/or restoring health. It is to be distinguished from **palliative** intent. In ethics consultations, it can be important to note its absence, for that means that it is time to **regoal**.

Curbside: medicalese for running a clinical question by a colleague at a less-than-official-consult level. It means "touching base" without the other party necessarily having to review the chart, examine the patient, and document the medical assessment and recommendations, though it may involve these elements in an unofficial capacity. Oftentimes, it will involve a treating physician seeking advice from a specialist, though not always. (One might hear, "We did a curbside and cardiology said not to worry about the valve before the procedure.") The term originally arose as physicians, on their way to the hospital parking lot, stopped at curbside to discuss cases.

Custodial Care vs. Skilled Care: the former provides an individual with assistance with life's routine, daily tasks: dressing, feeding, bathing, getting in and out of bed, and taking medications that could normally be self-administered. These tasks are personal rather than medical; they do not require a licensed caregiver. The latter involves medically necessary kinds of assistance which are more technical and therefore more costly. **SC** can only be delivered by, or under the supervision of, licensed and/or specially trained medical practitioners. They include: nurses, physical therapists, occupational therapists, and others. See **ADL (Activities of Daily Living)**

15. Le Page, "What Is CRISPR?," para. 1.

Cutter Incident: possibly the worst public health calamity in American history. In 1955, Cutter Laboratories, Berkeley, California, released a batch of vaccines for the public. Though the vaccines had been tested and had passed, they contained the virus: live and fully infectious. As a result, five children died, up to 200 were paralyzed to some extent, and an additional 40,000 came down with poliomyelitis in a nonparalyzing form. (The numbers vary; some accounts say ten children died.) The vaccines were recalled; government oversight was upgraded; and the manufacturing process was improved. Also: national health officials lost their jobs and Cutter Laboratories, although found not to be negligent, was required to pay damages.

Cyanosis (κυανός = blue): a condition in which skin or lips turn bluish, signaling that tissues are not receiving enough oxygen-laden blood.

Letter D

Data Mining vs. Data Dredging: the first of these two, which can be understood in a positive sense, is exploratory analysis designed to suss out hidden patterns in data. The second, by contrast, is the misuse of data mining. It skips the prespecification of a study protocol. It conducts many data analyses, watching for chance correlations. Late in the game, it tacks on a post hoc hypothesis as if it were a priori, that is, it pretends to find illumination in results arrived at blindly. Because there's no there *there*, such "findings" are highly unlikely to be reproduced. Which is why this is one of the "questionable research practices" frequently mentioned as contributing to the present-day research **replication crisis**. See **A Priori vs. A Posteriori**

Dead Donor Rule: stipulates that vital organs shall only be taken from deceased donors (determined by either neurological or cardiopulmonary criteria) and that their removal shall not be the cause of death. There is much uncertainty about what this entails, however, and the uncertainty is fundamental. "Brain dead organ donors are the principal source of transplantable organs. However, it is controversial whether brain death is the same as biological death. Therefore, it is unclear whether organ removal in brain death is consistent with the 'dead donor rule.'"[1] Yet even with this unclarity, the neurological criteria approach has many advocates. They point out that it allows for the harvesting of organs from bodies that continue to have circulation and respiration, something which serves to minimize ischemic damage to the targeted organs. And that angle gives rise to the question of whether the rule should require only the death of the cerebral, upper brain (rather than of the whole brain), for if so, that would expand the pluses of this alternative. Moreover, it would pave the way for including as donors babies born without an operational upper brain (**anencephaly**). But in the face of such considerations, many objections and admitted inconsistencies

1. Nair-Collins et al., "Abandoning the Dead Donor Rule?," para. 1.

43

remain. (Put forward in the late 1960s to reflect the existing medical-moral consensus, **DDR** was articulated as such by University of Texas Law School professor John A. Robertson.) See **Brain Death**; **Circulatory-Respiratory Death**; **Ischemia**; and **Uniform Determination of Death Act**

Death by Neurological Criteria, Determination of: see **Brain Death**

Death Panels: a highly controversial term which unites disapproval of euthanasia and fears about healthcare rationing with concerns about governmental overreach. Credit for the phrase goes to Sarah Palin, the 2008 Republican vice presidential candidate. In 2009, Ms. Palin alleged that the Affordable Care Act would "empower unelected bureaucrats to make decisions affecting life or death health care matters."[2] These shadowy decision-making agencies were labeled "death panels." Much effort went into showing that the ACA ("Obamacare") did no such thing. On the other hand, some argue that, properly directed, the term nevertheless accurately depicts an unhappy but inescapable fact of life. Thaddeus Pope, for example, maintains that in the present-day United States, "all sorts of tribunals are making life-and-death decisions not just every day, but even every hour of every day."[3] So the phrase persists, rather like "1984," as a handy way of warning about a dystopian future in which, one might say, "Big Brother is making all of your healthcare decisions." See **Health Care Rationing;** and **God Committee, The** (in **Part 2**).

Decision-Making Capacity (DMC): the ability of a patient to make medical-care-related choices. Four components are necessary. The patient must be able to: (1) understand his or her medical condition; (2) appreciate the consequences of the treatment possibilities; (3) reason through the advantages and disadvantages of these alternatives; and (4) communicate a choice in light of personal goals, values, and preferences. (A fifth component can be: the choice's consistency with the patient's history.) This capacity may come and go; and a patient may be able to make some decisions but not others. What matters is the patient's **DMC** at the time a particular choice is made. See **ACE (Aid to Capacity Evaluation);** and **MacCAT-T (MacArthur Competence Assessment Tool for Treatment); MMSE (Mini-Mental Status Examination)**

Decompensation: a turn for the worse. That is, among behavioral health specialists, it refers to the gradual or rapid decrease of an individual's

---

2. Palin, "Obama and the Bureaucratization of Health Care," para. 11.
3. Pope, "Top 10 North American Death Panels," para. 23.

cognitive processing, mental functioning, or psychological balance. In psychoanalytic theory, it is the above specifically because his or her defense mechanisms have been overcome by stress. However, decompensation is also commonly used to describe many physiological illnesses (e.g., decompensated cirrhosis and acute decompensated heart failure).

Deductive vs. Inductive Reasoning: as generally understood, the former starts with abstract generality and works toward concrete application: trees have roots; that's a tree; therefore it has roots. The inductive approach begins with multiple examples and reasons to an overarching conclusion. Every tree we've seen has roots; so our hypothesis is that all trees have roots. Science educators use these twin terms in this common parlance kind of way. However, do not expect present-day philosophers to follow suit. No, because among philosophers, deductive reasoning involves true premises, logical inference, and certain conclusions; and inductive reasoning involves true premises and probable conclusions. Yes, except for those times when the latter term simply refers to any argument which is not deductive.

Defensive Medicine: clinical self-protectiveness, ordering tests and/or pursuing a course of patient care, not for the patient's sake, but to minimize the risk of a malpractice lawsuit. Another angle is steering clear of anything high-risk. See **Overtreatment vs. Overdiagnosis** and **Parsimonious Care**

Defibrillation (dee-FIB-ri-LAY-shun): the use of a defibrillator to send an electric shock to the heart. The purpose is to disrupt an arrhythmia—that is, a heartbeat that is too fast, irregular, or too slow—so as to allow the heart to return to a normal rhythm. "This is the single most important intervention a rescuer can take in patients who have suffered cardiac arrest due to vfib or pulseless ventricular tachycardia."[4] Note: restarting a heart from zero is not in view here, though popular media have convinced the general public that that is what defibrillators do. "Defibrillators do not jump start the heart like jump starting a car; they stop it like rebooting a computer. . . . The defibrillator administers a shock to stop the heart if it is in an abnormal but shockable rhythm, enabling the heart's own system to reboot and hopefully restart in sinus rhythm (normal beat)."[5] For a patient whose heart has completely stopped, **Cardiopulmonary Resuscitation (CPR)** is called for instead. See **Ventricular Fibrillation** and **Ventricular Tachycardia**

---

4. Venes, *Tabor's Cyclopedic Medical Dictionary*, 631.
5. Hammett, "All about Defibrillators," paras. 9–10.

Deidentification: in research with human subjects, steps taken to keep participants' identities a secret. The **HIPAA** Privacy Rule requires that person-specific information be strictly protected. Specifically, any data that could reasonably be used to identify a participant must be removed or replaced. See **Confidentiality vs. Privacy**

Deinstitutionalization: the practice of moving mentally ill and developmentally delayed patients out of large, state-run asylums to receive services elsewhere, especially in presumably more humane, local settings. In American mental health policy and practice, the term generally refers to a federal government-sponsored initiative, begun in the 1960s and associated with President John F. Kennedy. Besides his imprimatur, its motivating factors included: the asylum scandals of that time; the availability of new psych meds; and the promise that community mental health clinics would be less costly. Observers point out that sufficient funds for those community centers never made it into the pipeline, and that that failure created a host of problems.

Delirium: acute and reversible, **D** is not a disease but a set of symptoms, the chief of which is a disturbance in **mentation** marked by a confused state of awareness and/or a reduced ability to focus on the here and now. Some of the symptoms are: disorientation, illusions, and hallucinations.

Deliverables, Medical: a buzzphrase for anything—results, goods, or services—produced in order to be passed along or transferred to intended recipients. Commonly used for the output or outcome of a healthcare-related project, educational program, or formal planning process. By extension, a patient's meds can be called deliverables.

Demarcation Problem: according to Karl Popper, this is the crucial challenge for philosophers of science: the difficult task of finding the line between science and nonscience, between genuinely scientific undertakings and findings, on the one hand, and their pseudoscientific substitutes, on the other. See **Falsification, Popper's Principle of** and **Logical Positivism**

Dementia: a progressive and irreversible decline in **mentation** characterized by memory deficits, impaired reasoning, and the clouding of conscious awareness.

Denial: as understood by behavioral health professionals, a defense mechanism employed to protect the conscious self against a too-painful set of circumstances. As such it is not unhealthy, at least not in the short run. It is also enshrined as stage one of the **Five Stages of Grief** (AKA the Kübler-Ross Model): Denial, Anger, Bargaining, Depression, and Acceptance ("DABDA").

Deontology: (δέον = that which is right, necessary, or binding; that which has to be done), one of the major theories of ethics. While it has many variants—some featuring rules, others moral intuitions—all have some expression of duty or obligation as a foundation; and all reject the idea that the morality of an action can be pegged to what it accomplishes. Take three familiar imperatives: "Follow your conscience and let the chips fall where they may"; "Obey God rather than the rulers of society"; and "Do the loving thing in each situation instead of the legalistic thing." However different these are from one another, each injunction prioritizes oughtness while discounting or ignoring outcome, and that is the key. Kantian ethics is usually offered as deontology's best example, but that requires explaining his **categorical imperative**; and in the context of his entire philosophy, that's not an easy thing to do! Explaining one unfamiliar concept in terms of another unfamiliar concept never is. Martin Luther King is more accessible than **Kant**: "Conscience asks the question, 'Is it right?' And there comes a time when one must take a position that is neither safe, nor politic, nor popular, but he must take it because conscience tells him it is right."[6] That's deontology in a nutshell. See **Consequentialism** and **Virtue**

Deprescribing: among pharmacists, this means dialing things down. That is, in light of the risks associated with **medication-related problems**, D is: identifying and then reducing or stopping selected prescription meds in light of possibly harmful drug-drug interactions (regarding which, senior adults are thought to be at higher risk). There are also concerns lest an Rx be maintained when: (a) it has not been shown to be effective; (b) it is no longer needed; (c) it duplicates another treatment; and/or (d) the burdens outweigh the benefits. See **Overmedication**; **Polypharmacy**; and **Prescribing Cascade**

Depression: (AKA major depressive disorder or MDD) a mood disorder characterized by feelings, for a period of at least two weeks, of sadness and/or loss of interest in activities previously enjoyed. Though how a person thinks and acts are also involved, the hallmarks of **D** are typically feelings of anxiety, emptiness, hopelessness, and worthlessness. One's normal daily routines can seem like immense burdens; life may seem as if it isn't worth the effort; thoughts of death or suicide may predominate.

---

6. King, "Proper Sense of Priorities," para. 14.

Designer Baby: a concept that takes hopes and fears about **test-tube babies** one step further. Whereas the latter are simply children conceived through **in vitro fertilization,** with **DB** the focus advances to the genetic engineering of babies with intentionally chosen traits, gender being one example. Choice of eye, skin, and hair color can come into view, along with grander qualities such as intelligence, temperament, and genetically influenced behavior predispositions. One common aim is the reduction of risk of debilitating conditions; but deaf parents choosing deafness for a future child counts as well.

Determinism: the view that everything takes place just as it does because of: causes or natural laws (as understood by the physical sciences); or influences outside the self (such as gods or demons); or a big scheme of things (such as the configuration of the stars or the routinizing influence of a social system). In any event, nothing comes about because of the conscious choice-making of individual human beings; and nothing "just randomly happens." Instead, events come along as if already locked into place, as it were. ▪ **Biological Determinism:** more specifically, the concept that individual and communal behavior is governed by our physiological constitution, so that, in Freud's words, "biology is destiny." ▪ **Genetic Determinism:** this is biological determinism moved down to the DNA level, meaning that "certain physical and behavioral traits are expressions of, and thus are necessarily determined by, the presence of particular genes or groups of genes in that individual's cells."[7] See **Freud, Sigmund**

Diabetes: (Διαβήτης = a passing-through, a siphon) a name that was first assigned by Aretaeus of Cappadocia, second century AD. It now indicates families of more conditions than are listed here, all having excessive urination as a common symptom. ▪ **Diabetes Mellitus:** the disease that the general public usually associates with "diabetes." With Type 1, the body makes too little or no insulin. Management involves diet, exercise, and typically, insulin shots. Type 2 is more common. Here the body is resistant and/or is not responding to insulin as necessary. Blood glucose levels have to be maintained, something that involves changes in lifestyle and oral medication; and if that doesn't work, then shots. ▪ **Gestational Diabetes Mellitus:** glucose intolerance arising during pregnancy because of changes in metabolism and insulin resistance. This usually goes away after delivery, though the patient may have an elevated risk for developing Type 2 at a point later on. ▪ **Diabetes Insipidus (DI):** unrelated to all of the above, this is a rare disease state involving a high urinary flow (the diabetes). It

---

7. Tubbs, *Handbook of Bioethics Terms,* 37.

is due either to: a lower-than-usual amount of antidiuretic hormone ADH (AKA vasopressin)—a condition called central **DI**; or a kidney disorder which prevents the kidneys from responding to ADH and from functioning properly—a condition called nephrogenic **DI**.

Diagnosis (διάγνωσις = know through; discern): the identification of the disease or condition that is causing a patient's medical difficulty. See **Prognosis**

Diagnosis of Convenience: an unjustifiable or insufficiently accurate medical diagnosis assigned to a condition for nonmedical reasons. Such reasons can include carelessness in satisfying the curiosity of a patient and sloppiness in recordkeeping. More troubling would be stretching the truth in order to receive payment from an insurance company. Deception in this latter case could count as insurance fraud. On a different note, faced with a sudden explosion of reports of "disease X" (think ADHD), a skeptical observer might ask if all of these cases are legitimate, or if **DC** might possibly be behind some of them. Compare with **Disease du Jour**

Differential Diagnosis: distinguishing a particular disease or condition from others that present similar clinical features.

Dilemma, Moral: (δί = two; λημμα = premise) technically, an either/or in which both possible courses of action are morally problematic. "Damned if you do, and damned if you don't" is the familiar way of putting it—although a choice involving the greater of two goods could also be regarded as a moral dilemma. Even so, only a few quandaries are dilemmas in this technical sense. Yet one commonly hears "moral dilemma" used in connection with any ethically confused or uncertain situation; and a downside to such usage is that it may, in limiting thinking to the two front-and-center alternatives, inhibit real problem-solving.

Directive vs. Nondirective Counseling: with the former, the therapist takes a proactive role: clarifying situations, explaining difficulties, and suggesting next steps. Or again, taking the client through a structured program, complete with an agenda and homework assignments. With the latter, **N-DC**, he or she is a forbearing, supportive companion rather than a guidance-dispensing expert; counselees may choose what to discuss, and are given the chance to come to insights in their own way and at their own speed. See **Rogers, Carl**

Discharge to the Street: see **Patient Dumping**

Disease de Jure: see **Disease du Jour**

Disease du Jour: (du jour = of the day) can refer to a matter of realistic concern: an epidemic in a context where hazards to public health are all too common ("Then suddenly Ebola was the disease du jour"). Alternately, it can be used as a put-down for the latest health scare to be promoted by, for instance, commercial interests, social media, a patient with **Illness Anxiety Disorder**, or whomever. Note: because of a confusion, one often sees "disease *de jure*"; but if that were a thing, it would be something else entirely, "a legally recognized disease." See **Diagnosis of Convenience**

Disease Mongering: as coined by health-science writer Lynn Payer in 1992, the effort to sell treatments, pharmaceutical or otherwise, by expanding or even inventing diagnoses, and by promoting the need for remedies for them. Payer framed the practice as twofold: persuading healthy people that they have a condition they didn't know about; and scaring mildly ill people into believing that their condition is worse than they had assumed. See **Medicalize**

Distance, Moral: the prominent meaning is the literal one: the question of whether geographic remoteness, or some other kind of apartness conceived geographically, should effect moral concern. Peter Singer advances the thesis that the moral claims of distant strangers have equal weight to those of people nearby. "It makes no moral difference whether the person I can help is a neighbor's child ten yards from me or a Bengali whose name I shall never know, ten thousand miles away."[8] For another view, Kwame Appiah provides an elegant disagreement to Singer in *Cosmopolitanism*; he counters that, really, there is great deal of distance between here and Bengali.[9] Then, for another separate-but-equally-important definition of **MD**, there is the matter of relative personal detachment and the view that ethical questions require an objective, big-picture perspective that only separation makes possible.

Divine Command Theory: the view that moral requirements have the power that they do because they come from a sacred source: typically God or the gods. That source has the right to require human obedience, it is believed; and it's a belief that has more plausibility if the deity is conceptualized along the lines of the traditional Creator, Sovereign, and Judge. That said, for some commentators, the first matter to discuss is, "Does God

---

8. Singer, "Famine, Affluence, and Morality," 231–32.
9. Appiah, *Cosmopolitanism*, 156–66.

approve of good deeds because they are good? Or are they good because God approves of them?" This is often referred to as the Euthyphro Dilemma because it was famously posed in Plato's *Euthyphro*. It's an interesting issue. But in actuality, the more pertinent questions are: "Are they good because God approves of them? Or are they good because of some other reason?"

DNR (Do Not Resuscitate): a doctor's order, written in advance. It instructs healthcare workers not to begin using emergency measures, such as **CPR**, when a given patient's heart or breathing have stopped. Also known as "No Code," it communicates the patient's wish to be allowed to die a natural death. However, it should never be taken as implying "withhold all treatment," for other forms of treatment should continue as appropriate, certainly including palliative care. One suggestion is that "AND" for "Allow Natural Death" would be preferable. ▪ **DNAR, Do Not Attempt Resuscitation:** a common alternative to **DNR**; it emphasizes to the laity that there is no guarantee that resuscitation will work and that therefore **CPR** is an attempt, nothing more. ▪ **DNI, Do Not Intubate:** some sources include **intubation** as one of the measures covered by **DNR**, and others call attention to a confusion between the orders. What is clear is that **DNI** rules out intubation and leaves open the use of chest compressions and cardiac drugs. Clearest of all would be "DNR/DNI/AND." See **Code**

Doctor vs. Physician: see **Physician vs. Doctor**

Double Effect: answers the question "How can a deed be good if it has a bad consequence?" There are multiple criteria in the answer, but the linchpin is the following. An action can have more than one consequence. If there's a good result and a bad one, then the action can be counted as good as long as the good result is the one that the agent was hoping for ("intending"). Importantly, this holds true—so the theory goes—even when it is perfectly obvious that the bad outcome will inevitably follow. The classic medical-ethics example is: administering heavy doses of sedatives to a palliative care patient for the purpose of alleviating pain, but with the full awareness that at such levels, the meds will surely hasten the patient's death. This "principle" or "doctrine" of **DE** makes sense when considered within the context of Roman Catholic ethical theory. Otherwise not so much. Statements of it strike some non-Catholics as unconvincing or even weaselly.

Down Syndrome: (AKA trisomy 21) this is a **congenital disorder** in which a baby is born with all or part of an extra chromosome 21. It is the most familiar of the chromosomal anomalies; it produces physical abnormalities; and of the genetic causes of intellectual disabilities in children, it is the most common. However, cognitive impairment varies widely from child to child and usually falls within the mild-to-moderate range, rarely reaching severe.

DPOAH: Durable Power of Attorney for Health Care. A document designating a patient's healthcare advocate or proxy, that is, the person who will oversee patient-care and make the necessary treatment choices if the patient ever loses the ability to do so him- or herself. (A "nondurable" power of attorney would be one that is nullified when the designator becomes incapacitated.)

Drug-Related Problems: see **Medication-Related Problem (MRP)** or **Drug-Related Problem (DRP)**

Dry-Labbing: a research shop term for scientific **fabrication** in which a bogus outcome is recorded without the specified experiment being performed. See **Research Misconduct**

DSM (Diagnostic and Statistical Manual of Mental Disorders): for mental health professionals, when it comes to personality disorder classification, this is "The Bible." Put out by the American Psychiatric Association, it is also consulted by psychologists, marriage and family therapists, and many others, especially in the United States. It provides the standardized means of identifying diagnoses and has important therapeutic uses as well. (A rival work, the International Classification of Diseases, is favored in Europe and elsewhere; and all American healthcare providers are required to use ICD codes when submitting medical claims.) The first iteration, the DSM-1, was published in 1952; the current edition, the DSM-5, appeared in 2013. Each new version has been criticized for tampering with the familiar categories of the one before.

Dual Diagnosis: within substance-abuse treatment programs, this is widely understood to mean a personality disorder and a substance abuse problem. However, in broader behavioral health circles, it can also refer to the co-occurrence of overlapping mental conditions, for instance depression and post-traumatic stress disorder. Another term, "co-occurring disorders," can mean that as well; or it can refer to a mental disorder coupled with an intellectual disability. See **Comorbidity**

Dual Relationship: in the counseling disciplines, the therapeutic role complicated by another significant association. In some settings, small towns for example, complicated relational overlap between counselor and counselee is unavoidable; and in a wide variety of contexts, it poses no ethical problem. But groups such as the American Psychological Association take the potential for moral difficulty seriously and warn against the impairment of a therapist's effectiveness, as well as the risk of exploitation or harm to the client.[10] ("Multiple relationships" means the same thing in this context.)

Due Care vs. Due Diligence: there's no sharp distinction here. The former is more qualitative and attends to the *patient* with the needs; the latter is more quantitative and focuses on the *needs* of the patient. Due Care is wholistic, and asks, "Are we providing this person with appropriate care, overall? Or is he or she just a number?" Due Diligence is detail-oriented, and asks, "Are we following through with all of the particulars? Or have we gotten careless?"

Dueling in the Chart: (AKA Chart Wars) "The practice of one member of the patient's care team criticizing other members of the care team in the patient's record."[11] Usually this involves an ongoing disagreement about treatment alternatives and/or their justifications.

Dumping: see **Patient Dumping**

Durham Rule: widely embraced in the United States for a short time, 1954 to 1972, and then mostly abandoned, this is one of the versions of the **insanity defense**. It holds that if a crime was "the product of" or "caused by" a mental disease or defect, then the perpetrator is not culpable. This bypasses such issues as whether the accused was capable of understanding that the act was illegal or immoral. Among the reasons that many states stopped using **DR** are concerns that it gives too much say-so to rival psychiatrists. "The Durham rule, therefore, perpetuated the dominant role of expert testimony in determining criminal responsibility, a task that many critics felt was best left to a jury."[12] The state that originally established this standard, New Hampshire (1871), is the only state still relying on it.

Duty: what is necessary in order to conform to, and be integrated with, the goodness of life in its ultimate context, more or less in spite of the ethical vagaries and moral contradictions of present experience. See **Authority, Moral**

Duty to Warn / Duty to Protect: taken together, this is the requirement that mental health professionals warn authorities about and/or protect intended victims from an imminent threat posed by a client. It is a duty

---

10. Behnke, "Multiple Relationships and APA's New Ethics Code," 66.

11. McCullough, *Historical Dictionary of Medical Ethics*, 101.

12. "Durham Rule," para. 6.

that supersedes the normal provider-patient confidentiality protections. The particulars vary from state to state, but in general: the obligation applies when a counselee poses an imminent threat to him- or herself; to the therapist; or to a third party—and it requires that notification be made to someone in a position to effect the outcome/avert the danger. Most likely that will be both law enforcement and the endangered third party, if there is one. As of 2020, in thirty-three states this duty was mandatory, either as codified in a statute or as indicated in common law; and in another eleven states, breaching confidentiality to report is permitted but is not mandatory. For the few remaining states, either there is no clear legal guidance on the issue, or there are different requirements for different types of mental health professionals. It was California's watershed court case, *Tarasoff v. Regents of the University of California* (1974 and 1976) that put this issue on the map. Initially the emphasis was on "warn." Since then, however, preference has gone to "protect" via the taking of other reasonable steps so as to not breach confidentiality—if that is possible. Turning to a different context (a medical one), **DTW** can also refer to the obligation to inform a patient about the possible negative consequences of a procedure or course of treatment. See **Informed Consent,** under **Consent,** and **Tarasoff Rule**

Letter E

Echocardiography (EK-ō-KARD-ee-OG-ra-fee): (AKA "Echo") the use of ultrasound to make visible the structures of the heart and any obstructions in specific arteries.

ECMO (Extracorporeal Membrane Oxygenation): providing a kind of artificial life support, an ECMO machine circulates blood out of a patient, adds oxygen and removes carbon dioxide, and then sends it back. This is necessary when a patient's heart and lungs cannot operate at a life-sustaining level. It is also used in **NICUs** for some babies with cardiac disease and during part of a coronary artery bypass graft (CABG).

Edema (οἴδημα = swelling): swelling or puffiness resulting from body fluid building up in the body's tissues.

Effect Modification: see Confounding vs. Effect (Measure) Modification

Efficacy, Effectiveness, and Efficiency: among epidemiologists (speaking of a vaccine, for example), "efficacy" refers to advantageous results in a controlled or ideal setting; "effectiveness" considers results in normal situations (in the field, as it were); and "efficiency" embraces additional real-world considerations such as affordability and cost-effectiveness.

Electroencephalogram (EEG) (ee-LEK-trō-en-SEF-a-lō-gram): appears as multiple squiggly lines on a piece of paper. These lines chart out the electrical activity of the brain (AKA brain waves). Administering an **EEG** involves having many electrodes attached at various points on a patient's scalp. It is the go-to procedure for diagnosing various brain disorders: epilepsy and sleep disorders are good examples; and there are many others. Note: in UK-influenced countries, the pronunciation uses a hard "c," so that it's "en-KEF-a-lo-gram."

Elopement vs. Wandering: when used of hospital patients and nursing home residents, the first means going AWOL. It is a deliberate venturing outside of the facility, possibly in an attempt to "make a break for it." The second typically refers to meanderings that remain within the facility or near its grounds. The wanderer may have dementia, for often there is no thought of making a getaway. Alternatively, **W** can be thought of as the more inclusive category, with **E** defined as a specific, purposeful kind of wandering.

Embolus: unwelcome debris in a blood or lymphatic vessel. An air bubble is a well-known example. All or part of a **thrombus** is more common.

Emergency Detention for Evaluation: there are two forms of **involuntary psychiatric treatment** available in all fifty states and Washington, DC, and this is one of the two. (The other form is **inpatient civil commitment**.) Commonly known as a "psychiatric hold" and in California as "5150," this is the crisis-stage confinement of an individual who meets certain criteria to a treatment facility for psychological assessment. The time frame is always limited and specified, such as for seventy-two hours. See **Lanterman-Petris-Short Act** and ***Parens Patriae* vs. *In Loco Parentis***

Emergency Medical Condition: three sorts of definitions would seem to be possible. One is conscientious and clinician-centered; the second is expeditious and patient-centered; and the third is a confusion of the two. As in: a first approach could emphasize what can reasonably be expected to happen if prompt medical attention is not forthcoming, with negative consequences specified so that a medical professional will know what to look for. A next option could embrace a "prudent layperson standard"—but in a particular and simplified way. If a prudent layperson believes that emergency services are necessary, then that settles it; they are. The American College of Emergency Physicians began promoting such a simple standard in 1994. It is no longer the ACEP's official position, that is true, but its influence lives on. See, for example, "What Constitutes a Medical Emergency?" from the Texas Association of Freestanding Emergency Centers.[1] The third alternative, which we find in many state health and safety codes, takes the medical specifications from the first definition but gives the responsibility for deciding to "a prudent layperson, who possesses an average knowledge of health

---

1. Texas Association of Freestanding Emergency Centers, "What Constitutes a Medical Emergency?"

and medicine."[2] The difficulty is that, except for in the most extreme of cases, assessing the former is beyond the competence of the latter.

Emergency Medical Technician (EMT): referred to as an "ambulance technician" or simply a "tech" in Great Britain, this is a person with special training in, and certification for, the provision of basic emergency care to persons suffering from sudden-onset illness or trauma. Typically the care is provided before and during transportation to a hospital or other medical facility. Terminology, certification, and/or licensure vary from country to country, and in the United States, from state-to-state. For example, the state of Texas has five levels of certification. At the top is Licensed Paramedic; below that are: EMT-Paramedic, Advanced EMT, EMT-Basic, and Emergency Care Attendant (ECA). It is common to regard paramedics as an advanced kind of EMT.

Emergent: needing both quick judgment and immediate action or treatment. Often used as the adjective for "emergency." See also **Emergent Consent,** under **Consent**

Emotivism: the metaethical position which holds that moral statements do not make objective claims but merely express the speaker's approval or disapproval. Thus: "murder is wrong" means "I don't like murder." In the mid-twentieth century, A. J. Ayer was an influential proponent. See **Logical Positivism**

Empiricism (ἐμπειρία = experience): the theory that knowledge arises from experience, especially sense perception, observation, and experimentation. One could say that empirical reasoning is inductive (as that term has traditionally been understood). It proceeds from the particular to the general, arriving at a conclusion after adding up the details. Among philosophers, the empiricists include **Aristotle, David Hume**, and **John Stuart Mill** (all in **Part 2**). See **Deductive vs. Inductive Reasoning; Rationalism;** and **Rationalism vs. Empiricism in Medicine**

EMTALA (Emergency Medical Treatment and Active Labor Act): enacted in 1986 in response to **patient dumping**, this federal legislation guarantees ready access to emergency services for all. It makes it illegal for a healthcare facility to deny medical attention based on an individual's insurance coverage or ability to pay, citizenship, and/or legal status. It applies to women in active labor and to all persons suffering from life-threatening conditions.

---

2. Public Health Department, "Emergency Care," para. 1.

And it remains in force until the emergent condition is stabilized or the patient needs treatment elsewhere.

Enabling Authority Model: among social workers in the UK, this term denotes a less centralized approach to caring for the elderly and those with mental illness, learning difficulty, or physical disability issues. Services need not be authority-run according to this model. The government's role is to stimulate and regulate private-sector organizations instead of, or at least in addition to, directly providing services.

Encephalitis (en-se-fuh-LĪ-tis): an infection and thus inflammation of the brain commonly caused by any one of roughly one hundred viruses.

Encephalopathy (en-SE-fuh-LAH-pa-thee): rather than a single disorder, it is a generalized condition of abnormal brain function or brain structure. The various types can be transient, recurrent, or permanent. The resulting loss of mental ability can be reversible, or static-and-stable—or it can be progressive, with cumulative loss of brain activity over time.

Endemic vs. Epidemic: the medical meanings of these terms—it is commonly observed—were first applied in the corpus associated with **Hippocrates**. There, the initial term (ἐν + δῆμος) refers to forms of sickness found "in" a given set of people, and the latter (ἐπί + δῆμος) to forms which are not as prevalent and which come "upon" a population seasonally, or else in some years but not in others. For a fuller and more complicated picture, consider "2,500-Year Evolution of the Term Epidemic."[3] See **Endemic vs. Sporadic**; **Epidemic vs. Pandemic**; and **Outbreak vs. Cluster**

Endemic vs. Sporadic: epidemiologists describe a disease or health condition as "endemic" to a geographic region or social group when it is perennially occurring or always present—and "sporadic" when it is random, infrequent, and unpredictable. See **Endemic vs. Epidemic**; **Epidemic vs. Pandemic**; and **Outbreak vs. Cluster**

Endoscopy (ἔνδον = within; σκοπέω = look for): using an endoscope, which is an optical, tubular instrument, to examine a hollow organ or body cavity. This can be done through a natural opening or an incision; colonoscopy, esophagogastroduodenoscopy (EGD), and bronchoscopy are examples. Forceps and scissors on the endoscope can be used to remove tissue for **biopsy**.

---

3. Martin and Martin-Granel, "2,500-Year Evolution."

Endotracheal Tube (ETT): a pliable plastic catheter (pipeline) that is run through the mouth and into the trachea (windpipe). A patient's breathing can then be supported, commonly by a ventilator. Endotracheal intubation is considered a "secure airway" in emergencies. E.g., if a patient is vomiting blood, it may be necessary to intubate in order to "secure" the airway, preventing breathing in blood. See **Extubation** and **Intubation**

Ends vs. Means: the contrast between purpose, result, or ideal, on the one hand, and process, tactics, or steps taken to get there, on the other. The claim, "the end justifies the means" is a way of asserting that a good intention or a worthy cause provides sufficient moral cover for blameworthy acts committed to advance it. In quite another direction, **Kant** famously argued that rational human beings must be treated "always as an end and never as a means only."[4]

Ensoulment: (AKA animation) in Western philosophy and theology, the moment at which a human soul (ψυχή) emerges in the developing embryo (ἔμβρυον). It is closely related to the question: When does life and when does personhood begin? Answers vary between and within traditions. And note: in some contexts "soul" refers to an entity separable from the body, but in many contexts something else is meant. The Pythagoreans believed in reincarnation and held that a preexisting soul was infused at conception. This is nothing like what we find in **Aristotle**; his soul is more like "a system of active abilities."[5] In his view, an embryo takes on these capabilities at forty days (for a male) and ninety days (for a female). Down through history, these matters have had a bearing on the question of **abortion**, though not as directly as one might suppose. At the present time, however, the prolife/prochoice divide overshadows and even overdetermines their consideration.

Epidemic vs. Pandemic (ἐπί + δῆμος = upon the people; πάν + δῆμος = all the people): among epidemiologists, an epidemic involves related cases of a disease occurring within a specific geographic area or population group, with a concentration greater than normal. It is often used as a synonym for "outbreak." But in technical discussions, epidemic and outbreak can be differentiated. The latter then refers to a disease-spread that is confined to a specific community or area, with the former referring to a rapid escalation of broader, public-crisis proportions. Then there's our other term, pandemic, which is used for an epidemic of yet far greater, that is to say, international

---

4. Kant, *Foundations*, 47.
5. Lorenz, "Ancient Theories of Soul," para. 29.

or even intercontinental, scope. See **Endemic vs. Epidemic; Endemic vs. Sporadic;** and **Outbreak vs. Cluster**

Epikeia (e-peh-KEE-eh) (ἐπιείκεια = reasonableness): the virtue enabling a person to discern the higher purpose behind a law or the original intent of its lawmakers. This is an idea advanced by **Aristotle** and **Aquinas,** that no law can cover every possible eventuality. Sometimes a norm will need to be reconsidered in view of previously unforeseen circumstances; sometimes, legal technicalities will need to be set aside for the sake of matters of greater importance. At such times, E shows the way. Note: pronunciations vary widely. See **Spirit of the Law and Letter of the Law**

Ethical Dilemma: see **Dilemma, Moral**

Ethical Distinction without a Moral Difference: by means of exceedingly fine line-drawing, describing a single phenomenon as if it were two significantly different phenomena. For example, among bioethicists, it is common to define a mercy killing as "involuntary euthanasia" when it is evident that the person has no wish to die, and "nonvoluntary euthanasia" when the desires of the person cannot be known—as with a person in a **persistent vegetative state** or a very young child. Yet some will ask whether such reasoning succeeds in producing an apparent distinction where there is no moral difference. (The view here is, no, there actually is a moral difference.) See **Vitalism**

Ethical Theories: see **Absolutism, Moral; Emotivism; Fallibilism, Moral; Relativism, Moral; Subjectivism;** and **Universalism, Moral**

Ethics in Patient Referrals Act: (AKA the Stark Law) the 1989 federal law that banned physicians from directing patients to health care facilities in which they or family members have a financial interest. It was named after sponsor Representative Pete Stark, Democrat from California.

Eudaimonism (εύδαιμονία = happiness) (yoo-DĪ-meh-ni-zehm): teleological ethical theories that have happiness (usually in the sense of well being or human flourishing) as their desired end.

Euthanasia (εὐθανασία = good death): (AKA mercy killing) deliberately, painlessly causing or permitting the death of a person in order to end grievous suffering, or the unwelcome advance of an incurable illness, or a dehumanizing condition such as a **persistent vegetative state.** (The humane killing of an animal is also labeled euthanasia.) Many distinctions are typically made. When the euthanizer causes the death, it is considered "active euthanasia," but when death occurs because he or she simply intentionally failed to prevent it, it is called "passive." Moreover, E is termed "voluntary" when it is known that the patient desires it; "involuntary" when it is clear or presumed that he or she does not; and "nonvoluntary" when a patient's wishes are unknown and consent is unobtainable—as with a very young child, or a person lacking decision-making capacity. It is possible to argue that differentiating between involuntary and nonvoluntary E creates an **ethical distinction without a moral difference**. But that is not the position taken here. See **Active and Passive Euthanasia**

Evidence-Based Medicine (EBM): The common assumption is that there's always been a relationship between the pure science of discovery and the applied science of patient care. Yet even through periods of major scientific breakthroughs, that relationship has remained loose and informal, if not even adversarial. So some might say that with **EBM**, pure science and applied science finally got married, as opposed to just flirting. That is, the relationship between research-results and their application to the actual practice of medicine was finally formalized. For prior to a generation ago, treatment decisions were usually based on inherited customs, professional expectations, isolated case studies, and the opinions of medicine's luminaries—as opposed to methodically and critically assessed findings of scientific investigation. Dr. David M. Eddy was a formative influence, credited with coining the phrase "evidence-based" in the 1980s. Other pioneers include Archie Cochrane, David Sackett, and Gordon Guyatt. Initially the changes called for were controversial; there was (and is) concern that remote policymaking and "cookie-cutter" protocols would ensue. Yet health insurance companies were interested and the time was ripe; so in almost no time, **EBM** came to be regarded as "something of a mantra in health care planning."[6] See **Empiricism**; **Rationalism vs. Empiricism in Medicine**; and **Variation in Care / Practice Variability**

Expanded Access Program: See **Compassionate Use / Expanded Access Program**

Extraordinary and Ordinary Medical Treatment: appears to be a straightforward contrast between interventions that "go above and beyond" and those that do not—but this is not the case. In line with centuries-old Roman Catholic usage, "extraordinary" is defined as not reasonably likely to provide a net gain of benefits over burdens—so therefore there is no moral obligation to pursue the treatment further. And "ordinary" means that it

---

6. Pinching, "Evidence-Based Medicine," 91.

is reasonably likely—meaning that, yes, there is a moral obligation. Two points: end-of-life care is usually in view here: any procedures that have a reasonable chance of helping extend life are morally required; but any that have no reasonable chance, are not. And second, impact on the family can be factored in. "If continued clinical management of a gravely ill patient is so psychosocially burdensome on the family . . . that it threatens the unity of the family, discontinuation is also ethically permissible."[7] Such a view has its critics.

Extubation: the removal of a tube, generally the endotracheal tube. ▪ **Terminal Extubation:** taking a patient off of ventilator life-support when he or she is not expected to survive without it. See **Endotracheal Tube (ETT)** and **Intubation**

7. McCullough, *Historical Dictionary of Medical Ethics*, 129–30.

Letter F

Fabrication: deceptive invention in scientific research, this is the first of the three practices specified in the official definition of **research misconduct**, often referred to as "the three cardinal (or deadly) sins." With this one, fiction is passed off as fact, something made up is presented as if it were legit. This can take place at the stage of proposing, conducting, or recording results. When an investigation that never took place is reported as if it did, the fabrication can go by the slang term **dry-labbing**. Compare with **Falsification; Plagiarism; Research Misconduct; Salami Slicing;** and **Text Recycling**

Factitious Disorder: once referred to as **Munchausen Syndrome** and **Munchausen Syndrome by Proxy**. The increasingly preferred terms are "factitious disorder imposed on self" and "factitious disorder imposed on another." Both are forms of mental illness; both center around medical symptoms that are not genuine. With the former, a person injures him- or herself, or plays up existent symptoms, or merely pretends to be sick—but with an obsessive investment in being ill and in playing the sick role. With the latter, a second person, such as a child or a dependent adult, is used (and/or abused) for the same purpose, the identity of the caregiver being irrationally, codependently wrapped up in the "illness" of the **identified patient**. In both scenarios, the underlying motivation is getting psychological needs met via the attention, sympathy, and/or medical care elicited. Note: all of the above is different than **malingering**, where the feigning of the illness is the means to some other end such as escaping from work or service, or securing a warm, dry hospital bed. ("Factitious" needs to be distinguished from "fictitious." Confusion is understandable, for the former often implies the latter. But factitious is from the same Latin root as "factory" and means "produced artificially rather than naturally.")

63

Failed Discharge: in the UK's National Health Service (NHS), this means that a patient (AKA a **bounceback**) has had to be readmitted within forty-eight hours after leaving the hospital because he or she was not medically fit when released. See **Safe Discharge**

Failure to Thrive (FTT): a baby or child not developing physically at the normal rate, as in, his or her weight is significantly lower than what the standard growth charts call for. ▪ **Geriatric Failure to Thrive:** a similar condition in senior adults, it is characterized by decreases in weight, appetite, and activity.

Fallibilism, Moral: ethical theories that agree that, although moral absolutes or universals do exist, or at least may exist, exactly what they require cannot be infallibly ascertained. This is a middle position between **universalism** and **relativism**. Practically speaking, it means that a person can hold meaningful moral convictions without being absolutely certain about them; revisions may always be called for. Compare with **Absolutism, Moral; Emotivism;** and **Subjectivism**

Falsification: a kind of scientific cheating, this is the second of the three practices covered in the official definition of **Research Misconduct**, often referred to as "the three cardinal (or deadly) sins." As distinct from **Fabrication**, here some part of the truth is deliberately fudged, twisted, or omitted—be it in the inflation of experimenters' qualifications, the mischaracterization of the investigation, the misreporting of the data, the misinterpretation of the literature, etc. Compare with **Dry-Labbing; Fabrication; Plagiarism; Research Misconduct; Salami Slicing;** and **Text Recycling**

Falsification, Popper's Principle of: whereas **Falsification** in research is unethical and to be avoided—a different use of the term is important in the philosophy of science. Karl Popper proposed that falsifiability is crucial and something to be pursued; it is the make-or-break characteristic of scientific theories. To be scientific, a hypothesis has to be testable to see if it falls apart under scrutiny; that is, it must be capable of being "falsified," challenged, and possibly found not to be true. A claim which cannot be tested is not a scientific claim, says Popper. See **Demarcation Problem**

Family Finding: a Child Protective Services model developed by Kevin A. Campbell, it majors in locating and involving relatives of children currently living in out-of-home care. The basic ideas are: that such children are in want of the permanency and emotional rootedness which biological families provide; and that bonding opportunities with extended family members will provide what is lacking. However, observers note that since child welfare is influenced by many variables, and since the contribution relatives can make is just one of those, the **FF** model should not be seen as a **panacea**.

Family First Prevention Services Act (2018): a Federal law designed "to help keep children with their families and to avoid entering foster care in the first place by putting funds toward at-home parenting classes, mental health counseling, and substance use disorders treatment."[1] The law provides for a dramatic shift in how Title IV-E resources can be utilized by the various states, territories, and tribal governments. Funds which previously were restricted to foster-care-related programs can now be appropriated for prevention services instead. On the other hand, the act favors family foster homes over larger, group residence alternatives, with a new time limit of two weeks of placement for the latter in many cases. See **Family Preservation vs. Child Placement**

Family Preservation vs. Child Placement: the two reigning paradigms in the field of Child Protective Services. For cases of abuse or neglect, advocates for the first model maintain that keeping the child in the home while bringing in oversight and support services is what is best for him or her. The other side argues that protecting the child is the top priority and that placing an at-risk child in foster care is the better alternative. See **Family First Prevention Services Act (2018)**

Fascinoma: a slang term for a rarely seen and unusually interesting case.

Fatality Rate: see **Case Fatality Rate (CFR) vs. Infection Fatality Rate (IFR)**

Feeder/Grower: an otherwise healthy baby who is in the **NICU** to learn to feed and to gain weight.

Feminist Bioethics: an orientation emphasizing: care-giving and care-receiving; vulnerability and mutuality; and relationships and emotional contexts. **FB** arose out of: (1) a dissatisfaction with the abstractness of male-sponsored ethical theories, which were faulted for their tendency to construe persons as morally isolated and emotionally barren decision-makers; and (2) concerns about disparities in healthcare professions, research, and therapy. Speaking in "a different voice"[2] and entering through "a different

---

1. Getz, "Closer Look at Family First," para. 2.
2. Gilligan, *In a Different Voice*.

door,"[3] feminist theorists approach issues in medical ethics from the standpoint of women's lived experiences. "Sensitivity to the needs of others and the assumption of responsibility for taking care lead women to attend to voices other than their own and to include in their judgement other points of view."[4] See also **Care, Ethics of**

Fideism (in Latin *fides* = faith): the view that religious faith is a sufficient source of knowledge; it does not need the assistance of reason nor is it subject to reason's challenges. Some versions can be quite sophisticated, and include representatives such as Søren Kierkegaard and Ludwig Wittgenstein. See **Athens and Jerusalem**

File-Drawer Problem: a research shopterm minted in 1979 by Robert Rosenthal, professor of psychology at UC Riverside. Since studies with negative or inconclusive findings are unlikely to be published, they tend to end up in the researcher's file drawer, as it were, not making it into the scientific literature. But then that literature is distorted by a publication bias. Donald Kennedy frames the issue thusly. "For years, we've been getting only part of the story on clinical drug trials. The successful ones get published and touted, but others that didn't work out so well may never see the light of day. ... The difficulty is that positive claims are sometimes made against a background of unrevealed negative results."[5] Which is why **F-DP** is frequently mentioned as one of the false-impression-generating factors contributing to the **replication crisis** in psychology and elsewhere.

First, Do No Harm: often expressed in Latin, *primum non nocere* or *primum nil nocere*. Contrary to popular opinion, it is not found in the **Hippocratic Oath**. True, a similar sentiment is found in another document associated with **Hippocrates**; but this particular phrase does not appear in a medical text until 1860, when it was attributed to Thomas Sydenham (1624–89). Generally thought of as representing the principle of **nonmaleficence**, many interpretations of it are possible. One interesting reading is from Classicist N. S. Gill: "The takeaway point of 'first do no harm' is that, in certain cases, it may be better to do nothing rather than intervening and potentially causing more harm than good."[6] See **Benign Neglect** and **Precautionary Principle**

---

3. Noddings, *Caring*, 2.
4. Gilligan, *In a Different Voice*, 16.
5. Kennedy, "Old File-Drawer Problem," paras. 1, 5.
6. Gill, "Is 'First Do No Harm' Part of the Hippocratic Oath?," para. 3.

Five Stages of Grief: as developed by Dr. Elisabeth Kübler-Ross and then adopted by pop psychologists, this is a pattern for how human beings come to terms with significant losses. The stages are: Denial, Anger, Bargaining, Depression, and Acceptance ("DABDA"). More recently, a sixth stage, Finding Meaning, proposed by David Kessler, has been taken up into the official paradigm. Caveats include: (1) Many readers of Kübler-Ross's book got the impression that the stages involved a temporal progression (first Denial, then Anger, etc.); it was only later that she made it clear that linear advance was not what she had in mind. (2) Psychologists point out that, as famous as her theory is, there is no evidence base for its claims. Still, supporters regard it as a helpful tool for alerting grieving individuals (and their therapists) that coping with loss is often a multifaceted process. See **Denial**

Five Wishes, The: created by Aging with Dignity, this is a popular and user-friendly kind of **advance directive**. It provides a way to record end-of-life preferences, including a person's choices about medical treatment. Legally recognized in forty-two states and the District of Columbia, it first appeared in Florida in 1996, and is now available in twenty-seven languages, as well as braille.

Flatten the Curve: a challenge associated with the COVID-19 health crisis. During the early months of 2020, an oft-published chart depicted two options for the number of new cases of the virus: one sloping up quickly and reaching much higher; the other (preferred) rising gradually and extending out farther. The hope was that, with public-health officials taking a sufficiently aggressive stance, and with the general public complying, the number of cases could be kept to a slower rate increase represented by the second, the "flattened," curve. That would allow more time for services to be provided, for capacities of medical facilities to be expanded, and for vaccines and other countermeasures to be developed.

Fomite: an inanimate object capable of passing along infectious agents from one source to another. Common examples include doorknobs, countertops, clothing, and—the chief exemplar—city park drinking fountains.

Forensic Nursing: a healthcare profession for situations in which medicine overlaps with law, crime, and/or trauma. Its twin foci are: providing compassionate medical care to victims of crime, on the one hand, while preserving evidence of the crime for law enforcement, on the other. Typical crimes include sexual assault, domestic violence, elder exploitation, and child abuse and neglect. But forensic nurses can also provide other services: death investigation, legal consulting, court testimony, correctional healthcare, and postdisaster community medical care. **Virginia Lynch** single-handedly invented this new medical subdiscipline in the 1980s. It was officially recognized as a nursing specialty by the American Nurses Association in 1995.

Foundationalism: a formal alternative in bioethics and other disciplines as well in which analyses are presumed to rise up from and to be supported by a "foundation." Serving as reflection's starting point, this substructure provides "a set of incontestable beliefs or unassailable first principles. . . . [which are] universal, objective, and discernable to any rational person."[7] That's the claim. But what we actually find is that these foundations are invariably the grand theological or philosophical thought-systems produced by thinkers like **Aristotle, Aquinas,** and **Kant** (all in **Part 2**). (Rawls's ethics, by virtue of its "original position," would seem to qualify as well.) The advantage in choosing one of these grand schemes is that they offer the orienting comfort of a big picture, a perspective on the nature of Being or of Appearance-and-Things-in-Themselves. The disadvantage is that—far from universal—the first principles of the system chosen will always be in disagreement with those of its rivals. Which brings us to the two alternatives.
■ **Nonfoundationalism:** seeing little need, or having no time, for exploring and resolving big-picture questions, nonfoundationalist bioethicists go right to work on moral problems, in medias res, as it were. **Principlism**, by virtue of the slightness of its nod to a common morality, qualifies.[8] ■ **Antifoundationalism:** takes things further. Not content to merely go without a thought-system, proponents argue that foundations are more trouble than they are worth. Or that they mostly provide places to hide. For postmodernists, for example, metanarratives are no longer credible. Existentialists, to take another example, go further still. They maintain that moral decisions, the authentic ones, have to be made with doubt and courage, in as much as they carry us to the boundary, that is, out to the edge of the sacred canopy that provides human choices with their ethical cover. See **Reflective Equilibrium**

Four Principles, The: see **Principlism**

Full Code: if a patient has a cardiac or respiratory arrest, **FC** authorizes the complete array of life-saving interventions necessary to revive and sustain the person's life. This can mean chest compressions and defibrillation; it can mean intubation and medications.

---

7. Grenz and Franke, *Beyond Foundationalism*, 23.
8. Beauchamp and Childress, *Principles*, 404–11.

Futility: a medical state of affairs in which further treatment will not provide an improvement to the patient in health, well-being, comfort, or prognosis. ▪ **Quantitative Futility:** the unlikelihood that an intervention will have a beneficial *effect*. ▪ **Qualitative Futility:** whatever the effect, the unlikelihood that it will actually make a *beneficial difference* for the patient. In some quarters, "futility" is considered old school and/or misleading. Suggested substitutions include "clinically nonbeneficial" and "not medically indicated." Nevertheless, futility is still widely employed in the literature. This includes *Bioethics*, 4th edition, formerly the *Encyclopedia of Bioethics*.[9] What is needed is terminology which allows for distinctions between prescription ("shouldn't be done") and description ("won't work"); between communitarian judgments, which include codes of ethics and standards of practice, and cosmopolitan claims, which purport to be broader-based; and between value-laden humanities' assessments and aspirationally neutral, "objective" scientific observations.

9. Youngner, "Medical Futility, 4:1951–56.

Letter G

Gamete (γαμετή): a reproductive cell having half the chromosomes that other cells have. A gamete can be either male or female, either a sperm or an egg (ovum), respectively. Fertilization results from the union of two gametes, a sperm with an ovum. This forms a zygote, which has the full set of paired chromosomes that are necessary for the development of a complete organism.

Gangrene (γάγγραινα): the death, or **necrosis**, of soft tissue in a localized part of the body. It is caused by a reduction in the flow of blood.

GCS (Glasgow Coma Scale): a frequently used tool for ranking a patient's level of consciousness, especially after a traumatic brain injury. In measuring how serious the situation is: **GCS** 8 or less indicates severe; **GCS** 9 to 12 indicates moderate; and **CGS** 13 to 15 means mild or minor. The lowest possible score, 3, suggests radical brain damage. At the other end, the highest rating, 15, means the patient is fully awake and responsive.

Genericism vs. Specialization: a topic debated by social workers in the UK with relevance elsewhere. The former represents the view that the heart of all social work is a solid foundation of generalist knowledge and skills which enables practitioners to provide services in a wide range of individual, family, and community situations. The alternative view is that a complex society is best served by professionals with training and experience in delimited and advanced specialties. Critics say this amounts to services in silos; but the specialists seem to have won the day.

Genetic Determinism: see **Determinism**

Gestation: the developmental period from conception to birth; the time during which an embryo/fetus develops into a child in the mother's womb.

Global Burden of Disease: See **Burden of Disease, Global (GBD)**

Golden Rule: see **Beneficence**

Graft-Versus-Host Disease (GVHD): injury to the recipient of a transplant caused by the "graft" (donor bone marrow or stem cells) attacking the "host" (the recipient). The disease is termed "acute" when arising in the first sixty days after the procedure, and "chronic" thereafter. Note the contrast: in **GVHD**, the graft rejects the host; in **transplant rejection**, the host rejects the graft.

Gram-Negative Bacteria: *E. coli* is one example. These microbes are named after Hans Christian Gram, the Danish bacteriologist who invented the Gram stain, a technique for identifying and classifying bacteria by dyeing their cell walls purple. So treated, most bacteria can be categorized as either gram-positive or gram-negative. The former keep their purple color, thus signaling that a certain kind of cell wall is present. With the latter, **G-NB**, either the cells do not have such a wall, or it is too thin to stain. This is of special concern in healthcare settings, and one reason is that **G-NBs** cause a number of infections. Moreover, their outer membrane works to shield them from many antibiotics, penicillin for starters.

Greyhound Therapy: see **Patient Dumping**

Guatemala Syphilis Experiments: egregiously immoral research conducted by the US Public Health Service from 1946 to 1948. The study was undertaken with the cooperation of Guatemalan authorities; and in fact, one claim is that Dr. Juan Funes, a Guatemalan public health official, suggested the idea while he was a visiting researcher in the United States.[1] Be that as it may, more than 5,500 uninformed and unconsenting Guatemalans were drafted into the program. Sex workers played an important role; but prisoners, mental patients, soldiers, orphans, and others were involved as well. Out of this larger group, 1,308 were deliberately infected with sexually transmitted diseases: syphilis, gonorrhea, and chancroid. The main purpose was to learn more about the effectiveness of penicillin and other medications in combatting STDs. Long forgotten about, the experiment was uncovered by medical historian Susan M. Reverby while she was researching the **Tuskegee Syphilis Study**. The federal government acknowledged the program in 2010, and President Obama and other administration officials offered their apologies.

---

1. Spector-Bagdady and Lombardo, "U.S. Public Health Service STD Experiments in Guatemala," para. 5.

Gunner: in med or law school, a slang term for the hypercompetitive student. Some have sharp elbows; others are just overly intense. A fitting motto might be, "There's only room in the spotlight for one."

Letter H

Harley Street: a street in London, long famous for its pricey, private health-care providers, which operate independent of the National Health Service (NHS). The PR hype puts it this way: "Harley Street Medical Area, with over 5,000 practitioners, boasts the largest concentration of medical excellence in one location anywhere in the world."[1]

Harm Reduction Model: in fields such as social work and public health, an approach aimed not at "solving" but at "managing." In view are, one might say, the kind of social problems that are not about to go away—drug abuse, for example. Instead of eradication, with **HRM**, the goal is shifted to limiting negative consequences. Thus: needle exchange programs. Opponents object that they enable and increase drug addiction. But proponents reply that (a) the sharing of needles leads to the transmission of deadly diseases, and that by reducing needle sharing, these programs produce a net reduction in harm; and (b) they are more realistic.

Harvard Criteria for Irreversible Coma: in 1968, an ad hoc committee from Harvard Medical School sought to identify crucial hallmarks for a definition of irreversible coma. "The Harvard criteria included unreceptivity, unresponsiveness, no movements or breathing, no reflexes with further delineation of brainstem reflexes, and a flat electroencephalogram (repeated after 24 h with no change). The apnea test involved disconnection of the ventilator for 3 min. Hypothermia or any other central nervous system depressant had to be excluded."[2] The intent, successfully carried out, was to establish irreversible coma (or what is now called **brain death**), as a new

---

1. HSMA, "About." The quote is the caption content under "2017" in the timeline at the bottom of the page.
2. Wijdicks, "How Harvard Defined Irreversible Coma," para. 1.

73

criterion for death. See **Dead Donor Rule** and **Uniform Determination of Death Act**

Hasselhoff: one of the weirder examples of British **medicalese**, this one applies to cases which are themselves, well, weird, because a patient offers a bizarre explanation for how his or her medical difficulty came about. The inspiration for the term came from television personality David Hasselhoff, who claimed that his injury resulted from hitting his head on a chandelier while shaving.

Hawthorne Effect: the changed behavior of research participants when they are aware they are being observed.

Healthcare Provider Fatigue: see **Provider Fatigue**

Health Care Rationing: the responsibly managed and directed distribution of health care resources, i.e., asking and answering, "Who gets what?" There have always been times when the need for medicinal goods and services has exceeded the supply. At such times, the alternatives can include: an unsystematic distribution (such as "first come, first served"), or an unethical one, or again an irrational one. **HCR**, preferable to all of those, means conserving and allocating resources according to ethical, systematic, and rational criteria. And now that medical science is making available hitherto unimaginable goods and services, with the possibility that some may be maximally expensive but minimally beneficial, oversight of research, development, and dispensation assumes an increased urgency. See **"Who Gets the Kidney?"** and **God Committee, The** (in **Part 2**)

Health Insurance Portability and Accountability Act: see **HIPAA (Health Insurance Portability and Accountability Act)**

Heart Attack: see **Myocardial Infarction**

Heart Failure: see **Congestive Heart Failure (CHF)**

Hemorrhage (αἷμα = blood; ῥηγνύναι = to burst)**:** the flow of blood from a ruptured blood vessel. "The term is usually used for episodes of bleeding that last more than a few minutes, compromise organ or tissue perfusion, or threaten life."[3]

Herd Immunity: the protection against a particular disease conferred on everyone in a group when a large enough segment is resistant to it (either

---

3. Venes, *Tabor's Cyclopedic Medical Dictionary*, 1108.

because of vaccination or because of a previous exposure). When many are immune, it reduces the chances that the disease will reach the few who are not.

Hernia: the pressing-through of an organ or tissue at a weak spot or through an opening. This may be benign or a medical emergency (e.g., if herniated bowels are trapped and cannot return to the abdomen, they may become "strangulated" so that blood flow ceases—which would be a surgical emergency). ▪ **Herniation, Cerebral:** elevated pressure inside the skull, either broad or localized, forcing brain tissue into a proximate area. Swelling or bleeding from a head injury, stroke, or brain tumor are typical causes. It can be fatal if not treated adequately and promptly.

Hickam's Dictum: see **Occam's (or Ockham's) Razor vs. Hickam's Dictum**

HIPAA (Health Insurance Portability and Accountability Act): in the United States, the federal legislation that mandates the securing and shielding of protected health information, notably with regards to keeping patient information confidential. Signed into law by President Bill Clinton in 1996, the act was intended: to insure health insurance continuity for workers whose employment status changes; to reduce the cost of healthcare by bringing consistency to the electronic transmission of data; to reduce waste, fraud, and abuse; and to heighten the availability of long-term care services and insurance. See **Confidentiality vs. Privacy** and **Deidentification**

Hippocratic Oath: a historically important distillation of the ethical precepts of **Hippocrates**, it is not the source of the famous dictum, **First, Do No Harm**. Nor is it likely to have been composed by the man himself, but by his followers. And why? One theory is that at some later point, when the school that Hippocrates had founded was beginning to admit outsiders, a pledge was drawn up to guide their entry and/or ensure their loyalty. On this theory, the oath was not a timeless declaration for all physicians everywhere but a screening tool for a particular set of circumstances. Be that as it may, the oath undoubtedly touches on matters of perennial significance, and contemporary practice is guided by its spirit, if not always by its letter. Promises include: not to facilitate an abortion or suicide; to leave surgery to the surgeons; not to take advantage, especially sexual advantage, of patients; and to keep confidential what ought not be spread abroad. See **Spirit of the Law and Letter of the Law**

HIV: human immunodeficiency virus. See **AIDS (Acquired Immune Deficiency Syndrome)**

Hospitalist: a physician who specializes in the care of patients in a hospital. The term was coined in 1996 by Robert Wachter and Lee Goldman. They introduced it in an article in the *New England Journal of Medicine* to indicate a new paradigm for inpatient medicine.[4]

House Officer: the equivalent of a resident. A physician or surgeon of a hospital (the "house") whose provision of care for patients is being overseen by an attending physician and who is receiving additional training in a particular specialty. See **Resident Physician**

Human Challenge Trial: the planful administration of a disease-causing agent to research subjects in order to study its effects. (It is said they are "challenged" with it.) Oftentimes a portion of the participants are also given a candidate-vaccine while others receive a placebo. HCTs can be controversial, and with any high-risk disease, unless an effective drug is at hand to treat it, they are unethical.

Humors (Χυμοί): in ancient Greek, medieval, and renaissance medicine, the four humors were understood to be the basic fluids of the body: blood (αἷμα), yellow bile (ξανθή χολή), black bile (μέλαινα χολή), and phlegm (φλέγμα). Being too hot, too cold, too wet, or too dry upsets the balance between them, which results in disease. (Note: Χυμοί is a common Greek term often translated as "juices.") See **Galen** and **Hippocrates** (both in **Part 2**).

Huntington's Disease: an inherited condition, it is a neurodegenerative disorder responsible for an intensifying decline in movement, behavioral, and cognitive facility; and it is fatal. The name comes from Dr. George Huntington, an American physician, who published the medical paper describing its symptoms in 1872. More recently, scientists have learned that it is caused by a mutation in one of the genes on chromosome 4, a mutation which can be detected by genetic testing before early symptoms appear.

Hypochondria: see **Illness Anxiety Disorder**

Hypoglycemia (ὑπογλυκαιμία): (AKA low blood sugar) occurs when the level of glucose in a person's blood drops below normal. A problem for many people with diabetes, it can cause unconsciousness and can be fatal.

Hypoxia and Hypoxemia (ὑποξία and ὑποξαιμία): failures of the body to get enough oxygen. The latter is a lower-than-normal level of oxygen in the blood, specifically in the arteries. It can be a sign of a breathing or circulation

---

4. Wachter and Goldman, "Emerging Role of 'Hospitalists,'" 514–17.

problem, though not always. It can also be caused by carbon monoxide poisoning, for one, which does not technically involve a failure of breathing or circulation. Instead, a separate molecule displaces oxygen on hemoglobin. The other term, the first one, is also a lower-than-normal level of oxygen, but this time it is in the body's tissues. However, it can be used to indicate both conditions as well. ▪ **Altitude Hypoxia:** at higher elevations, oxygen molecules are less concentrated, and hypoxia can be the result. See **Pulse Ox**

Letter I

Iatrogenesis (ἰατρός = physician; γένεσις = origin): an injury or illness resulting from medical treatment. ("In the U.S., 0.67% of patients admitted to a hospital die because of health care associated error.")[1]

Identified Patient: a family therapy term referring to an obviously troubled member of a family. Often it is someone the counselor is being asked to "fix," be it a delinquent teen, an alcoholic husband, or whomever. But the savvy counselor will wonder if the **IP** is manifesting the dysfunctional family's repressed tensions and conflicts. If so, it is the entire family that needs fixing, not just the one with the "problem."

IHSS: can refer to "In Home Support Services," a state of California social services program for low-income elderly, blind, or disabled individuals, children included. It is an alternative to out-of-home care options such as nursing homes. **IHSS** can also mean "idiopathic hypertrophic subaortic stenosis," an obstruction of blood flow out of the left ventricle of the heart.

Ileostomy: creating a surgical opening (στόμα = mouth) in the lower abdomen, after which a section of the small intestine (*ileum*) is brought to the abdominal wall to connect to the surgically created opening. Stool comes out and collects in a drainage bag.

Illness Anxiety Disorder: (AKA hypochondriasis and health anxiety) an inordinate concern about one's own health in the form of a belief about having, or a fear about getting, a serious or life-threatening illness. Actual physical symptoms, if present, are blown out of proportion; and medical reassurance has no impact or at least no lasting impact. Behavior can be either avoidant or hypervigilant. Compare with **Factitious Disorder;**

---

1. Venes, *Tabor's Cyclopedic Medical Dictionary*, 1192.

Malingering; Munchausen Syndrome and **Munchausen Syndrome by Proxy;** and **Valetudinarian.**

Illness Perception: the understanding and beliefs that a patient has about his or her illness. It influences a patient's emotional response, coping behavior, treatment adherence, and functional recovery.

Imago Dei: The Latin phrase for "image of God." A foundational Judeo-Christian concept derived from Genesis 1:26, "Then God said, 'Let us make man in our image, in our likeness.'" One prominent application is as follows: Human beings cannot be understood in any this-worldly frame of reference alone, for each one bears an imprint, a stamp of approval, as it were. This means that there is a sacredness to personhood. Regardless of physical attributes, mental abilities, or societal recognition, each person is worthy of respect, and infinitely so.

Immunization: see **Vaccination**

Incidentaloma: a slang term for an abnormality discovered by chance. For instance, a tumor detected in a diagnostic test for some other, unrelated condition would count as an **I**. But a benign condition could count as well.

Index Case vs. Patient Zero: two epidemiological terms, one formal and one informal, both meaning the first person known to have contracted a transmittable disease (during an **outbreak**) or inheritable condition. **IC** can also mean: in an epidemiological study, the first person to be written up; or within the medical literature, the first in a series of cases to be documented. In both of these latter contexts, it is unimportant that the case be the first chronological instance of the disease. **PZ** was coined in the 1980s because of a mix-up. When an early HIV patient was deidentified as Patient O (the letter O standing for Out-of-California), that O came to be misread as the number 0. A reporter went with it and brought "Patient Zero" into vogue. It is now used in descriptions of malware attacks and various other spreadable calamities. See **Deidentification**

Indian Child Welfare Act: a federal law enacted in 1978 to provide protections to Native American children. For children living on a reservation, when it comes to involuntary custody cases, the tribal government has exclusive jurisdiction; plus it has presumptive jurisdiction over Native American children living elsewhere. Rationales include: that the placing of tribal children in nontribal foster care settings jeopardizes the survival of Native American culture; and that what counts as neglect and abuse in the dominant culture may not reflect the unique values of Indian families. One example cited is that of parents leaving a child in the sole custody of a grandmother—which social services then interprets as "neglect," even though in Indian culture the grandmother is as much a member of the family as the mother and father are. Thus the need for tribal autonomy when it comes to the fates of tribal children.

Indicated, Medically: providing a valid reason or meeting the criteria for using a certain test, medication, procedure, or surgery with a particular patient. ▪ **Indications:** "the facts, opinions, and interpretations about the patient's physical and/or psychological condition that provide a reasonable basis for diagnostic and therapeutic activities aiming to realize the over-all goals of medicine: prevention, cure, and care of illness and injury."[2] ▪ **Not Indicated:** not called for but not harmful, either; so, in the case of a test, a physician could possibly order it anyway. Not to be confused with **contraindicated**.

Inductive Reasoning: see **Deductive vs. Inductive Reasoning**

Infarction: the death of an area of tissue or of an organ. It occurs when the flow of blood is impeded, either by a **thrombus** or an **embolus**.

Informed Consent: see **Informed Consent,** under **Consent**

Inoculation: see **Vaccination**

Inpatient Civil Commitment: (AKA involuntary hospitalization) this is one of the two forms of **involuntary psychiatric treatment** utilized in all fifty states and Washington, DC. It involves court-ordered confinement-for-treatment in a psych ward. It is for an individual who, after an initial **emergency detention for evaluation** (the second form), continues to qualify under the state's civil commitment criteria. (Compare with **outpatient civil commitment**, which is not available in all states.) See **Lanterman-Petris-Short Act** and *Parens Patriae* vs. *In Loco Parentis*

Insanity Defense: in court cases, the argument that the defendant should not be held responsible for the crime in question because of a psychiatric disorder. This is classified as an "excuse defense" as opposed to a "justification defense." The types of **IDs** are sometimes listed as: the **M'Naghten Rule;** the **Durham Rule;** and the **American Law Institute Model** (AKA "the Brawner Rule"). But there are also the Irresistible Impulse Defense—and

---

2. Jonsen et al., *Clinical Ethics*, 12.

last and least, the infamous **Twinkie Defense**. Roughly half of the states in the United States use the M'Naghten Rule, and the other half use the more recent ALIM. The exceptions are: New Hampshire, which uses the Durham standard; and Idaho, Kansas, Montana, and Utah, where pleading not guilty by reason of insanity is currently not an option.

Insulin: a hormone produced by the pancreas. Used to treat type 1 and type 2 **diabetes**, it lowers the glucose in a person's blood by promoting its absorption into certain kinds of cells.

Integrative Medicine: with definite similarities to the **Biopsychosocial-Spiritual Model**, this approach makes much of: (a) its proactive stance toward health in opposition to a reactive stance toward disease; (b) its commitment to the doctor-patient partnership; (c) its preference for natural and/or less aggressive or intrusive remedies whenever beneficial; and (d) its willingness to draw selectively from complimentary and alternative therapies such as acupuncture, biofeedback, meditation, and yoga—not instead of but alongside of Western medicine's standard offerings.

Intracerebral Hemorrhage: this is the escape of blood inside the skull (cranium), specifically within the brain tissue proper. Although not especially common, it is a quite serious form of **intracranial hemorrhage**, often resulting from head trauma due to an accident (though also from some strokes). The flow of blood increases pressure inside the brain and, depending on the location, can cause significant brain and nerve damage, and even death.

Intracranial Hemorrhage: this is any kind of bleeding inside the skull (cranium). Place names: if it locates between the tough, outer covering of the brain and the skull, it is an epidural hematoma; slightly further in, it is a subdural hematoma; even closer, it is a subarachnoid hemorrhage. And if it is down in the brain tissue itself, it is an **intracerebral hemorrhage**. The location and the amount of bleeding determine the degree of seriousness. Broadly speaking, epidural hematomas are more deadly than subdural hematomas. See also **Intraventricular Hemorrhage**

Intraventricular Hemorrhage: bleeding located in or around the brain's ventricles, spaces that contain the cerebral spinal fluid, that places damaging pressure on nerve cells. Babies born prematurely and those with a low birthweight are at a higher risk for this problem.

Intubation: (AKA endotracheal intubation and EI) the insertion of a tube through the mouth (or the nose) and into the trachea, or windpipe. It provides an open and secure airway and allows the patient to be hooked up to a ventilator. It also provides a conduit for administering the kinds of drugs that lungs can accommodate. But note: although this is the preferred treatment for the short-term (one to two weeks by some estimates) for longer periods, a tracheostomy (AKA a "**trake**") is less problematic. With-drawal is called **extubation**. See **Endotracheal Tube (ETT)**

In Vitro Fertilization: the process by which an egg is removed from a mother's body, fertilized, and then transferred to the uterus of either the biological or the surrogate mother-to-be. One angle of bioethical signifi-cance is that, in allowing direct assessment of **zygotes** (egg + sperm) so as to select the best one, it is a form of eugenics.

Involuntary Holds: see **Involuntary Psychiatric Treatment** and 1799 **Medical Hold, 5150 Psychiatric Hold, 5250 Psychiatric Hold, 5260 Psy-chiatric Hold, 5270 Psychiatric Hold, 5300 Psychiatric Hold,** and 5585 **Psychiatric Hold** (under **Numbers**)

Involuntary Psychiatric Treatment: the specialized treatment of a person with a behavioral health disorder without his or her consent, as autho-rized by state civil commitment laws. Often this involves confinement in an inpatient mental health facility, though not always. In the United States, forty-seven states and Washington, DC, have three arrangements available: **emergency detention for evaluation; inpatient civil commitment;** and **outpatient civil commitment.** In three states—Connecticut, Maryland, and Massachusetts—the first two options are available but not the outpatient al-ternative. In the UK, it is called "**Sectioning**." See **Lanterman-Petris-Short Act,** *Parens Patriae* vs. *In Loco Parentis,* and 5150 **Psychiatric Hold, 5250 Psychiatric Hold, 5260 Psychiatric Hold, 5270 Psychiatric Hold, 5300 Psychiatric Hold,** and 5585 **Psychiatric Hold** (under **Numbers**)

Irony (εἰρωνεία = pretended ignorance)**:** a term with a wide range of mean-ings. One that has a direct bearing on ethics is Reinhold Niebuhr's famous definition. He introduces it while describing the differences between the pathetic, tragic, and ironic dimensions in historical situations and political experiences. Pathos, he says, relates to sufferings which are relatively mean-ingless; we feel pity, but no guilt can be assigned and there are no life-lessons to be drawn. With tragedy, sufferings are experienced and there is a reason: some measure of guilt has been shouldered because of a superseding duty, or some important value has been sacrificed for the greater good. "The ironic situation is distinguished from the pathetic one by the fact that the person involved in it bears some responsibility for it. It is differentiated from tragedy by the fact that the responsibility is related to an unconscious weakness rather than to a conscious resolution."[3] Niebuhr sees American history as replete with ironic difficulties, for the nation's wisdom, strength, and virtue have been carriers of unconscious vanity and pretense.

Ischemia (ἰσχαιμία = to retard the blood): inadequate flow of blood, and thus of oxygen and nutrients, to tissue, an organ, or a part of the body, usually because of blockage, narrowing, or the constriction of blood vessels.

Is-Ought Problem: see **Hume, David** (in **Part 2**)

I-Thou Encounter: in one of the more consequential distinctions in twentieth-century thought, Martin Buber differentiated between "I-It experiences" and "I-Thou encounters."[4] This distinction profoundly affected philosophy, theology, psychotherapeutic practice, and much else. As Sarah Scott sums it up, "An 'I-It' relation *experiences* a detached thing, fixed in space and time, while a 'I-Thou' relation *participates* in the dynamic, living process of an other."[5] That is, in instances of the former, an other is reduced to an object-as-object; whereas with the latter, one truly and fully encounters a person-as-person. Buber, a Jewish philosopher, was commonly thought of as an existentialist. Like most of the leading existentialists, he rejected the label.

---

3. Niebuhr, *Irony of American History*, viii.

4. Buber, *I and Thou*.

5. Scott, "Martin Buber," para. 24 (emphasis original).

Letter J

Japanese Medical War Crimes: when biowarfare was outlawed by the Geneva Protocol in 1925, the Japanese Imperial Army became intrigued. Apparently the thinking was: this international ban sets biological weapons apart as ultra-dangerous—which means they ought to be explored. Thus it came to pass that from 1937 to 1945, Unit 731 emerged as a massive military program devoted to developing and deploying weapons, bacteriological and chemical. Cruel and ethically heinous experiments on human subjects were standard operating procedure, including vivisections and much else. In time, bubonic plague bombs were "field tested" on Chinese cities. An attack on civilians on the West Coast of the United States was planned for September 22, 1945, but the war ended before the go-date arrived. Some of the program's principals were taken into custody by the Soviet Union. In 1949, twelve were tried as war criminals in the Khabarovsk War Crimes Trials. In the West, however, it was a different story. Unlike the **Nazi medical war crimes**, the Japanese operation was entirely hushed up. The Soviet trials? They were dismissed as disinformation. And here's one reason why: the man in charge of Unit 731 was microbiologist Lieutenant-General Shirō Ishii. After his arrest by the United States, he was granted immunity in exchange for fully cooperating, that is, for furnishing information for America's own biological warfare program.

Jessica's Law: a common way of referring to any legislation that seeks to protect children from sex offenders that follows the model of Florida's Jessica Lunsford Act (2005). That law was named after a nine-year-old girl who was raped and murdered by a convicted sex offender, John Couey. Though he was under legal obligation to report his location, Couey had not done so. A jury found him guilty of murder, and he was sentenced to death plus three consecutive life sentences; however, he died before his death sentence could be carried out. The typical **JL** increases the length of prison time for

84

convicted sex offenders, and for those released, requires a GPS ankle device. See **Laws Named after Victims**

Joint Commission, The: formerly the Joint Commission on Accreditation of Healthcare Organizations, this is the outfit that accredits healthcare institutions in the United States. Independent and not-for-profit, it maintains an evaluation process designed to help hospitals, labs, and other healthcare organizations and programs focus on, measure, evaluate, and improve their services. Most states rely on it, but not all. Some states have their own in-house assessment procedures, and there are rival organizations which have also been granted "deeming authority" (authorization to accredit) by the Centers for Medicare and Medicaid Services (CMS).

Jonathan's Law: a New York law (2007) that ensures that parents and guardians have access to information about the health and/or safety of a child of theirs in a state facility. Specifically, when there's been an accident or injury, parents are to be notified within twenty-four hours, provided a copy of the incident write-up, and offered an opportunity to meet with an official representative. Agencies covered are: the Office for People with Developmental Disabilities; the Office of Mental Health; and the Office of Alcoholism and Substance Abuse Services. The impetus for this law came from the death of thirteen-year-old Jonathan Carey. Jonathan had autism; he was badly mistreated at a state-run, live-in school; and his parents were denied access to the relevant records. Moved to a different school, he ended up being killed by an attendant, suffocated while restrained in the back of a transport van. See **Laws Named after Victims**

July Effect: in the United States, med school graduates begin their teaching-hospital residencies in July. Conventional wisdom holds that these trainees make the most mistakes when their learning curve is the steepest, mid-summer. However, studies have not consistently borne this out, and the theory has been called an urban legend. In the UK, a similar situation goes by a grislier name, "the killing season." See **Black Wednesday**

Justice: traditionally arrayed under four subheads: (a) Distributive Justice, which portions out society's sources of human fulfillment and their attendant costs; (b) Retributive Justice, which addresses crimes and their morally appropriate punishments; (c) Corrective Justice, which addresses civil damages and their fair recompense; and (d) Commutative Justice, which covers interactions between people, such as those involving wages and prices. Famously **J** is also one of the four major ethical principles in **principlism**, albeit the least-well defined of the lot. Beauchamp and Childress's handling begins, "Common to all theories of justice is a minimal requirement traditionally attributed to Aristotle: 'Equals must be treated equally, and unequals must be treated unequally.'" Good enough. But then six general theories of distributive justice follow; and even though "all six are usually considered competitive,"[1] the reader is never offered a preference or an essence or a synthesis—nor again an explanation for why not. On such a sandy foundation, applications are made. Some would argue that what is missing is a broader context, whether historical, political, philosophical, or theological. One discussion worth considering is Alasdair MacIntyre's.[2] Another is Reinhold Niebuhr's classic pairing of justice with democracy which finds, "Man's capacity for justice makes democracy possible, but man's inclination to injustice makes democracy necessary."[3]

Justification, Moral: as understood here, the process by which morality turns into ethics. This happens whenever a person, called upon to provide warrant for a moral claim, makes a fully engaged effort "to establish one's case by presenting sufficient reasons for it."[4]

Justification of Acts vs. Justification of Policies: a surprising but, upon reflection, worth-pondering distinction. It is based on the recognitions that: (a) there are few norms that do not admit of exceptions; and (b) conduct that is not problematic in particular situations can nevertheless sometimes end up in tension with legal or institutional strictures set in place because of "public considerations and consequences external to the private relationship between a physician and a patient." Which means, "Public rules or laws sometimes justifiably prohibit conduct that is [nevertheless] morally justified in individual cases."[5] Beauchamp and Childress cite physician-assisted hastening of death as their example. See **Legalism, Physician-Assisted Suicide,** and **Spirit of the Law and Letter of the Law**

Just-So Story: anthropologists, sociobiologists, and others use this term critically. For in a just-so story, a narrative connects a result to a cause, providing a tidy explanation for some much more complex natural or cultural phenomenon. The narrative is typically too neat, too simple, and impossible to trace down. And oftentimes its intended effect is to stave off further reflection if not to conceal an indefensible arrangement of some kind. ("In

---

1. Beauchamp and Childress, *Principles*, 250, 253.
2. MacIntyre, *Whose Justice?*
3. Niebuhr, *Children of Light*, xiii.
4. Beauchamp and Childress, *Principles*, 390.
5. Beauchamp and Childress, *Principles*, 406–7.

fact, the executives' just-so story of the 1990s nursing shortage masked the active role that hospital management played in creating a supply-demand imbalance and the strong likelihood that ratios would—as they ultimately did—ameliorate the problem.")[6]

Just War Theory: historians now recognize similar norms from earlier times and geographically diverse locales: ancient Egypt, China, and India. That said, **JWT** has long been treated as a Western tradition, promoted by **Aristotle**, taken up by **Augustine**, and then carried forward by medieval scholarship. And no, the concept had no connection with "holy war." Instead it was mostly understood as the least-bad option for channeling the evils of combat. Its classic formulation was issued by **Aquinas**. He held that to be "just" a war must be waged: (a) by a legitimate authority; (b) for a just cause; and (c) for the purpose of installing good or displacing evil.[7] To those three, tradition has appended a fourth: (d) using proper means. Other criteria can be and have been added in as well. Pacifists, however, object to all this, calling it a moral failure. One point they make is that, whatever usefulness the criteria may once have had has been completely done away with by the hyper-destructive and increasingly impersonal character of modern weaponry. Certain hardened skeptics, on the other hand, argue that bringing a values overlay to combat situations is counterproductive and unnecessary—or naïve and unworkable. Some Protestant ethicists, without agreeing with the skeptics or the pacifists, would counter that **JWT** is an **Athens and Jerusalem** compromise—and therefore not binding.

---

6. Stryker and González, *Up, Down, and Sideways*, 213.

7. Aquinas, *Summa Theologiæ* 35, 2a2æ. 40, I.

Letter K

Kari's Law: in 2013, Kari Hunt Dunn was murdered by her estranged husband in a Marshall, Texas, motel room. Her nine-year-old daughter kept trying to call for help by dialing 911, but the phone system required that an initial "9" be dialed in order to access an outside line. This measure mandates that motel- and office-style, multiline telephones be set up for direct 911 calls. Passed in Texas in 2015, a federal version was adopted in 2018. See **Laws Named after Victims**

Karly's Law: this Oregon law requires that when suspicious physical injuries are observed during a child abuse investigation, photographs must be taken immediately and a medical examination must be conducted within forty-eight hours. **KL** was named in honor of Karly Sheehan, who died in 2005 as a result of horrific child abuse and neglect. Authorities had investigated her situation on more than one occasion, called in because Karly would say, "My dad hits me." Their conclusion was that her injuries were not caused by child abuse. The end came when she was beaten to death by her mother's boyfriend. He had been the abuser all along but investigators hadn't seen it. See **Laws Named after Victims**

Kendra's Law: the New York state law named after Kendra Webdale. She was killed in 1999, pushed by Andrew Goldstein onto the subway tracks in front of an oncoming train. Goldstein had a diagnosis of schizophrenia but was off meds at the time. The law, billed primarily as a public safety measure, was designed for individuals with a history of rehospitalization, noncompliance with outpatient treatment regimens, and/or violence so as to pose a danger to self or others. It provides for the "assisted outpatient treatment" of a qualifying individual for up to twelve months, renewable. See **Involuntary Psychiatric Treatment; Laura's Law; Laws Named after Victims;** and **Outpatient Civil Commitment**

Ketoacidosis, Diabetic Ketoacidosis (DKA): a potential complication of **diabetes mellitus,** which is life-threatening without prompt treatment. Precipitating factors include starvation, prolonged alcohol abuse, or infection. When a body isn't producing enough **insulin** to use glucose, its normal source of energy, it begins to burn fat instead. Burning fat produces ketones which, when they build up in the blood, make it more acidic. Further, without insulin to allow glucose to enter the cells, blood levels of glucose rise to high levels, overpowering the kidneys' ability to resorb glucose. More water is pulled into the urine, which left unchecked creates dehydration alongside the acidosis. Left untreated, **DKA** can lead to a diabetic coma or death. **Ketosis:** a mild form of **K** which is sometimes used as a controversial weight-loss technique to burn fat.

Kristen's Law: in cases involving a fatal overdose, this Rhode Island ordinance targets the drug trafficker. It is named after Kristen Coutu, the twenty-nine-year-old who unintentionally took a lethal dose of fentanyl, thinking it was heroin. Passed in 2018, the law holds those who unlawfully sell illicit substances accountable for the deaths-by-overdose that result. The sentence can be up to life behind bars. See **Laws Named after Victims**

Letter L

Lanterman-Petris-Short Act: a landmark piece of legislation for the state of California. When it was passed in 1967, it set a new standard for behavioral health confinement policies throughout the United States. In a nutshell, the law humanizes state procedures for involuntary civil commitment and sets up protections against the inappropriate (unlimited or not subject to review, for example) confinement of persons with mental illnesses, developmental disabilities, and others. See **Involuntary Psychiatric Treatment** and **5150 Psychiatric Hold, 5250 Psychiatric Hold, 5260 Psychiatric Hold, 5270 Psychiatric Hold, 5300 Psychiatric Hold,** and **5585 Psychiatric Hold**

Laura's Law: specific to California and only for those counties that choose to opt-in, the measure authorizes the use of the civil courts to mandate outpatient mental health treatment services for individuals who meet the criteria. The qualifying individual would be one who: (a) has a mental illness severe and persistent enough that he or she needs treatment; (b) poses a danger to self or others; and (c) is either unwilling or unable to voluntarily accept the treatment needed. The law was named after Laura Wilcox, a nineteen-year-old who was shot and killed by an assailant with a severe but untreated mental illness. See **Kendra's Law; Laws Named after Victims;** and **Outpatient Civil Commitment**

Laws Named after Victims: there are many of these measures and generally they were enacted in response to a tragic death. Typically a horrific crime was committed, often involving a child; and the incident captured the public's imagination. Critics insist that such laws tend to be the result of a misdirected or "knee-jerk" policy-making process. Some ordinances are of parochial or temporary interest. Others have a significance that is broad, or lasting, or both. See the following: **Buster's Law; Casey's Law; Caylee's Law; Chelsea's Law; Clery Act; Jessica's Law; Jonathan's Law; Kari's Law;**

Karly's Law; Kendra's Law; Kristen's Law; Laura's Law; Leandra's Law; Marsy's Law; Megan's Law; Sami's Law; and Simon's Law. See also **Amber Alert** and **Code Adam**

Lazarus Phenomenon vs. Lazarus Sign: not to be confused! The first can be explained colloquially as a patient coming back from the dead. Medically it is the return of spontaneous circulation (**ROSC**) at some nonimmediate time (in most cases ten minutes or less) after cardiopulmonary resuscitation (**CPR**) has been stopped and the patient has been pronounced dead. But the same term has been applied to other scenarios, for example, a renal-graft patient surviving against steep odds. What the second term (AKA "Lazarus Reflex") refers to is something entirely different. "Dramatic movements of the arms across the torso, which are occasionally observed in brain-dead patients after they have been disconnected from mechanical life support. These movements may be misinterpreted as signs of life, when in fact they are merely involuntary reflexes."[1] Each of these phrases takes its name from Lazarus, the man who, although dead for four days and buried in a tomb, was raised to life by Jesus (John 11:43–44).

Leandra's Law: (AKA New York's Child Passenger Protection Act) makes it a felony to drive with someone fifteen years old or younger in the car if intoxicated (under the influence of alcohol, or drugs, or both). The measure was named in honor of Leandra Rosado, an eleven-year-old who was killed when the car driven by the mother of one of her friends went out of control and flipped over on the highway. Passed in 2009, and considered one of the strictest DWI (driving while intoxicated) laws in the country, **LL** also requires anyone convicted of a DWI offense to use an ignition interlock devise, which is an automobile breathalyzer, in his or her vehicle. See **Laws Named after Victims**

Legalism: in the West, this term has been understood in light of its usage in Christian ethics. There it means an excessive or misguided reliance on the Law, the stipulations of the Old Covenant. This is viewed as the futile attempt to find favor with God, not through faith but "through works," that is, through moral endeavor. And that discussion nearly always raises the question of **antinomianism**. That said, **L** is not solely a Christian concept. In general usage, it can refer to a number of misguided, inauthentic, or irresponsible behaviors: the effort to set up rules for every occasion; or the mindless adherence to ethical formulae with little concern for the persons involved or for circumstantial exceptions; or again, the kind of dodge by

---

1. Venes, *Tabor's Cyclopedic Medical Dictionary*, 1370.

which ethical questions are "de-moralized" and treated as matters for legal/judicial determination alone. By contrast, **L** has a place in Chinese history which is entirely different. For there it refers to an administrative philosophy for organizing the populace, one that some scholars find to be comparable to the teachings of Machiavelli. See **Situation Ethics** and **Spirit of the Law and Letter of the Law**

Libellus de dentibus: see **Eustachi, Bartolomeo** (in **Part 2**)

Locard's Exchange Principle: in forensic science, this is the axiom that "every contact leaves a trace," that is, that criminals and crime scenes leave indicators on each other. Regarded as the father of modern forensic science, Frenchman Edmond Locard (1877–1966) created the first police laboratory and advanced the use of fingerprints in identifying criminals. His principle prompts the call for the disciplined gathering of crime scene evidence for scientific investigation.

Logical Positivism: as popularized by English philosopher A. J. Ayer (1910–89), this science-obsessed view holds that only statements which can be empirically verified are meaningful. Since metaphysical, religious, and ethical claims cannot be borne out scientifically, they are nonsignificant wastes of time. One problem with Ayer's verification principle, however, something pointed out by Alvin Plantinga and others, is that it itself cannot be empirically verified. See **Demarcation Problem** and **Falsification, Popper's Principle of**

LOS: length of stay.

LOT (Limitation of Treatment): restricting the types of medical interventions to be used in a patient's care. Often considered are: not resuscitating (**DNR**), not intubating (**DNI**), and not escalating the care the patient. Questions about **withholding and withdrawing life-prolonging treatment** are also in view.

Love: the ultimate ethical standard in Christian ethics and in some other traditions as well. In a Christian perspective, the fact that God *is* love and also *commands* love means that it arises from a nature-and-obligation (**Is-Ought Problem**) dynamic, lifted by Jesus into a universal inclusiveness. God's love shows itself as both redemptive action to free his people from bondage and to accept the wayward wanderer who has returned, but also as a creative goodness poured out on all, the just and the unjust alike. In correspondence to such divine goodness is a love-ethic expressed as a polarity between targeted benevolence for insiders and for redeemable sinners (potential insiders), on the one hand, and an indiscriminate, proactive goodness-for-all, including those who "insult you, persecute you and say all kinds of evil against you" (Matt 5:11), on the other. Love is therefore the moral absolute; it both "hopes all things" but also "endures all things" (1 Cor 13:7)—even those things that are apparently beyond hope. Compare with **Agape** and see **Situation Ethics**

LTAC (Long-Term Acute Care) Hospital: a transitional facility for patients needing an extended recovery period. Many of these patients have been treated in and released from an ICU; they continue to need care, but not at that intensive level. Whereas traditional hospitals offer a wide array of specialized services, such as ERs and maternity care, LTAC hospitals limit themselves to treating a reduced number of conditions. Their patients typically have serious, medically complicated health challenges; and they require treatment that is more technical than a **SNF** can provide. Stays average twenty to thirty days.

Letter M

MacCAT-T (MacArthur Competence Assessment Tool for Treatment): the most widely used of the standardized assessment approaches. Lengthy and comprehensive, it is a structured interview which measures the four legally relevant components of **decision-making capacity**: understanding, appreciation, reasoning, and the ability to communicate a choice. It considers a patient's healthcare decision-making "competence," not in the abstract as many other tools do, but with reference to the patient's actual decisional context. Instruments like this can be useful when capacity is difficult to determine, and they are definitely valuable when a case ends up in court. Yet note: use of wording here could lead to some confusion because "competence" is technically a legal determination to be made at the court-level, whereas "capacity" is a functional assessment to be made by a physician for treatment purposes.

Macroallocation vs. Microallocation: the former is system-wide choice-making which asks which goods and services do we want available in our healthcare institution, agency, or national service? The latter, by contrast, is individualized; it asks either "Which of the available treatments will Patient X receive?" or "Which of these candidate-patients will receive Treatment Y?" When supply of resources is outstripped by potential demand and rationing is in view, the contrast is sometimes put as "rationing at the bedside vs. in the boardroom (or at the policy level)," or, again, as "patient vs. population." See **Health Care Rationing**

Magnetic Resonance Imaging: see **MRI (Magnetic Resonance Imaging)**

MAID (Medical Assistance in Dying—Canada): the law, passed in 2016, that allows a doctor or a nurse practitioner (where the province permits) to facilitate a person's death. (Canada is the first country to open this role to nurse practitioners.) The national health care system covers the costs. The government website explains:

> There are 2 types of medical assistance in dying available to Canadians. They each must include a physician or nurse practitioner who: [1] directly administers a substance that causes death, such as an injection of a drug—this is becoming known as clinician-administered medical assistance in dying; it was previously known as voluntary euthanasia—or [2] provides or prescribes a drug that the eligible person takes themselves, in order to bring about their own death—this is becoming known as self-administered medical assistance in dying; it was previously known as medically assisted suicide or assisted suicide.[1]

See **Euthanasia** and **Physician-Assisted Suicide**

Malingering: pretending to be sick but not, as with **factitious disorder,** driven by psychological needs—that is, not because of mental illness. Instead, **M** is a kind of con job, if you will. The objective can be as simple as being the center of attention. But other objectives can include: acquiring prescription pain meds, receiving a financial payment (as in insurance fraud), avoiding work or military service, or forestalling jailtime. Behaviors can be the same as those associated with factitious disorder. A critical difference is that benefits are sought, or obligations are avoided, deliberately and not because of an irrational compulsion.

Malpractice, Medical: negligence, either by commission or omission, by a health care provider: (a) resulting in the injury or death of a patient, because (b) the care provided failed to meet the medical community's accepted standard of practice. See **Negligence, Medical** and **Omission vs. Commission, Sins of**

Mandatory Reporting: mandated reporters are professionals (and others such as child care workers) who have regular contact with members of vulnerable populations: children, certainly, but also dependent adults and the elderly. They are required by law to notify a specified state or local agency of suspected instances of abuse, neglect, domestic violence, or financial exploitation. Laws vary from state to state. ▪ **Mandatory Reporting of Infectious Diseases by Clinicians:** the legal requirement that a condition with serious public health consequences be reported by a healthcare professional or a

---

1. Government of Canada, "Medical Assistance in Dying," lines 45–53. (The quote has been reformatted for dictionary consistency.)

laboratory at the time it is diagnosed. Each state has its own protocols and maintains its own **reportable diseases** list. This mandate is longstanding. Michigan was the first state to require that health authorities be notified of specific infectious conditions—and that was in 1883. By 1901, all states had followed suit. See **Tarasoff Rule**

Marsy's Law: officially the California Victims' Bill of Rights Act of 2008, approved by California voters as Proposition 9, this law confers new rights, seventeen in all, on victims of crime. Included are restitution for the crime, notification of court proceedings, and protection from the accused, which includes notification of his or her release from prison—or escape. For the accused, it makes parole less likely. Intended to be a sweeping and comprehensive bill of rights for victims and their families, **ML** served as a model for many other state legislatures which sought to pass similar legislation. It was named after Marsalee ("Marsy") Nicholas, a senior at UC Santa Barbara at the time she was murdered by an ex-boyfriend in 1983. The ex was arrested but then a week after the crime Marsy's brother and her mother, having no idea that he was out on bail, encountered him at a local grocery store. The brother, Henry Nicholas, became a driving force in the effort to pass **ML** nationwide. See **Laws Named after Victims**

Mastectomy: the removal of a breast, commonly as a treatment for or a prophylaxis against breast cancer. There are different types: (a) Simple or Total, removing the entire breast; (b) Modified Radical, removing both the breast and the lymph nodes; (c) Radical, removal of the breast, more of the lymph nodes, and the muscles beneath the breast; (d) Partial, removal of the cancerous part of the breast tissue and some of the normal tissue surrounding it (a Lumpectomy is a kind of partial mastectomy, but with less tissue being removed, usually only the mass); and (e) Subcutaneous, all of the breast tissue is removed, but the nipple is spared.

MCA (Middle Cerebral Artery) Stroke: A particular kind of **stroke**. The middle cerebral artery is the largest of the brain arteries and the most common location of an ischemic stroke. See **Ischemia**

Medicalese: the insider lingo used by healthcare professionals. It is an amalgam of technical medical terminology, informal expressions, sets of initials, and nicknames, which are often shortened formations. For example, "**Onk**" and "**Bronk**" (pronounced as such but written as "Onc" and "Bronch") mean "the oncology department," and "perform a bronchoscopy," respectively.

Medicalize (or **Medicalizing**): to reframe life's ordinary events and experiences as medical problems so as to treat them, perhaps pharmaceutically. For some, this is an ominous and insidious process designed to expand medicine's social control. For others, it is a product of a shallow society in which everything must have a fix, preferably a quick one, and nothing can be left for individuals to work out for themselves. See **Disease Mongering**

Medically Fragile Home: not what it sounds like. It is a living facility optimally set up for a medically fragile child or adult—that is, one with "a chronic physical condition which results in a prolonged dependency on medical care for which daily skilled nursing intervention is medically necessary."[2] Examples include foster care homes and specialized group residences.

Medically Unexplained Symptoms (MUS): the official diagnosis for a continuing physical problem which, after sufficient medical examination, cannot be matched up with any known medical condition.

Medical Surveillance Monthly Report: see **Burden of Disease, Global (GBD)**

Medication-Related Problem (MRP) or **Drug-Related Problem (DRP):** anything associated with prescription meds, or the lack thereof, that negatively impacts a patient's health and/or treatment. It can be a prescription error, a side effect, or a harmful drug-drug interaction. It can be a right drug/wrong dosage mix-up. Untreated conditions count as **MRPs** as well. See **Deprescribing; Overmedication vs. Overprescription; Polypharmacy;** and **Prescribing Cascade**

Medi-Medi (Dual Eligibility): covered by both (a) Medicare, the United States' national health insurance program for seniors sixty-five years and older and certain others; and (b) Medicaid, the state and federal health insurance program for limited-income individuals, and, again, certain others.

Megan's Law: this New Jersey ordinance requires authorities to make information about registered sex offenders available to the public. The impetus was the 1994 rape and murder of Megan Kanka, a seven-year-old, by a sex offender who lived across the street. **ML** provided a template for subsequent legislation in other states and at the federal level. See **Laws Named after Victims**

2. NMDOH, "MFW Families," para 1.

Meningitis: meningitis is an inflammation usually due to, and colloquially referring to, infection of the protective membranes of the brain or spinal cord (μῆνιγξ, "meninges"). Most cases in the United States are caused by a viral infection, but bacterial and fungal infections can be sources as well. There are different kinds of M. In some instances, an infected person can recover without treatment in just a few weeks. However, M can also be life-threatening. ▪ **Bacterial Meningitis:** a very serious illness that must be treated with antibiotics immediately. In the United States in earlier days, infants and children were affected more than adults; because of vaccines, this changed in the 1990s. Now it is primarily a disease affecting adults. ▪ **Meningoencephalitis:** inflammation, usually caused by infection, of the brain and the surrounding tissues.

Mentation: the activity of reasoning and thinking. (Examples: "On examination, the patient had slowed mentation" and "The patient has sufficient mentation to make a decision").

Metabolic Disturbance/Disorder: abnormal chemical reactions disrupting the body's normal metabolic (μεταβολή = change) processes by which food is converted to energy, etc.

Metastasis (μετάστασις): (me-TAS-ta-sis) the spread of malignant cancer cells from their primary site to other parts of the body. ▪ **Metastatic Cancer:** (AKA a metastatic tumor) a cancer that has traveled from its primary site to other, relatively distant parts of the body, moving through the bloodstream or the lymph system to form tumors in new areas.

Micro/Mezzo/Macro: a tripartite schema common in American social work circles. Applied to spheres of practice, micro refers to traditional services offered to individuals and families, mezzo to social work in neighborhoods, parishes, organizations, and in city or county programs, and macro to activist and policy endeavors in state, national, and international arenas, and also to research conducted in universities and thinktanks. These levels are not mutually exclusive; the same social worker can provide services in more than one zone. In addition, the trichotomy can have many other applications as well, as a way of categorizing therapeutic modalities (theories of counseling), for example.

MICU: Medical Intensive Care Unit.

Middle Axioms Theory: a major Christian ethics concept, associated with John Bennett but best described by his colleague, Paul Tillich:

The difficulties, stressed by Continental theology, in applying the absolute principles of the Christian message to concrete political situations, were met by American theological ethics in a rather ingenious way. One found that between the absolute principle of love and the ever-changing concrete situation, middle axioms exist which mediate between the two. Such principles are democracy, the dignity of every man, equality before the law, etc. They are not unchangeable in the sense in which the ultimate principle is, but they mediate between it and the actual situation. This idea prevents the identification of the Christian message with a special political program. It makes it, on the other hand, possible for Christianity not to remain aloof from the actual problems of man's historical existence. In this way American theology has created a new approach to Christian social ethics, and has made the Christian message relevant not only to the relation of God and the individual person, but also to the relation of God and the world.[3]

Minimally Conscious State (MCS): severely diminished personal awareness but with an observable degree of being tuned in—or of being able to tune in—to self and/or surroundings. The ability to interact at the "Can you squeeze my hand?" level would be one example. So, there is sentience, but only limited or inconsistent presence and/or responsiveness. (Compare with the less-conscious **persistent vegetative state**.) A caveat is in order, however. Continuing progress in brain science may supersede all of the above. "Functional neuroimaging and electrophysiological studies suggest that some degree of consciousness or awareness that has not been or could not be determined by behavioral evaluations alone may be present in some of these patients who, hence, have covert consciousness."[4] Which means our understanding of disorders of consciousness in general, and the **PVS** and **MCS** categories in particular, may need to be revised.

MMSE (Mini-Mental Status Examination): a test of cognitive function. It wasn't designed to gauge decisional capacity, but it is a familiar tool and it is often used in that way.

M'Naghten Rule: the first of the insanity-defense standards, it emerged in Victorian England as a result of the M'Naghten court case of 1843. Insanity is a matter of suffering from "a disease of the mind" or "a defect of reason" so that the acts committed were not understood by the defendant to be either:

3. Tillich, *Theology of Culture*, 167.
4. Kondziella and Koehler, "Disorders of Consciousness," para. 1.

(a) illegal; or (b) wrong. Still widely used around the world, roughly half of the states of the United States adhere to it, though different jurisdictions interpret it differently. See **American Law Institute Model; Durham Rule; and Insanity Defense**

MODS: there are two different terms referenced by this one acronym; one is a score and the other is a syndrome. ▪ **Multiple (Modified) Organ Dysfunction Score** is one of the level-of-illness scoring systems, along with APACHE II, SAPS II, and SOFA. APACHE II and SAPS II are based on routinely measured physiologic variables, while SOFA and MODS are organ-failure-based. By one means or the other, the point is to measure risk of mortality in the ICU and hospital. Moreover a score can be used for the allocation of care. ▪ **Multiple Organ Dysfunction Syndrome**: (AKA Multiple Organ Failure [MOF], Total Organ Failure [TOF], and Multisystem Organ Failure [MSOF]) indicates the shutdown of two or more organ systems—such as the cardiovascular and renal systems—of an acutely ill patient. Often this will be occasioned by critical injury, severe illnesses, or sepsis.

MOLST (Medical Orders for Life-Sustaining Treatment): the equivalent of a **POLST** form. It was created in New York state and is also used in Connecticut, Maryland, Massachusetts, Ohio, and Rhode Island.

Moral Agency vs. Moral Patiency: moral agents are those who can make moral judgments and take moral actions for themselves. Moral patients are the foci of those judgments and the recipients of those actions. "Moral agency is the capacity to do right or wrong, whereas moral patiency is the capacity to be a target of right or wrong."[5]

Moral Complicity: see **Complicity, Moral**

Moral Dilemma: see **Dilemma, Moral**

Moral Distinction without a Moral Difference: by means of exceedingly fine line-drawing, describing a single phenomenon as if it were two significantly different phenomena. Among bioethicists, when the practice of palliative/terminal sedation and **physician aid in dying** are discussed, some will ask whether there's a real ethical dissimilarity between the practice of the one and the practice of the other—or simply a perspectival or linguistic one.

Moral Distress vs. Moral Injury: the first refers to the subjective response to a conflict between what should be done and what can be done in a

---

5. Gray and Wegner, "Moral Typecasting," 505.

high-pressure medical institution. Andrew Jameton was the first to give it a label, in 1984. He described it as knowing the right thing to do when that right thing is just about impossible. The initial focus was on nurses who stand at the busy intersection of what a doctor wants, what a hospital allows, what professional and ethical standards require, and what a patient actually needs. At that intersection, Cynda Rushton observes, nurses are "forced to go against their 'moral compass' on a regular basis."[6] But now, because of the recent shifts in the American healthcare landscape, doctors are experiencing **MD**, as are others. The second concept, **MI**, is associated with psychiatrist Jonathan Shay and his work with Vietnam veterans. Shay focused on the character-damaging consequences of participating in wartime atrocities, specifically those ordered by military higher-ups in life-or-death situations. Thus the points of origin of these two terms are quite different. Yet as their definitions evolve, in clinical discussions there seems to be considerable overlap. Even so, nuances persist, as we see in the question, "When does moral distress become moral injury?"[7]

Moral Treatment: a model for caring for the mentally ill that began in the late 1700s and spread widely in the 1800s. Up until that time, the mentally ill, and certainly those without resources, were confined to cruel madhouses. Innovators began calling for a treatment model that combined humane care with heightened expectations. The patient would now be expected to behave, sit at table, etc. Instead of treating sufferers like animals, they were now to be cared for like children in need of strict oversight; and the road to their cure would involve the inculcation of self-discipline. However, in time, **MT** lost its appeal. One reason is the model's success led to a decrease in smaller, therapeutic asylums and an increase in overcrowded warehouses; and once that happened, the return of the "madhouse" was inevitable. But another reason involves a paradigm shift; the idea that moralistic paternalism contributes to mental health recovery fell out of favor. (It is often pointed out that in its original context, "moral" did not suggest what the English word means today. But if a humane but demanding authority figure is working to inculcate self-discipline in his charges—"moral" seems the appropriate word.) See **Pinel, Philippe** (in **Part 2**)

Mortality Rate: a basic epidemiological term. When tied to a specific cause, it places the number of people who die from that condition or event in comparison with the total population overall. The result is commonly expressed

6. Rushton, "Moral Distress," para. 1.
7. Macdonald, "When Does Moral Distress Become Moral Injury?"

per 1,000, or for rarer causes, 100,000. See **Case Fatality Rate (CFR) vs. Infection Fatality Rate (IFR)**

MRI (Magnetic Resonance Imaging): a medical imaging technology for capturing the visual likeness of an anatomical organ or tissue. X-rays and CT scans are different in that they make use of radiation—and so does ultrasound, which uses soundwaves. MRI technology works by introducing a strong magnetic field and a radio frequency pulse; and, when the pulse is turned off, by measuring the release of electromagnetic energy. The advantage is that, for some internal structures, MRIs provide sharper images than the alternatives do. The first MRI scan of a human body took place in New York in 1977.

Multiple (Modified) Organ Dysfunction Score: see MODS

Multiple Organ Dysfunction Syndrome: see MODS

Multiple Sclerosis (MS): a potentially disabling disease that affects the brain and spinal cord. The body's immune system attacks and damages the sheath (myelin) that protects the nerve fibers of the central nervous system. As a result, communication between the brain and the rest of the body is disrupted. Symptoms include weakness, numbness, vision difficulties, and loss of coordination.

Munchausen Syndrome and **Munchausen Syndrome by Proxy:** traditional names for mental illnesses that are now increasingly labeled "factitious disorder imposed on self" and "factitious disorder imposed on another"—and, when the other in question is a child, "medical child abuse." However, these two former designations continue to appear in the literature. See **Factitious Disorder** and **Malingering**

Muscular Dystrophy: a group of more than thirty different, genetic diseases that cause progressive weakness, either generalized or localized, and the deterioration of skeletal muscles responsible for movement. Duchenne **MD** is the most common form; it primarily affects boys.

Myocardial Infarction or **Acute Myocardial Infarction (MI):** commonly called a heart attack, and also known as coronary thrombosis, this is a sudden loss of the function of a portion of the heart to which blood supply has been reduced. If the flow to the area is not restored quickly, damage to the heart muscle is imminent, and the resultant loss of forward propulsion of blood into the arteries can be, and often is, fatal. Serious as it is, however, an **MI** is not to be confused with, and is not as life-threatening as, **cardiac arrest**.

Letter N

Narrative Bioethics: an approach which gives personal testimonies a crucial place in ethical decision-making. Human beings are storytellers; our unique journeys are best appreciated by those who are willing to hear our own accounts of them. What is more, any stop along life's way (in a hospital for instance) should not be viewed ahistorically: it's a moment in an ongoing story. As a consequence, narrativists are less interested in philosophical consistency than they are in narrative fit: the right choice for a patient will be the most meaningful one. "At its best, it provides an alternative means of justifying ethical decisions which focuses on the relational and communicative dimensions of moral situations."[1]

Nasogastric Intubation: the sending of a thin "NG" tube through the nose, down the esophagus, and into the stomach.

National Institute for Health and Clinical Excellence (NICE): the organization which provides guidelines for the British National Health Service (NHS). Set up in 1999, it is an independent and yet government-funded agency. Critics fault it for being a sluggish bureaucracy, and for being needlessly restrictive and inhumane to boot. Moreover, it is also a convenient target for those in the United States who oppose socialized medicine in general and/or the rationing of drugs and treatments in particular. See **Death Panels**

National Notifiable Diseases Surveillance System (NNDSS): a program of the CDC which coordinates the gathering, analyzing, and disseminating of public health data. Reports of cases of notifiable diseases are voluntarily submitted to the CDC by state, territory, and other authorities. These are

---

1. McCarthy, "Principlism or Narrative Ethics?," 67.

compiled within a "system of systems" of disease-specific programs. See **Reportable Diseases vs. Notifiable Diseases**

Naturalistic Fallacy: as articulated by British philosopher G. E. Moore (1873–1958), this is the pegging of a moral quality, such as "good," to a natural quality, such as "pleasure." When the latter is used to provide a defining feature of the former, confusion is the result. That said, the following points need to be made. First, it is generally agreed that Moore's use of the word "naturalistic" is misleading, for his complaint applies to all concepts which are not inherently moral, whether supernatural or natural. Second, as William Frankena suggests, the word "fallacy" is unhelpful as well.[2] Third, Moore's actual argument is subtle and technical. To wit: for any ethical definition such as "good is whatever brings pleasure," if a meaningful question can be asked, "But *is* whatever brings pleasure *good*?" then the meaningfulness of the question shows that the matter is not wrapped up, which in turn proves that the initial definition fails to define—making it, in Moore's view, a "fallacy." Fourth, the way the fact-values distinction is treated here can profitably be compared to the handling of the "**Is-Ought Problem**" by **David Hume** (who is found in **Part 2**). But fifth, too often "naturalistic fallacy" is used as a banner under which to do battle against straw man versions of **natural law** theory.

Natural Law: a venerable ethical theory, the twin pillars of which are: (a) moral norms arise out of human nature and/or the order of the natural world; and (b) the criteria for recognizing them are available to the general populace (as opposed to, say, religious insiders only). These norms are not subsidiary to a legislating authority such as the state. And they are not products of individual or class experience, nor again of communal or sectarian tradition. They may be thought of as depending on, or as needing clarification from, an outside source, but if so, it would be wrong to imagine that they function as imports from a separate realm. Written on the heart, they are at the heart of what it means to be *human*; and any human being as such is capable of appreciating their demands. Although there are many expressions of **NL** theory, everyone's favorite proponent is **Thomas Aquinas**. His version begins by pairing morality with human rationality. "Law is a kind of direction or measure for human activity through which a person is led to do something or is held back. . . . Now direction and measure come to human acts from reason. . . . We are left with the conclusion, then, that law is something that belongs to reason."[3] This confidence in natural reason's role

2. Frankena, "Naturalistic Fallacy," 464.

3. Aquinas, *Summa Theologiæ* 28, 1a2æ. 90, I.

in the moral life lives on in Roman Catholicism today, the official catechism of which attests, "Objective norms of morality express the *rational* order of good and evil."[4] See **Aquinas, Thomas** (in **Part 2**)

Nazi Medical War Crimes: heinous research conducted by physicians on concentration camp prisoners, including children, during World War II. The subjects were unwilling participants, and the experiments can easily be recognized as medical torture and as crimes against humanity. Twenty-three doctors were brought to justice in connection with the Nuremberg Trials. (The Nuremberg Code was adopted during this judicial process.) Seven leading figures were executed, including Karl Brandt, Adolf Hitler's escort physician. But there were doctors who got away. The notorious Josef Mengele fled to Argentina and was never apprehended. Others were among the 1,600 Nazis with marketable skills who were finagled into the United States with records whited out. They were brought in under the cover of Operation Paperclip, the program that found a place for Wernher von Braun in America's space program. See **Japanese Medical War Crimes**

Necessary vs. Contingent: a time-honored philosophical distinction between what could not possibly be otherwise and what could be otherwise. It is necessarily true that all pentagons have five sides; it is contingently true that the Pentagon is the headquarters for the US Department of Defense.

Necrosis (νέκρωσις): the death of cells, tissues, or organs. It can be caused by **ischemia**, an undersupply of blood. See **Gangrene**

Negative vs. Positive Autonomy: The former is the principle which provides grounds for a patient to refuse a form of care. It comes proximately close to being an absolute right. That is, although there may be exceptions, modern medicine puts a premium on the authority of patients to set limits to the medical attention that they receive. The latter, **PA**, would be grounds for demanding treatments, were the two sides of autonomy commensurate, but they are not. Patients are autonomous decision-makers, but they cannot demand the moon. The reasons why they cannot are many and varied, but they start with: medical professionals have standards of their own and an **NA** of their own. See **Autonomy, Respect for**

Negligence, Medical: action or inaction by a medical professional that deviates from, or violates, "the accepted medical standards of practice" or "the applicable standard of care." When injury to a patient has been caused by

4. The Catholic Church, "Catechism of the Catholic Church," #1751 (emphasis added).

negligence, or "substandard conduct," there can be grounds for a malpractice claim. See **Abandonment, Patient; Continuity of Care;** and **Malpractice, Medical**

Neonatal Intensive Care Unit: see **NICU (Neonatal Intensive Care Unit)**

Neural Tube Defects: a group of malformations of the brain or spinal cord
occurring early during embryonic development. The two most common are
anencephaly and **spina bifida.**

NICU (Neonatal Intensive Care Unit): the area of the hospital devoted to
providing advanced and heightened care services to newborn babies who
are premature or seriously ill. See **Apgar Score System**

Nonmaleficence: often paired with **beneficence,** this is one of the four pillars of **principlism.** James Tubbs observes that it is "widely considered to
be the most fundamental moral norm of healthcare."[5] As such, it is often
expressed as **First, Do No Harm,** a phrase capturing the spirit of the **Hippocratic Oath** without being found in its letter. What **N** requires is clearer
when the emphasis is placed on refraining from actions that result in greater
harm overall, that is, not ending up with burdens outweighing benefits.
Which leads to the following: "There has been considerable debate about
where the negative duty of nonmaleficence ends and the positive duty of beneficence begins, especially because the former has been regarded in most
Western societies (at least since the Enlightenment) as prior or more clearly
obligatory."[6] On this, see **Beneficence.** Also see **Benign Neglect; Harm Reduction Model; Precautionary Principle;** and **Spirit of the Law and Letter
of the Law;** and **Hippocrates** (in **Part 2**)

Nonsentient: lacking sense perception; unconscious.

NSTEMI vs. STEMI: the first stands for "non-ST segment elevation myocardial infarction," a less serious kind of heart attack. It results from either a
lesser blockage of a major coronary artery or a greater blockage of a minor
one. A **STEMI** is definitely more serious, for in that case the blockage is
more detrimental, with blood having been shut off to a significant portion
of the heart muscle. These two are only distinguishable after medical evaluation and repeated electrocardiogram findings and other testing.

---

5. Tubbs, *Handbook of Bioethics Terms,* 114.
6. Tubbs, *Handbook of Bioethics Terms,* 114.

Nudging: the deliberate but covert sequencing or staging or verbal inflection of alternatives so as to influence the choice a patient makes, without being out-and-out directive or coercive. In medicine this means helping people make healthy decisions, be it in terms of the lifestyle patterns of a populace, or the treatment choices of an individual. In the latter instance, best-case scenarios have health professionals presenting options to patients in ways that, while influencing their final decisions, also respect, and ideally reinforce, their freedom of choice. Critics, however, see lack of candor, manipulation, and paternalism. The view here is that **N** represents medicine's awkward search for a correction to an overemphasis on patient **autonomy**.

Letter O

Occam's (or Ockham's) Razor vs. Hickam's Dictum: Medieval philosopher William of Ockham's philosophical principle cashes out as: the mere fact of being complicated does not make a hypothesis superior; if there are two equally explanatory theories, and one is simpler, then the simpler one is to be preferred. Commonly applied in medical contexts, the idea is: a single diagnosis which fully accounts for a patient's multiple symptoms is preferable to multiple diagnoses. However, this "Keep It Simple, Stupid" approach is often counterposed with **HD**, promulgated by John Hickam, an American professor of medicine. He famously said, "A patient can have as many diseases as he or she damn well pleases." That is, an individual's many health complaints may well have many causes, rather than a single omni-cause.

Omission vs. Commission, Sins of: this is a distinction derived from traditional Christian ethics although its significance for Christian devotional practice is even greater. At its simplest, the former are right deeds left undone; and the latter are wrong deeds done. Pressed further, the contrast can be as broad as a particular doctrine of sin allows for, meaning that attitudes could be included right along with acts. The verse most frequently cited for the sins of omission is, "Everyone who knows what is the right thing to do and doesn't do it commits a sin" (Jas 4:17 JB). Compare with **Active vs. Passive Euthanasia** and **Acts and Omissions Doctrine**

"Onk," usually written as "Onc": oncology, the hospital section or department devoted to patients with cancer.

"On the Floor": hospital slang for where the patients are. That's the meaning when a nurse manager says, "I would rather get out on the floor and see the patients." Sending a patient "back to the floor" after a procedure has the same meaning.

Organ Support: the range of care techniques known as "life support" while a patient is alive are referred to as "organ support" once he or she has died.

Orientation Times Three: questions to gauge a patient's level of awareness: Who ("Can you tell me your name?"), Where ("Do you know where you are?"), and When ("Do you know what year it is?"). "Orientation Times Four" adds the relevant event, that is, Why ("Do you know why you are here [in the hospital]?"). And note: A&Ox3 is shorthand for "patient is awake, alert and oriented" (x3 means "times three") "regarding person, place, and time." Variations such as A/A/Ox3 mean the same thing.

Outbreak vs. Cluster: for epidemiologists, the first term refers to a sudden occurrence, at a higher concentration than normal, of related cases of a disease within a particular social group or geographic region. As such, it is interchangeable with "epidemic." However, when the two terms are technically distinguished, "epidemic" means an outbreak with a serious-to-severe public impact, and "outbreak" means an increase that is confined to a specific area or community. The second term, "cluster," by contrast, is a broader category. It encompasses all groups of proximate disease occurrences: whether or not a relationship (such as a common source of infection) is known or suspected, and whether or not a baseline has been ascertained. See **Endemic vs. Sporadic** and **Epidemic vs. Pandemic**

Outpatient Civil Commitment: (AKA assisted outpatient treatment) this is a form of **Involuntary Psychiatric Treatment** recognized (though not necessarily implemented) in forty-seven states (all except Connecticut, Maryland, and Massachusetts) and Washington, DC. The specifics are: a court orders a treatment regimen for an individual with a behavioral disorder while he or she continues to live "in the community," that is, outside a psychiatric facility and more or less on his or her own. See **Lanterman-Petris-Short Act; Laura's Law;** and *Parens Patriae* vs. *In Loco Parentis*

Overdiagnosis: see **Overtreatment vs. Overdiagnosis**

Overmedication vs. Overprescription: the latter is the problem of drugs or treatments being ordered too much (quantity) or too often (frequency). Opioids, antibiotics, and antidepressants are commonly referenced. The former is the negative consequences of their actual overuse and/or abuse. One common theme is that patients who feel overmedicated (that is, feel that their meds are interfering with their normal functioning) tend to nonadhere. Another is that senior adults are particularly at risk. See **Deprescribing; Medication-Related Problem (MRP)** or **Drug-Related Problem**

(DRP); **Overtreatment vs. Overdiagnosis; Polypharmacy;** and **Prescribing Cascade**

Overprescription: see **Overmedication vs. Overprescription**

Overtreatment vs. Overdiagnosis: the former can be used to mean "more than is necessary." However, in medical contexts, it usually means "unnecessary and inappropriate," as in giving medical attention to a condition that would go away on its own; or utilizing healthcare services for reasons that have nothing to do with either **evidence-based medicine** or patient preferences. Overdiagnosis, by contrast, is **medicalizing** a condition—making it official, so to speak—when it is not likely to cause the patient any problems and/or when it will probably resolve itself. Screening to achieve an early detection of an abnormality is often mentioned as a gateway to overdiagnoses, which can lead to overtreatments. Contrast with **Benign Neglect; Overmedication vs. Overprescription;** and **Parsimonious Care**

Letter P

Painting the Mice: a shopterm for deceptive research practices. The phrase comes from a high-profile instance of scientific fraud which was exposed in 1974. For his experiment in transplantation immunology to succeed, medical researcher **William Summerlin** (in **Part 2**) needed white mice with black patches. He used a black felt-tip pen, et voilà!

Palliative Care: end-of-life treatment aimed at relieving symptoms and controlling pain, so as to improve the quality of life (**QOL**) of a patient, rather than trying to achieve a cure. Contrasts with curative treatment. See **Symptom Management**

Panacea (Πανάκεια = a Greek goddess): the source of our English word is one of the deities called upon at the beginning of the **Hippocratic Oath**. Her name means all-healing. A **P** is a cure-all, and by extension, a solution for every difficulty.

Pandemic: see **Epidemic vs. Pandemic**

Paradigm (παράδειγμα = pattern, example, precedent): a standard framework, small or grand, for conceptualizing or investigating something. One example would be the grand worldview of Sir Isaac Newton. "The Newtonian paradigm is materialistic and atomistic in nature. It sees the world as a set of isolated objects that interact in a linear, cause-and-effect fashion."[1] All **Ps** end up determining which sorts of questions researchers ask and which sorts of answers they seek. The fame of the term, along with the idea that scientific paradigms shift suddenly and according to a recognizable pattern, we owe to philosopher of science Thomas Kuhn.[2]

---

1. Systems Innovation, "Newtonian Paradigm," para. 5.
2. Kuhn, *Structure of Scientific Revolutions*.

Parasuicide: the broader definition is any purposeful but nonfatal attempt at harming oneself, whether or not death was the intended goal. However, it is frequently used more narrowly to mean specifically only those cries-for-help-type, suicidal gestures, where death is pretended to be, but not actually, sought.

***Parens Patriae* vs. *In Loco Parentis*:** (Latin = father of the nation vs. in place of a parent) both legal doctrines trace back to English common law. The former originally indicated the protective role of the king over his subjects. In time it came to represent the state's prerogative to step in on behalf of children and incapacitated adults. As such it provides the basis for the **involuntary psychiatric treatment** of individuals who pose a danger to themselves or others. The second doctrine is different. Among its distinct features are: (a) it assumes temporary rather than permanent oversight; and (b) it involves responsibilities which can be shouldered by entities other than, or in addition to, the government. Educators are the prime example.

Parsimonious Care: medical attention characterized by a restrained and frugal stewardship. Endeavoring to ensure the judicious use of available resources, it aims at balancing medical effectiveness with efficiency and cost-consciousness. See **Defensive Medicine** and **Overtreatment vs. Overdiagnosis**

Paternalism: "a type of medical decision making in which health care professionals exercise unilateral authority over patients."[3] At such times, the doctor is essentially a benevolent dictator, presuming that the decisions made are in the patient's best interest. The rub is that, generally speaking, it is in a person's best interest to be self-determining whenever possible; but paternalism requires a parent-child relationship, by definition. Note: when decisions are made on behalf of a patient who lacks **decision-making capacity**, that is often categorized as soft or weak paternalism. Hard or strong paternalism is when a patient's preferences are slighted and patient **autonomy** is disregarded—even though the patient is fully capable of making his or her own treatment choices.

Pathogenicity vs. Infectivity and Infectiveness: the former is a disease-causing organism's ability to cause a disease, to make a body actually get sick. The latter two are closely related to **P**, but are concerned with infection—whether the host gets sick or not. Infectivity is the ease, as it were,

---

3. Venes, *Tabor's Cyclopedic Medical Dictionary*, 1751.

with which a pathogen establishes a beachhead, survives, and multiplies in a host. Infectiveness is its ability to travel, to spread to new hosts.

Pathogenicity vs. Virulence: two terms which are sometimes used synonymously. Or again, the latter can simply indicate the degree of the former. If they are distinguished further, **P** refers to the ability of a pathogen to cause a host to get sick; and **V** to the power, the severity of the resultant disease. See **Pathogenicity vs. Infectivity and Infectiveness**

Patient Dumping: if a hospital has the ability to provide medical services to an individual, but prematurely discharges or transfers him or her to another facility, and if the reason is that the person is unable to pay, or is troublesome and/or nonadherent, that is **PD**. (Flatly declining admittance in the first place is as well.) The transfer out can be to another healthcare facility, a homeless shelter, or even to a convenient bus stop (thus the related terms "Greyhound Therapy" and "Discharge to the Street.") See **Abandonment, Patient** and **EMTALA (Emergency Medical Treatment and Active Labor Act)**; contrast with **Black Alert**

Patient Zero: see **Index Case vs. Patient Zero**

PEG Tube: the "percutaneous endoscopic gastronomy tube" is a feeding tube sent through the skin and into the stomach. It is a common way of providing food, liquids, and meds to patients who are unable to take them by mouth for an extended period of time. PEG tubes can also be palliative. For example, a cancer patient might have a small bowel obstruction, which would mean that he or she could not eat whatsoever. However, a palliative PEG tube would allow for the satisfaction of eating, with the food then removed from the stomach via suction. ▪ **PEG-J Tube:** a similar set-up but with an extension routing through the PEG tube and into the jejunum.

Penetrance: in genetics, the frequency, as a percentage, with which individuals with an inheritable condition, or genotype, manifest its clinical symptoms, or phenotype. As in: if individuals who have a genetic mutation show its problematic characteristics 100 percent of the time, it is fully penetrant.

Perioperative: around the time of surgery. There are three phases involved: preoperative, intraoperative, and postoperative. ▪ **Perioperative Care:** providing for patients before operation, during operation, and after operation. ▪ **Perioperative Cardiac Event:** undergoing noncardiac surgery can bring with it the risk of major perioperative cardiac events: cardiac death, nonfatal

myocardial infarction or acute myocardial infarction (MI) or nonfatal cardiac arrest.

Periviability vs. Previability: the initial term literally means around the time of viability. In the field of prenatal medicine, it refers to that earliest stage of maturation at which a preterm newborn will have a reasonable chance of a life without severely compromising conditions. The second term means prior to that point, when survival is unlikely. See **Viability, Fetal**

PERK (Physical Evidence Recovery Kit): in forensic science, a package of items used for conducting a sexual assault investigation, one which involves collecting, documenting, and protecting the evidence. It is also known in some jurisdictions as a "Sexual Assault Kit," and sometimes referred to as a "Rape Kit."

Pernicious: (per-NISH-us) in normal parlance, when used of a person, it means intentionally hurtful and villainous. In medicine, when used of a condition, it means extremely damaging and potentially life-endangering— with no villainy implied. ▪ **Pernicious Anemia:** a serious condition which stems from the body not absorbing enough of the vitamin B12 needed to make healthy red blood cells. It was once regarded as deadly but is now treatable with B12 shots or pills.

Perseveration: in psychiatric/psychological contexts, the compulsive and unnatural repetition of a word, phrase, or gesture. It can be a symptom of a brain injury or a behavioral disorder.

Persistent Vegetative State: "persistent" means lasting for a month or more; "vegetative state" means biologically alive but without any tuning in—or being able to tune in—to self or surroundings. So, the autonomic nervous system maintains basic body functions, and reflexive movements like yawning, grunting, and the rolling of eyes are possible. But unlike with a **minimally conscious state (MCS)**, the patient has no ability to make simple, voluntary responses to external stimuli, and does not have even a very limited conscious awareness. (Alternate designations to **PVS** have been suggested because of misgivings about seeming to reduce a person to the level of a vegetable—that is, not just less than human but even less than an animal— and "Unresponsive Wakefulness Syndrome" is one of those proposed alternatives. But **PVS** persists in the literature.) A caveat is in order, however. Advances in brain science call into question all of the above. "Functional neuroimaging and electrophysiological studies suggest that some degree of consciousness or awareness that has not been or could not be determined by behavioral evaluations alone may be present in some of these patients who, hence, have covert consciousness."[4] Our overarching understanding of disorders of consciousness, and of categories such as **PVS** and **MCS**, may need to be revised, therefore.

Persons and Personhood: "the word 'person' is now widely used in medical ethics to denote someone who (or which) has full *moral* status of the sort that moral agents accord themselves. 'Personhood' is the possession of such full moral status. . . . In specifying the attributes of personhood, or the criteria by which we may differentiate entities that are persons from those that are not, vigorous philosophical and theological debate continues."[5] The position here draws inspiration from the Judeo-Christian tradition in relating the moral status just mentioned to something higher. Personhood is identified with being created in the *imago Dei*, the image of God. All persons—those able to make their own autonomous decisions and those less or unable to do so—have been created with an indelible imprint, a permanent stamp of approval, as it were. In other words, all persons are sacred. As such, they point beyond themselves to life's goodness in its ultimate context. But then they are also capable of making desecrative and inauthentic choices— in ways that no impersonal thing can. Yet irrespective of the choices made, the innate sacredness remains, so that to be a "person" is to be enduringly worthy of respect. That said, with due appreciation for the moral complexity of, for example, beginning-of-life and end-of-life situations, situations in which tragic tradeoffs are sometimes unavoidable, whether a principle of respect for persons should trump all other ethical considerations is another matter, one about which, as was said, debate continues. See **Authenticity; Autonomy, Respect for;** and **Principlism**

P-Hacking: a shopterm for a cluster of problematic research practices believed to be behind the present-day research **replication crisis**. One problematic strategy is to affix a hypothesis after the data are known—affix it selectively and misleadingly (AKA **data dredging**). Another starts with a hypothesis (which would be good) but then proceeds to run analyses, keeping them going as long as it takes for an acceptable result to be achieved. Then, sleight-of-hand style, only the successful run-through gets reported; everything else is kept from view. A third alternative is to make use of midcourse methodological corrections. These provide ways to give the data a significance that they wouldn't have without the string-pulling of the research puppeteers.

4. Kondziella and Koehler, "Disorders of Consciousness," para. 1.
5. Gillon, "Persons and Personhood," 186 (emphasis original).

Pharmacological Calvinism: a phrase coined in 1972 by psychiatrist Gerald Klerman to represent the view, which he opposed, that happiness in life has to be worked for and that using prescription meds to escape anxiety or depression is immoral. Klerman's complaint was that many Americans in his day regarded drugs as a "crutch," and saw treating stress with tranquilizers as a cop-out.[6] That basic concept was then popularized by Peter Kramer in *Listening to Prozac* in 1993. Kramer broadened the focus from meds for relief and included meds for emotional enhancement and personal transformation. As before, **PC** was depicted as the party-pooper idea that "if a drug makes you feel good, it must be morally bad."[7] (Note: for a thoughtful analysis, see the article by Sperry and Prosen.[8] A look at the practical issues can be found in a chapter by Stein.[9]) However, most historians would counter that other figures better fit the position being delineated than John Calvin does. See **Calvin, John** (in **Part 2**)

Physical Dependence: the body's adaptation to a substance in the form of either tolerance or withdrawal, or both. Tolerance means that higher doses are required to achieve the desired effect; withdrawal that physical and/or mental symptoms occur if the drug is discontinued. With these two adaptations, **PD** overlaps with **addiction** but the two conditions are not synonymous: (a) addictions to behaviors such as gambling, sexual activity, etc., are possible without **PD**; and (b) dependence on a substance like caffeine or nicotine is possible without addiction. Nevertheless, it is common for **PD** to accompany addiction.

Physician-Assisted Suicide: (AKA Death with Dignity, End of Life Option, Physician Aid in Dying, Physician-Assisted Hastening of Death, and **Active Shortening of the Dying Process**), this is a hotly debated concept; and which name should be used to identify it is part of the debate. The **American Medical Association (AMA)** continues to use the traditional terminology, **P-AS**, and defines it as follows. "Physician-assisted suicide occurs when a physician facilitates a patient's death by providing the necessary means and/or information to enable the patient to perform the life-ending act (e.g., the physician provides sleeping pills and information about the lethal dose, while aware that the patient may commit suicide)."[10] Oregon was the first state to pass a Death with Dignity statute; it took effect in 1997.

6. Klerman, "Psychotropic Hedonism vs. Pharmacological Calvinism," 3.

7. Kramer, *Listening to Prozac*, 274.

8. Sperry and Prosen, "Contemporary Ethical Dilemmas in Psychotherapy," 54–63.

9. Stein, "Pharmacological Enhancement," 1–12.

10. American Medical Association, "Physician-Assisted Suicide," para. 1.

Since then, seven other states and the District of Columbia have followed suit. The AMA is organizationally opposed to **P-AS**, but not all its members are. See **Justification of Acts vs. Justification of Policies** and **MAID (Medical Assistance in Dying—Canada)**

Physician vs. Doctor: "a physician is a medical doctor, either an MD or DO, who has completed graduate training to provide health care. A physician may be referred to as a doctor. However, not all doctors are physicians. An individual with a PhD, such as a doctoral degree in economics, is referred to as a doctor. So while all physicians are doctors, not all doctors are physicians."[11] Note: the term "doctor" dates back to the early Christian church when teachers of the Scriptures were given that title (in Latin *docere* = to teach). Moving forward, in the medieval universities, the doctoral degree emerged as a license to teach. At the time, the principle fields of instruction were theology, law, and medicine.

Phytoremediation: a biotech term that refers to using living plants to control and treat areas polluted by contaminants. Green plants and their related microbes work to isolate, degrade, and/or remove toxins or hazardous materials from oceans, groundwater, soil, or air. See **Bioremediation**

PICC: the "peripherally inserted central venous catheter" is a long, thin kind of IV tube, inserted into the upper arm and directed to a large vein near the heart. The purpose is to eliminate frequent "needling." Moreover, it can be used as a longer-term venous access, making possible in-home antibiotic treatment that would otherwise require perhaps multiple weeks in the hospital.

PIMP (Put In My Place): actually meaning something closer to "put on the spot," this is medical slang. Most commonly, it refers to an attending physician quizzing a med student with a tough question or series of questions for the purpose of making the student look stupid and feel powerless. But it applies throughout the medical community: anytime someone with a higher status, under the pretense of asking a question, bullies someone with a lower status. Think of it as medical hazing.

Plagiarism: academic or scientific stealing of credit for someone else's work, this is the third of the three practices included in the official definition of **research misconduct**, often referred to as "the three cardinal (or deadly) sins." With **P**, an investigator fails to properly acknowledge words or ideas from another source or sources, giving the impression that the material is

11. Whitlock, "Doctors, Residents, and Attendings," paras. 6–7.

original when in fact it is not. The failure can be deliberate or inadvertent. ▪ **Reverse Plagiarism:** Whereas with the above the ethical violation consisted in pretending someone else's work is your own, here it is pretending that your own material is someone else's, that is, purporting to cite an outside source for your own fabricated material. The purpose is to provide support for a claim, but the support is fictitious. (Example: "Never say that you're quoting a celebrated psychiatrist when actually the words are yours, not the other person's." —M. Scott Peck, *The Road Less Traveled*, 402)[12] ▪ **Self-Plagiarism:** (AKA **Text Recycling**) presenting and taking credit for one's own work—the same or substantially similar—a second time or more, but without admitting it. This is a contested concept; some commentators argue that it isn't unethical. Yet illustrations of what can be problematic include: a student handing in the same term paper for multiple courses; a professor amplifying a publications record without conducting additional research; and the issue of copyright infringement. Yet the Office of Research Integrity concedes that **S-P** does not fall within its definition of research misconduct. At the same time, the ORI points out that journal editors in the biomedical sciences are taking steps to oppose the practice. See **Fabrication; Falsification; Research Misconduct; Salami Slicing;** and **Text Recycling**

Pneumonia (πνεύμων = lung): an inflammation of one or both lungs commonly caused by an infection. The air sacs of the lungs may fill with fluid or pus, causing a cough with phlegm or pus, plus fever, chills, and difficulty in breathing. A variety of organisms, including bacteria, viruses, and fungi, can cause the infection, which can range from mildly serious to life-threatening. The most at risk are: infants and young children; people sixty-five and older, and people with health issues or weakened immune systems. ▪ **Pneumonitis:** inflammation of the lung(s) due to a cause other than infection.

Point-of-Care Testing, POCT: (AKA bedside testing) diagnostic analyses undertaken in the actual healthcare setting, at or near the patient—rather than in an offsite lab facility, as was formerly customary. The major advantage is shortened turnaround leading to improved patient outcomes. The major challenges have to do with quality control. Instruments have to be maintained, and in-house personnel have to be kept in sync with advances in technology, so as to stay compliant with clinical standards and regulatory requirements. ▪ **POCUS**, "Point of Care Ultrasound," is becoming more and more common.

---

12. There is no p. 402 in *The Road Less Traveled*. Without this footnote, the quote would be reverse plagiarism.

POLST (Physician, or Provider, Orders for Life-Sustaining Treatment): a medical order recording a patient's preferences regarding end-of-life care. It is intended to be immediately recognizable by health care providers in all settings, most notably emergency medical technicians (EMTs) responding to a medical emergency—something that is not true of an **advance directive**. Signed by a doctor and, depending on the state, the patient or surrogate, it should (ideally) reflect a careful conversation about treatment options—although, bureaucracies being what they are, conversations do not always take place. It is also known as a **MOLST**.

Polypharmacy: the problem of adverse effects and other unintended consequences for someone who is taking too many different meds. They can be of all sorts: prescription drugs, over-the-counter products, nutritional supplements, home remedies, etc. Abused and illegal drugs can also be a part of the picture. Negative consequences can include problems of cost and nonadherence; but harmful Rx-Rx interactions are the uppermost concern. And for that, senior adults are the most likely to be at risk, for they are the ones who are most likely to have multiple health conditions that are being treated by multiple practitioners; and with some of those, such as specialists or ER physicians, there may not be consistent medical supervision. "Polypharmacy is a clinical challenge because the health care system is geared toward starting medications, not reducing or stopping them."[13] See **Deprescribing; Medication-Related Problem (MRP)** or **Drug-Related Problem (DRP); Overmedication vs. Overprescription;** and **Prescribing Cascade**

Populate (a patient's note): to fill in information, such as clinical history, medications, etc., to a patient's electronic health record (EHR). ("Populating a note with incomplete information creates problems down the line.")

Posturing: the involuntarily and abnormally rigid arms and legs of a patient can be important signals of severe brain damage. Called posturing, the two contrasting forms are: decorticate and decerebrate. The most obvious difference is that with decorticate, the arms are clinched up against the chest, and with decerebrate, they are thrust out to the sides. These forms of rigidity are indicators of how badly the brain has been damaged and are used in assigning the patient a score on the **Glasgow Coma Scale**

Pragmatic Bioethics: sharing with **consequentialism** a rejection of **moral absolutism** and a focus on outcomes, this approach is distinctive for its commitment to progress. Ethical norms are still in the making, still being

---

13. Farrell and Mangin, "Deprescribing," 7.

improved upon. Inspired by Darwinian evolution, the scientific method, and philosophers such as William James and John Dewey, bioethicists of the pragmatic persuasion are committed to shared, "democratic" decision-making, and to keeping the conversation between physician and patient open-ended. Significantly, they are liable to speak less in terms of right and wrong, or good and bad, and more in terms of ethical preferences. Morality is "purpose-driven." It is a matter of experimentation and/or construction, moral norms functioning like scientific hypotheses or even like tools, revisable in light of "what works." **PB** is particularly attractive for clinicians impressed by ground-shifting achievements in science and technology. (Note however: "pragmatic" can also mean simply "practical, unconcerned with theory.") "Life is a moving affair in which old moral truth ceases to apply."[14]

Precautionary Principle: in environmental ethics: faced with the possibility of serious-to-catastrophic damage to, say, an ecosystem, and with scientific analyses unable to determine the precise level of risk, the wise course of action is to err on the side of environmental preservation. See **Benign Neglect; First, Do No Harm; Nonmaleficence;** and **Sustainable Development**

Prescribing Cascade: one Rx followed by another and then another, because the first med produced a side effect, or interacted with another drug, and the symptoms were misdiagnosed as a new medical problem. So a second remedy was prescribed, and so on. See **Deprescribing; Medication-Related Problem (MRP)** or **Drug-Related Problem (DRP); Overmedication vs. Overprescription;** and **Polypharmacy**

Presenting Problem and Chief Complaint: synonyms for the unwelcome symptom(s) that motivate(s) a client or patient to seek help. In medical contexts the two are interchangeable, while in mental health circles the former predominates. But that's just in the United States. In Europe and Canada, the preferred term is "Presenting Complaint." And then there is "Reason for Encounter" (RFE). This has been a broad category for anything—problematic or otherwise—that brings someone into contact with a healthcare service. In the UK, general practitioners continue to use RFE.

Pressors: drugs such as dopamine, epinephrine, and norepinephrine, which increase blood pressure of patients in shock. Pressors can act on the heart or on the blood vessels. See **Vasopressors**

---

14. Dewey, *Human Nature and Conduct*, 239.

Prima Facie: (Latin = at first face) in ethics, a way of taking the temporal dimension seriously. For it refers to a norm, usually a duty, which is binding for the time being, until life moves on and a countervailing norm comes to light, or changed circumstances or unforeseen difficulties in application set the entire matter in a different light. At such a time, further reflection will be necessary to arrive at an up-to-date and more comprehensive understanding of what is required.

Primum Non Nocere or **Primum Nil Nocere:** see **First, Do No Harm**

Principlism: the name attached by others to the approach of *Principles of Biomedical Ethics* by Tom Beauchamp and James Childress. That highly influential text centers around four main principles: **Autonomy, Respect for; Nonmaleficence; Beneficence;** and **Justice.** The four, having been drawn straightforwardly (and some would say, naïvely) from "the common morality," are put to work within a **reflective equilibrium** methodology, "while incorporating tools to refine and correct unclarities and to allow for additional specification of principles, rules, and rights. As ethical reasoning progresses, a body of more specific moral guidelines is formed."[15] One reason **P** has been adopted so widely is that, since it has no time for a search for an adequate theoretical orientation, there is no problem in combining it with many other approaches, philosophical and religious. A second is that the ethicist is ushered very quickly into the solving of urgent moral problems. Yet therein lies the strength and the weakness of this program: for anyone who finds its solutions unconvincing, **P** has nothing else to say. See **Burden vs. Benefit** and **Foundationalism**

Procedural Care: short-term medical attention before and after a surgical or other intervention, with an emphasis on preparation ahead of time and observation afterwards. ▪ **Periprocedural Care:** care prior to, throughout, and subsequent to a procedure. For example, "Anesthesiology is the practice of medicine dedicated to the relief of pain and periprocedural care of patients before, during and after invasive procedures."[16]

Proctocolectomy: (PROK-tō-kō-LEK-tō-mē) surgical removal of the rectum (the "procto") and the colon. It is the standard surgical method for addressing ulcerative colitis when other medical treatments have failed or when complications have ensued.

15. Beauchamp and Childress, *Principles*, 411.
16. American Medication Association, "Anesthesiology Programs," para. 3.

Prognosis (πρόγνωσις = foreknowledge): a forecast of the anticipated development and outcome of a disease and of the patient's chances of recovery.
See **Diagnosis**

Prolonging Life vs. Prolonging Death: a distinction made necessary by
life-extending advances in medicine and technology which make it possible
to add days, weeks, and years to a person's life. In some cases, all it amounts
to is an unnatural stretching out of the dying process. An example would
be the patient, hooked up to machines, whose "current or projected condition will result in an intolerable inability to engage in valued life tasks or
to derive sufficient pleasure from doing so, understood from the patient's
perspective."[17] In earlier times, life and death were clearly delineated; now
however, the bio-techno-medicalization of aging has instituted a drawn-out
living-dying gray zone unprecedented in human history. The **PL/PD** contrast is a shorthand challenge to the assumption that "longer is better." See
Futility; Natural Law; and **Nonmaleficence**

Propagated Outbreak vs. Common Source Outbreak: the one is decentralized, the transmission taking place mostly person-to-person; the other is
centralized, the spread moving outward from a single, shared disease locus.
▪ **Point Source Outbreak:** a kind of **CSO** in which the spread window is
limited and all the cases arise within a single incubation period. A particular
meal or event are good examples.

Provider Fatigue: closely related to, and sometimes used interchangeably
with, both **burnout** and **compassion fatigue**. Here, **PF** is taken to be the
more inclusive category, overlapping the other two. That is, it is depletion
because of both impersonal/structural and intimate/interpersonal factors—both long hours, heavy caseloads, and insufficient support, on the one
hand, and personal involvement with the sufferings, struggles, and negative
emotionalities of people in need, on the other. But note: **PF** is also used:
(a) as an ironic way of referring to, say, a medical team's exasperation after
multiple encounters with a difficult patient; and also (b) in the nontechnical,
ordinary sense of physically tired healthcare employees. (For example, one
might hear, "Because of cutbacks and extended shifts, provider fatigue can
result in an increase in medication errors.")

Prudence: an underrated virtue, it is variously defined but is often associated with caution, circumspection, and/or enlightened self-interest. Classi-
cally, it was one of the four cardinal or "hinge" virtues, and it had to do with

---

17. Jones and McCullough, "Extending Life or Prolonging Death," 521–22.

reading a situation and knowing what needed to be done next. As such, it was the gatekeeper—**Thomas Aquinas** (in **Part 2**) would render it "the charioteer"—of the other qualities of personal excellence. If we turn to **Aristotle** (in **Part 2**), in his *Nicomachean Ethics* we find that wisdom (σοφία) and prudence (φρόνησις) are virtues of the intellect. Wisdom has the higher responsibility of recognizing unchanging first principles; it has no worries about practical matters in the here-and-now. Aristotle tells us,

> Prudence, on the other hand, deals with human affairs, and with matters that admit of deliberation: for the prudent man's special function, as we conceive it, is to deliberate well; but no one deliberates about what is invariable, or about matters in which there is not some end, in the sense of some realizable good. . . . But prudence is concerned with practice; so that it needs knowledge both of general truths and of particular facts, but more especially the latter.[18]

One suggestion is that the methodology of **principlism**, with its emphasis on weighing and balancing, and its ideal of **reflective equilibrium**, can best be understood as a kind of prudential processing very close to what Aristotle had in mind.

Pulse Ox: a "pulse oximeter" is a medical gizmo that measures a patient's blood oxygen level. It does this by beaming infrared light into the capillaries of an earlobe, finger, or toe. See **Hypoxia and Hypoxemia**

Pyelonephritis (PIE-lo-neh-FRY-tis): an inflammation of the kidney and renal pelvis. It is usually caused by a bacterial infection from the lower urinary tract that has spread to the kidneys. Acute **P** can be life-threatening.

---

18. Aristotle, *Nicomachean Ethics*, 123–24.

Letter Q

QALY (QUAWL-ee): the "quality-adjusted life year" concept attempts to objectively measure something which is generally thought of as difficult, if not impossible, to assess: the value of one year of a person's life relative to his or her health. The measurement is arrived at by estimating the number of years a patient should continue to live because of a particular treatment or intervention—and by estimating the quality, in terms of degree of health, of those years. It is important in the UK's state-run health system, yet it was banned from use in Medicare by the Obama-era Affordable Care Act in 2010. American insurance companies are increasingly relying on it in their economic evaluations, however. In a write-up of its use with new pharmaceuticals, the *Wall Street Journal* summarized, "It puts a dollar figure on a year of healthy life, calculates how much health a drug restores to a patient, then prices drugs accordingly."[1]

Quality Assurance, Hospital: the systematic and comprehensive oversight of institutional operations to ensure that patients are being provided with essential treatment services and that they are not being given contraindicated services. The purposes of this oversight are: to maintain the confidence of patients, future patients, and the public at large; to support staff morale; to improve work processes and efficiency; and to render the organization competitive in the health care marketplace.

Quality of Life (QOL): well-being as subjectively experienced together with the objective conditions that make it possible. **QOL** is one of the key considerations in clinical ethics decision-making, because many interventions cannot be evaluated without a thoughtful assessment of their potential impact on a patient's capacity to continue enjoying normal relationships and activities, and ultimately on his or her sense that life continues to be

1. Roland, "Obscure Model Puts Price," A1.

worth living. This is particularly important in cases involving a patient lacking **decision-making capacity** and for whom no **surrogate decision-maker** can be found. Meaning that treatment choices have to be made without person-specific input. In such circumstances, if there is moral uncertainty, a hospital ethicist or ethics committee can be consulted. Decisions will be made with due consideration given to the potential diminishment or enhancement of the patient's life satisfaction. **QOL** is often contrasted with length of life under less favorable conditions, on the one hand, and with **sanctity of life**, on the other.

Quarantine and Isolation: a pair of measures for protecting the public from serious health risks, the Centers for Disease Control and Prevention (CDC) distinguishing between them in this way: "Isolation separates sick people with a contagious disease from people who are not sick. Quarantine separates and restricts the movement of people who were exposed to a contagious disease to see if they become sick."[2] Yet one readily finds other sources confusing **Q** with **I** or treating the two as one action: **QI**. In the United States, authority over such public health responses is divided between the states, the federal government, and the federally recognized tribal governments. And note: animals and plants can be subject to quarantine as well—fruit across state lines and dogs after a dog bite being prime examples.

Quarantine Fatigue and Social Distancing Fatigue: two informal terms for delayed reactions to lifestyle restrictions imposed during the COVID-19 pandemic of 2020 and thereafter. Technically, **QF** would apply to shelter-in-place restrictions; and **SDF** to out-and-about mandates (such as requiring face masks and maintaining a "social distance" from others of at least six feet). However, the two are used interchangeably to capture a social-psychological polarity: emotional exhaustion from the prolonged stress, on the one hand, while on the other, a fed-up rebelliousness borne of disbelief in, impatience with, or youthful disregard for, public-health policies. See **Quarantine and Isolation**

Quaternary Care Center: a major medical center, usually university-based and heavily endowed, that is capable of supporting sub-sub-specialists and experimental therapy beyond the level of a **tertiary care center**. Such a hospital will be the locus of cutting-edge science and/or translational research, the results of which are then introduced into practice very early on.

---

2. CDC, "Quarantine and Isolation," para. 1.

Queuing: in the UK, a "queue" is a line of people. Within the National Health Service (NHS), **Q** is understood to be a well-established, if regrettable, means of meting out services. "Queuing represents one form of rationing which Rudolf Klein calls rationing by delay (as opposed, e.g., to rationing by denial or by price). In the National Health Service it is most obviously manifested in hospital waiting lists for elective (meaning non-emergency) admissions. . . . Hospital waiting lists have been a fact of life throughout the history of the NHS."[3] And they continue to be. "The number [of people] waiting longer than 52 weeks was at the highest level for more than a decade, the NHS England statistics show. In July [2020], some 83,203 were waiting more than that length of time."[4]

---

3. Maxwell, "Queuing," 209.
4. PA Media, "Hospital Waiting List Numbers," paras. 3–4.

Letter R

Radiation Therapy: a way of treating cancer by delivering high-energy radiation to malignant (cancer) cells to control or kill them. The radiation targets the genetic material that determines how the cells grow and divide. X-rays, gamma rays, or charged particles are examples of the types of radiation that are involved. And there are different methodologies: with external-beam **RT**, a beam is delivered by a machine; with internal **RT**, also called brachytherapy, radiation is implanted in or near the problem area; and with systemic **RT**, an agent, such as radioactive iodine, is swallowed or injected.

Rationalism: the theory that knowledge is a product of the mind's ability to think truly. Its mode of operation is deductive (as that term has traditionally been understood); that is, it proceeds logically from a general truth or first principle to a specific illustration or particular application. An example is the familiar syllogism: "All men are mortal; Socrates is a man; therefore Socrates is mortal." Among philosophers, the rationalists include **Plato** and **Kant** (in **Part 2**), as well as Descartes and Spinoza. See **Deductive vs. Inductive Reasoning; Empiricism;** and **Rationalism vs. Empiricism in Medicine**

Rationalism vs. Empiricism in Medicine: a famous and longstanding divide with roots in ancient Greek and Roman practice. At that early point, representing the rationalist pole, Thessalus and Polybus, the son and the son-in-law of **Hippocrates** (in **Part 2**), founded the Dogmatic school of medicine. They taught that what matters are the hidden causes of diseases, and that reason and reason's theories are the best guides for understanding those underlying causes and for treating the resultant diseases. In opposition, the adherents of the Empiric school preferred experience and observation. They were skeptical about hidden causes and rejected debatable ideas such as the theory of the four **humors**. Instead, they chose to focus

on plainly evident causes, that is, on what was readily perceivable about patients' conditions. Serapion of Alexandria and Philinus of Cos are credited
with founding the Empiric school. See **Empiricism** and **Rationalism**

Rationing: see **Health Care Rationing**

Reablement: a social work term, especially in the UK and Australia. One
problem for persons recovering from an illness or accident or coping with a
disability can be a lack of some of the skills necessary for independent, day-
to-day living; this can be an issue for senior adults as well. **R** is assistance in
reacquiring these skills—or in developing them for the first time.

Reasonable Person Standard: a way of assessing a person's behavior by
comparing it to what the average individual of normal intelligence would
do under the same circumstances. In medicine, questions about **RPS** are
often associated with discussions of **informed consent**: when it comes to
undergoing a medical procedure or participating in a scientific experiment,
what and how much information would a "reasonable person" need to know
to make a fully responsible decision?

Red Flag Law: (AKA extreme risk protection order or gun violence restrain-
ing order) it authorizes police to take firearms away from, or to prevent their
purchase by, a person found to be a credible threat to self or others. As of
2020, seventeen states and the District of Columbia had red flag laws, and
no two are the same. A federal version is in the works. But basically, family members, mental health professionals, law enforcement, or others can
present evidence in court saying that someone poses an "extreme risk," with
the defendant having the right to oppose their efforts, as one would expect.
After weighing the evidence and counterevidence, if appropriate, the judge
can issue a temporary civil order.

Reductionism: any approach that claims to explain a broader, more complex, or more significant reality as "nothing more than" something narrow-
er, simpler, or less important. For example, arguing that ethics is personal
preference, pure and simple, so that "murder is wrong" really only means
"I don't like murder," would be reductionistic. But note: the argument that
a finding of one field of science can be better rendered in the categories of
another field—that chemical or biological realities can be better explained
by the theories of physics—would be reductionistic as well.

Reflective Equilibrium: an ethical-coherence model introduced by John
Rawls in *A Theory of Justice*, taken up by Tom Beauchamp and James

Childress in *Principles of Biomedical Ethics*, and available in various inter-pretations. The versions differ regarding the presuppositions they begin with, be they moral intuitions, or considered judgments, or widely shared ethical convictions. But whichsoever they are, the method calls for testing them in light of the principles or rules they support, on the one hand, and on the other, the particular cases or situations to which they apply. Where inconsistencies appear, adjustments can be made until a conceptual harmo-ny is achieved. Commentators note that advantages of this model include: it allows reason to advance in multiple directions at once; it doesn't allow counterexamples cited by critics to become automatic deal-breakers; and it demonstrates that "it is not necessary to build moral theories on necessary or a priori premises."[1] (Nor on a unified, general ethical system, we would add.) All that matters are: whether our starting points are ones we are will-ing to own; and whether we can persevere until equilibrium is achieved. See **Foundationalism**

Refractory: unresponsive, or not yielding readily, to attempted forms of treatment.

Regoal: to let go of previous goals-of-care and to draw up new ones more appropriate to changed circumstances.

Relational Bioethics: an orientation which places a premium on the inter-personal solidarity of doctor and patient. This is what ensures **continuity of care**; and it also helps to keep the doctor and patient working toward com-mon goals. For this view maintains that medicine's difficult questions are best answered when personal connections—meaningful, healthy ones—are pursued as sources of healing in and of themselves. Not to be overlooked is the importance of the supportive presence of family and significant others as well. **RB** has special attraction for: (a) those who believe that loneliness and wellness are opposing conditions; (b) those who are not comfortable with recent developments in medicine that have reduced the time doctors get to spend with their patients; and (c) clinicians who recognize that patient-trust cannot be taken for granted; it has to be earned, and the best way to do that is to treat the patient not as a bundle of symptoms but as a person. "Whether we are conducting research abroad or sitting down at the bedside in the hospital, we are fellow human beings and we can meet. There is a possibility for connection. . . . Relational ethics acknowledges the quality of the con-nection, and examines what gives rise to feeling acknowledged, respected,

---

1. Richardson, "John Rawls," para. 39.

and well cared for in the course of our (professional) lives."[2] Compare with
Care, Ethics of and **Feminist Bioethics**

Relativism, Moral: ethical theories that argue that the binding quality of
moral precepts is "relative" to their context. That is, things that are right or
wrong within a particular situation or societal perspective need not be right
or wrong from the vantage point of another situation or cultural milieu.
Moral values need not "carry over"—which is the opposite of what **universalism** holds. The important point is: for the relativist, there is no mega-
perspective permitting anyone to sit in judgment on all the various value
systems. Instead, morals are similar to mores, or tribal customs, if you will.
The upshot of this is that convictions and actions can only be critiqued from
within. Taken to its logical extreme, **MR** means that for any controversial
event—say, an officer-involved shooting—in order to know whether it was
justified or not, "you had to be there," as the saying goes. Compare with
Absolutism, Moral; Emotivism; Fallibilism, Moral; and **Subjectivism**

Renal Insufficiency: a medical condition in which the kidneys are not
operating adequately. The problem can be chronic or acute; and it can be
partial or total (which is renal failure).

Replication Crisis: starting after 2010, a cloud began to form over peer-re-
viewed research—especially in psychology but also with dire consequences
in medicine—regarding the credibility of purportedly "scientific" findings.
The problem was that, too often, when subsequent attempts were made to
confirm important studies, similar procedures failed to obtain similar results. Why? The problem seems to be that, while not being guilty of outright
fraud, researchers have been using questionable research practices. (Those
practices are usually regarded as having been produced, not so much by
deliberate dishonesty and malfeasance, but more often by unconscious bias,
research naïveté, and problems in the system.) Be that as it may, the practices in question have colorful names: **data dredging, file-drawer problem,
p-hacking,** and **Texas sharpshooter fallacy**. In 2005, John Ioannidis wrote
an instant classic, "Why Most Published Research Findings Are False."[3] And
while his title is over the top, the article itself performed the important service of shining new light on a serious issue. See **Research Misconduct**

Reportable Diseases vs. Notifiable Diseases: in the United States, the
terminology is different than in the UK. In stateside usage, the former are

---

2. Dabis, "Introduction to Relational Bioethics," 2–4.
3. Ioannidis, "Why Most Published Research Findings Are False."

conditions which (because they pose a serious public health risk) medical professionals, hospitals, and laboratories are mandated to report to state and territorial jurisdictions. The latter, by contrast, are those conditions which states and other authorities voluntarily report to the CDC, to facilitate the monitoring of disease trends and the crafting of public health initiatives. And note: "Every national notifiable disease is not necessarily reportable in each state. In addition, not every state reportable condition is national notifiable."[4] In the UK and some other countries, mandatory-to-report conditions go by the latter term rather than the former. That is, **NDs** are the ones that medical practitioners and laboratories are legally required to report. See **Mandatory Reporting** and **National Notifiable Diseases Surveillance System (NNDSS)**

Research Misconduct: beginning in 1974 and continuing throughout the 1980s, a number of instances of deceptive misreporting of data by scientific investigators came to light. The cumulative impact of these public disclosures prompted the US Public Health Service to begin a corrective process, one that specifically targeted a narrow band of practices. The resulting definition of **RM** is as follows:

> Research misconduct means fabrication, falsification, or plagiarism in proposing, performing, or reviewing research, or in reporting research results. (a) **Fabrication** is making up data or results and recording or reporting them. (b) **Falsification** is manipulating research materials, equipment, or processes, or changing or omitting data or results such that the research is not accurately represented in the research record. (c) **Plagiarism** is the appropriation of another person's ideas, processes, results, or words without giving appropriate credit.[5]

Compare with **Replication Crisis,** and see **Dry-Labbing; Fabrication; Falsification; Plagiarism; Salami Slicing;** and **Text Recycling**

Resection / To Resect: surgery to cut out and remove part or all of a damaged organ or other part of the body, especially a tumor. Whereas to excise means to remove the entire structure, resection can mean all or part.

Resident Physician: (AKA **House Officer**) graduating from med school means that a person has an MD or DO degree and is therefore now a

---

4. CDC, "National Notifiable Diseases Surveillance System," para. 3.

5. Office of Research Integrity, "Definition of Research Misconduct," lines 1–7 (bold emphasis mine).

"doctor"—but a doctor still in training. Residency is the additional three to seven years of supervised experience in one of the medical specialties. First-year residents are routinely referred to as "interns" and their first year as an "internship." And while any intern may legitimately refer to him- or herself as a "resident," only first-year residents are ever called interns.

Respiratory Failure: the failure of the lungs to transfer oxygen from inhaled air to the blood, and to transfer carbon dioxide from the blood to exhaled air. The problem can be in the tiny air sacs in the lungs (alveoli), or in the brain centers controlling breathing, or again in the muscles that expand the lungs. A number of medical conditions can result in **RF**: asthma, burns, chronic obstructive lung disease, drug overdose, emphysema, extreme obesity, heart failure, multiple physical injuries, muscle disease, near-drowning, nerve disease, premature birth, profuse bleeding, severe infection, and/or surgery.

Return of Spontaneous Circulation: see **ROSC (Return of Spontaneous Circulation)**

Reverse Plagiarism: see under **Plagiarism**

Right to Die: in the first instance, the focus was on the entitlement to die *naturally*, that is, (a) not to be kept alive against one's wishes; (b) in conditions more burdensome than beneficial; and (c) in reliance on extraordinary measures. So, it meant personal freedom winning out over the imposition of artificial life support and over a medical team's paternalistic disregard for human **autonomy** and **quality-of-life** concerns. In some circles, the above now comes under the **right to refuse treatment**. For more recently, **RtD** has been cited in discussions of euthanasia, suicide, and **physician-assisted suicide**. And in these contexts, it is viewed as an entitlement to actively end one's own life either directly or at the hand, or with the assistance, of others. See **Active Shortening of the Dying Process** and **Advance Directive**

Right to Refuse Treatment vs. Right to Treatment: the former refers to a right to say no to unwanted medical care, and generally it is understood as an absolute negative right. So, per the principle of **autonomy**, it applies to care that is expected to be in the patient's best interests and even to life-and-death decision-making. The latter term, by contrast, often has the care of behavioral health patients in view. A facility such as a psychiatric hospital, which has admitted and thus assumed responsibility for a resident, is thereafter legally obligated to provide appropriate and adequate treatment for him or her. Concerns include that involuntarily institutionalized persons not receive substandard treatment; and that residents of public facilities not receive medical care inferior to those in private facilities. However, **RtT** can also be used in other contexts. For example, in the ER it indicates the entitlement that all persons have to receive emergency medical services irrespective of their ability to pay.

Right to Try: a green light provided by federal and state laws for patients with life-threatening illnesses to request experimental therapies. These are as-yet unproven treatment options sought in the hope that they might provide some clinical benefit. Colorado adopted the first **RtT** law in 2014; forty other states followed suit. The Federal Right to Try Act was passed in May 2018. Less strict than some of the state laws, it is limited to drugs that have passed the first (of three) of the Food and Drug Administration's (FDA) clinical trial phases. And significantly, it shields manufacturers and physicians from liability. **RtT** provides an alternative pathway to the FDA's Expanded Access Program (EAP). In fact, a major reason for these laws is that the red tape of the EAP was daunting and time consuming; **RtT** was meant to provide a workaround. See **Compassionate Use / Expanded Access Program**

Risk: the probability of some potential harm in combination with its seriousness. Risks are rated "higher" or "lower" depending on how likely they are to occur, factored together with how great the envisioned harm would be.

Risk-Benefit Analysis: weighing the positives against the negatives in treatment alternatives. In reference to individual patients, "burden-to-benefit" is a common way of saying the same thing. Not to be confused with **Cost-Benefit Analysis (CBA)**

Risk Management, Hospital: identifying, assessing, and averting risks in the organization. These can include: hazardous conditions; diagnostic, surgical, or medication errors; and breaches in patient privacy.

Risk Score Calculator: a simple instrument for estimating a person's risk of, for instance, having a myocardial infarction or a stroke, based on major risk factors. It can also, in some cases, be taken as indicating who are the best candidates for preventative measures. There are many different calculators for many different diseases, as well as for candidates for organ transplants, etc. Frequently mentioned are: the Framingham, the ASCVD (Atherosclerotic Cardiovascular Disease), and the Reynolds Risk Calculators.

ROSC (Return of Spontaneous Circulation): the restoration, after **cardiac arrest**, of a patient's heart rhythm signaled by a discernible pulse or measurable blood pressure. Other signs include a return of breathing—a gasp or coughing—and/or movement. Getting a heart to start beating on its own again is the whole purpose of CPR. However, though it's a crucial step along the way, **ROSC** is not the end of the story, for there is no guarantee that the patient will survive to his or her release from the hospital. See **Cardiopulmonary Resuscitation (CPR)**

Rule-Utilitarianism: consequentialist ethical theories unite in holding that right and wrong are determined by outcomes—and this is one of those theories. What sets **R-U** apart is that: (a) it focuses on the greatest good for the greatest number of people; and then (b) it asks which enduring norms (rather than which situational acts) produce the best results. See **Act-Utilitarianism; Consequentialism;** and **Bentham, Jeremy** and **Mill, John Stuart** (in **Part 2**)

Letter S

Safe Discharge: release from a medical facility once the patient is medically stable and no longer needs inpatient attention, and with a plan for appropriate care from that point forward. In such a plan, the patient's posthospital destination and ongoing care needs should be identified, with arrangements made for any additional, necessary health care services. See **Failed Discharge** and **Patient Dumping**

Salami Slicing: sectioning the results of a study into smaller packages, called "least publishable units," to maximize the number of submittable manuscripts. The consensus view is that, however common, the practice ought to be avoided. This is particularly true in the biomedical sciences. In the arts, humanities, and social sciences the downside is not as obviously serious. See **Text Recycling**

Sami's Law: first a New Jersey and then a federal (2019) enactment, this measure protects customers of ride-sharing services. It requires Lyft- and Uber-type vehicles to display a barcode and illuminated identification signs; and it makes driver misrepresentation a crime. The law was named after Samantha Josephson, a college student in South Carolina. She accepted a ride from, and was murdered by, an imposter she thought was from Uber. See **Laws Named after Victims**

Sanctity of Life: the view that life is worthy of being respected, protected, and prolonged. With a figure like Mahatma Gandhi, this reverence extends to all living beings: "To my mind the life of a lamb is no less precious than that of a human being. . . . The more helpless a creature, the more entitled it is to protection by man from the cruelty of man."[1] Some present-day animal rights activists hold a similar view. However, when it is human life that is

---

1. Gandhi, *Autobiography*, 235.

in view, proponents of **SoL** typically maintain that the continued physical existence of each person has an unconditional priority which supersedes all other considerations. Unfavorable circumstances (such as those which might prompt someone to say, "I would never want to live unconscious and be kept alive by a machine") do not matter; life must be maintained. That said, two points are worth remembering. (1) There are positions that are not so extensive and which appeal to the principle in some more limited way, as in discussions of **abortion** or **physician-assisted suicide**. And (2) in the religion of the Jains, respect for life extends beyond the human-and-animal level. Monks take great pains not to harm the smallest of insects; and Jains are taught to avoid injuring plants as much as possible. So with **SoL**, establishing a minimum or maximum is exceedingly problematic. See **Quality of Life (QOL)** and **Vitalism;** and **Schweitzer, Albert** (in **Part 2**)

SAPS II (Simplified Acute Physiology Score II): like **MODS** and **SOFA**, a newer classification system for measuring the seriousness of disease for patients admitted to ICUs. Preferred over **APACHE II** in many places.

Scheduled Drugs: the Controlled Substances Act of 1970 was designed to revamp the manufacturing, importing, exporting, distributing, and dispensing of controlled substances. To that end, many drugs were assigned to categories according to their medical usefulness and their potential for abuse and/or dependency. From highest potential for harm to lowest, the categories are: Schedule I—having no medical usefulness, plus a high probability for abuse and addiction (heroin, etc.); Schedule II—having recognized medical usefulness but also a high potential for misuse and a risk for severe physical or psychological dependence (oxycodone, etc.); Schedule III—low-to-moderate possibility of physical or psychological dependence (like codeine); Schedule IV—low (in comparison to I, II, & III) risk of dependence or abuse (such as Valium); Schedule V—meds that include reduced quantities of certain narcotics (cough syrups being a good example). Some wonder, however, whether "It's possible that our scheduling system no longer makes sense."[2]

Schizophrenia (σχίζω = split; φρήν = mind): a mental disorder which compromises a person's ability to think, feel, act, and function in the world. Primary symptoms are: delusions, hallucinations, and incoherent speech— possibly coupled with extremely disorganized behavior, or again with an unduly diminished level of activity or emotional expressiveness.

2. Emba, "Opinion," para. 9.

Scrupulosity: a term that arose out of the traditional Roman Catholic sacrament of penance. There it referred to the hyper-moralism of penitents who would enter the confessional, possibly several times a day, to admit to the same sins, over and over. Today, it has been taken up by psychologists; they understand it to be a form of Obsessive Compulsive Disorder, one in which a person's pathological anxiety manifests itself as guilt over religio-moral obligations and sins. See **Spirit of the Law and Letter of the Law**

Scut Work: slang for the uninteresting, unpleasant, nonmedical chores required in patient care. Traditionally used for any task assigned to a doctor-in-training, a nurse—or actually any hospital employee—which the assignee regards as not what they signed up for. However, in recent years the term has been applied by clinicians to newly imposed rigamarole, such as electronic record keeping, that takes away from face-to-face contact with patients.

Sectioning: in the UK, this is what being involuntarily committed to a mental facility is called. Detention of persons with "any disorder or disability of mind" is authorized by the Mental Health Act (MHA) 1983. The particulars of said detention depend on which section of the act is being applied. For example, Section 2 authorizes an assessment period of up to twenty-eight days; and Section 3 authorizes a treatment period of up to six months. Being sectioned for shorter periods of time are also possible. Section 5(4), authorizes a nurse to detain a hospital patient for up to six hours. See **Involuntary Psychiatric Treatment**

Self-Regulation Model of Illness (SRMI): (AKA the common sense model of illness representation) first described in 1980 by Howard Leventhal and colleagues, this model is a way of appreciating the subjective take an individual has on his or her illness as distinct from what is indicated by the objective clinical evidence. Such an illness representation is based on how the condition is liable to impact the patient's ability to continue with his or her normal level of functioning.

Semmelweis Reflex: a cognitive bias named after **Ignaz Semmelweis** (found in **Part 2**). It refers to the irrational, seemingly automatic rejection of new evidence or information when it contradicts received knowledge and/or an existing paradigm.

Sepsis (σῆψις = putrefaction): especially serious to patients who are critically ill, this condition results from a body's overreaction to an infection. The immune system launches infection-countering chemicals into the bloodstream, normally a good thing; but too much produces an overwhelming inflammatory state that induces low blood pressure. Which means that the amount of blood reaching crucial organs and limbs is restricted. ▪ **Septic Shock:** sepsis at its worst. This is when, on top of everything else, blood pressure drops dangerously low and requires medications to raise it. It is the leading cause of death in ICUs in the United States. (There are multiple scoring systems and specific clinical rubrics for sepsis which are not discussed here.) See **Asepsis**

Sequelae: in medicine, this plural of sequela refers to a longer-lasting, follow-on medical condition subsequent to and/or caused by a different problem or injury.

Serious (Condition): the patient is very ill and might have unstable vital signs outside the normal limits. Indicators for recovery are questionable. (**Critical** is worse than serious.)

Seroprevalence: an estimate of the pervasiveness of an infectious agent in a population arrived at by testing to determine the number of people who have antibodies for it in their bloodstream. It is commonly stated as a percentage or as the rate per 100,000.

Shoehorn: a slang term favored by bioethicists which means: maneuvering something into a context in which it does not reasonably or comfortably fit. For example, "Lowering compensation to research subjects to protect them from 'undue inducement' is a misguided attempt to shoehorn a concern about exploitation into the framework of autonomy."[3]

Shopterm: a jargony word used quasi-seriously by insiders in a business, interest group, academic association, or scientific discipline.

Shotgunning: medical slang common in Great Britain. It applies to a doctor, having no idea what might be wrong with a patient, ordering a wide array of tests on the off-chance that one might actually detect something. See **Sutton's Law**

Simon's Law: named after Simon Crosier, this legislation (2017 in Kansas; 2019 in Missouri) prohibits healthcare providers from limiting life-sustaining care for minors without the authorization of a parent or guardian. It further mandates written disclosures of patient-care policies, such as futility guidelines. Simon was born in 2010 in a Missouri hospital. Diagnosed with

---

3. Lamkin and Elliott, "Avoiding Exploitation," 52.

trisomy 18, a genetic anomaly, he lived three months. His mother, Sheryl Crosier, was shocked to learn that he had been given **DNR** status and had been assigned nutrition as a comfort measure—without her knowledge and approval. These steps had been in keeping with hospital guidelines; and at the time they were legal in Missouri (Kansas, too). But no longer.

Situation Ethics: the view that the moral demands of **love (agape)** are so decisive, and that the circumstantial realities in which moral questions arise are so important, that ethical reflection need not look elsewhere. All that's needed is "love plus the situation"—that's the basic idea. It should be pointed out that situationism was an idea whose time had come and gone until Joseph Fletcher paired it with sixties-era sexual revolution sensibilities in *Situation Ethics—The New Morality*.[4] Then it sprang back to life. Fletcher contrasted his approach with a stony **legalism**, on the one hand, and a guidance-free **antinomianism**, on the other—and many readers found this compelling. In contemporary bioethics, **SE**'s relevance lives on as comparisons are made to **casuistry**. And in fact, Fletcher anticipated as much. "This neocasuistry is, like classical casuistry, case-focused and concrete, concerned to bring Christian imperatives into practical operation."[5]

Slow Code: highly controversial, a deliberate slowdown in what would otherwise be treated as an emergency. (See **Code**.) In a situation in which CPR is believed to be of no medical benefit, performing a **SC** means that the medical team goes through the motions without making a sincere effort to resuscitate the patient. ▪ **Show Code:** performance of CPR, not for the benefit of the patient, but for nearby stakeholders, such as members of the family. Slow Code and Show Code can be used interchangeably. ▪ **Short Code:** CPR of a more limited duration than normal, either as a trial to confirm that, in fact, resuscitation is not possible, or as a symbolic gesture or even a pretense, making it the same as the above.

SNF, "Sniff" (Skilled Nursing Facility): one type of nursing home. The difference between a SNF and a regular nursing home has to do with level of care, though length of stay can be a factor too. A **SNF** will commonly be staffed by a number of licensed healthcare professionals: registered nurses, vocational nurses, speech pathologists, physical therapists, and doctors. Facilities can provide either short- or long-term care, but are most often looked to for posthospital follow-up or transitional medical services. Nursing homes, on the other hand, offer indefinite-length or long-term custodial

4. Fletcher, *Situation Ethics.*
5. Fletcher, *Situation Ethics*, 148.

care; a doctor might be on staff, but very likely will not be; and most of the care will be provided by nurses' aides. One complication is that there are nursing homes which are Medicare- and Medicaid-certified; this brings with it additional requirements. Compare with **LTAC (Long-Term Acute Care) Hospital and Subacute Care**

Social Prescribing: as understood in the UK and Scandinavia, this is when a health provider directs a patient to an involvement or activity for health and well-being purposes: certain community-based options, yes, but traditional social services, no. Gym workouts, art classes, food clubs, and peer support meetings are good examples. And so is going for a walk in the park.

SOFA (Sequential Organ Failure Assessment): another one of the severity-of-illness scoring systems, along with **APACHE II, SAPS II,** and **MODS**. Although APACHE II and SAPS II are based on routinely measured physiologic variables, **SOFA** and MODS are organ-failure-based scores.

Solution-Focused Model: (AKA Solution-Focused Brief Therapy) an approach to mental health counseling. There is little time spent delving into major personality problems, their complicated history, and the client's self-frustrating behaviors. Instead the focus in on where the client would like to end up and what he or she is already doing right that can be utilized as a springboard for getting there. Building on client goals and strengths, the idea is to achieve positive changes after just a few sessions—with some versions putting the number at four or five.

Somnolence: sleepiness/drowsiness, normal or otherwise.

Source Control: all surgical and nonsurgical steps taken to eliminate the source of an infection, control its spread, and restore a patient to a previous state of health.

Spina Bifida: (Latin = split spine) a birth defect involving the neural tube, the embryonic precursor of both the brain and the spinal cord. During the third and fourth weeks of pregnancy, the spine and spinal cord can sometimes fail to develop or close as they should; and when that happens, the end result is that at birth a portion of the spine is exposed. However, no two cases of **SB** are the same, and the problem can range from mild to severe. Together with **anencephaly, SB** is the most common of the **neural tube defects**.

Spinal Stenosis (στενός = narrow): a narrowing of the open spaces in the spinal column which results in pressure on the spinal cord and the nerves that extend to the arms and legs.

Spirit of the Law and Letter of the Law: one of the more profound distinctions in all of moral philosophy, this theme originated with the Apostle Paul's "the letter kills, but the Spirit gives life" (2 Cor 3:6). For **Augustine**, it provided the basis for his response to the Pelagians. They preached that obedience and righteousness are natural human possibilities, not needing God's grace but only his law in order to be fulfilled. Augustine disagreed. It is not enough, he argued, to observe that "God gave the law, instituted the teaching, delivered good precepts. For all this, apart from the Spirit's aid, is indubitably the letter that killeth: only when the life-giving Spirit is present, does he cause to be written within, and loved, that which when it was written externally the law caused to be feared."[6] Far removed from Paul and Augustine, this same basic distinction lives on whenever the issue is that the literal requirements of a norm fail to correspond to the essential goodness of life in its ultimate context. See **Epikeia** and **Scrupulosity**

Spirituality: the search for, or the awareness of, the depth dimension in human experience. In that dimension are found life's meaning and its mystery. Commonly thought of as the realm of God or gods or spirits, it is a dimension that evokes from any who would draw near both fascination and dread (Rudolf Otto), and that summons responses of both courage and doubt (Paul Tillich). Ambiguities between mystery and meaning—and in fact between losing one's life and finding it—are fundamental to all true **S.**

Spontaneous Remission: the sudden, medically inexplicable improvement or disappearance of a disease, typically cancer. Although distinctions can be made, **SR** can also be referred to as "spontaneous healing" or "spontaneous regression."

Sporadic: see **Endemic vs. Sporadic**

Standard of Care vs. Standard Operating Procedures: two standards, the former constituting the baseline for a professional practice. It requires "the provision of services in a manner consistent with care, as another professional with similar training and experience faced with a similar care situation would provide. Standards of care set minimum criteria for job proficiency."[7] The second category, **SOPs**, are the multifarious, written-

---

6. Augustine, "Spirit and the Letter," 219.

7. Gura, "Differentiating," para. 1.

up descriptions of how to sequence tasks and perform essential activities within an office, organization, or event. They are aimed at uniformity and efficiency. And unlike **SoC**, they do not apply across a profession; for in theory, there could be as many sets of written procedures as there are enterprises. They are common in hospitals and in research. For example, "Labs must have written **SOPs** when work involves the use of hazardous materials (chemical, radioactive, and biological) or physical hazards."[8]

Stat: (Latin *statim* = immediately) calls for something to be done at once, without delay.

Stealth Euthanasia and Covert Euthanasia: two terms favored by **vitalism** activists, some of them, who oppose much that is common in contemporary end-of-life patient care. In their minds, a culture of death reigns in the United States—hidden behind the deceptive arguments of doctors and bioethicists. The claim is that in hospice and palliative care settings which are under the influence of this culture of death, patients are intentionally being euthanized. This is not a view espoused here. See **Euthanasia**

Stent Cases: can often refer to court cases in which the federal government seeks to prove healthcare fraud against cardiologists for unnecessarily placing stents in patients who did not need them. (The coronary artery stent is a small, cylindrical cage positioned to prevent an artery from closing.) One objection to these federal cases is that they pit government-hired doctors against the ones being charged, when actually "government doctors are no more reliable than private ones."[9] The result is prosecution based on "the criminalization of medical judgment."[10]

Step-Down Unit: (AKA transitional care unit or intermediate care unit) a section of the hospital dedicated to providing medical services and care observation, with less concentration than the ICU but with greater focus than the general wards. The two most important factors are: (a) nurse-to-patient ratio; and (b) the technical ability of the nurses and technical capacity of the unit to provide organ support. A "step-down bed" is similar but need not be located within a specialized unit.

Stroke: an interruption or reduction in the flow of blood to the brain. Most strokes (80 percent) are caused by blocking up and are called "ischemic." Fewer (approaching 20 percent) are caused by bleeding and are called

8. Iowa State University, "Standard Operating Procedures," para. 1.

9. Clark and George, "Court Corrects a Medical Injustice," A13.

10. From the title of George et al., "Stent Cases."

"hemorrhagic." Strokes can sometimes be the cause of various disabilities, either temporary or long-lasting; it depends on which part of the brain was involved and on how long and how fully the supply of oxygen was reduced. Also called a cerebrovascular accident. See **Ischemia**

Struck Off: a British slang term which applies to various professions: doctors, nurses, lawyers, teachers, and social workers. It means being disbarred, removed, or having one's professional license revoked. ("A doctor who was struck off the UK medical register in 2013 for misconduct has been allowed back on.")[11] See **Wakefield, Andrew** (in **Part 2**)

Stuporous: having diminished responsiveness to external stimuli and requiring vigorous, repeated, or unpleasant stimulation to be brought back to conscious awareness.

Subacute Care: an intermediate level of medical services between a skilled nursing facility (**SNF**) and a hospital. It is intended for patients whose acute illness, traumatic injury, or progressive disease requires specially skilled nursing care, technical treatment, or rehabilitation services. Yet these patients are medically stable enough not to need the more intense, high-tech diagnosis or monitoring of a traditional hospital.

Subarachnoid Hemorrhage: see **Intracranial Hemorrhage**

Subclinical: not available for medical detection. A condition can be insufficiently advanced or insufficiently severe for symptoms to be displayed (as yet). Or again, its carrier can be asymptomatic. **Typhoid Mary**, for example, had a **S** case of typhoid fever.

Subjective: in clinical contexts, subjective findings are the matters shared by the patient during an interview regarding what he or she has felt or experienced, as distinct from the objective findings which are garnered by the clinician. For example, palpitations are subjective and felt by the patient, whereas heart rate is an objective finding ascertained by the clinician. So in these settings, subjectivity and objectivity are thought of as complementary. But in a more general context, it was once common to understand subjectivity as meaning limited to, and distorted by, an individual's needs and circumstances—an objective view being assumed to be unbiased, and thus more accurate. However, in recent times, one often finds that these two terms have been given the opposite valuations, so that subjectivity is considered trustworthy and objectivity dubious.

11. Dyer, "Doctor Who Was Struck Off," 368.

Subjectivism: in ethics, the view that morality is a matter of personal preference, and that moral claims are expressions of personal convictions. So, "Murder is wrong," means that the person speaking disapproves of it (and/ or has strong negative feelings about it). Moral claims, according to subjectivists, never take us "out there" beyond the interiority of the individual. And thus wrong-for-you can't ever imply wrong-for-anyone-else. Compare with **Absolutism, Moral; Emotivism; Fallibilism, Moral; Relativism, Moral;** and **Universalism, Moral**.

Substituted Judgment vs. Best Interest Standard: the twin paradigms for making healthcare decisions on behalf of a patient when the patient lacks **decision-making capacity**, and when there is no **advance directive** or other reliable information to go on. With **SJ**, one person speaks for another, echoing, as it were, what the other would say if he or she were able communicate. This only works if there is a **surrogate decision-maker** who can say, "Knowing Aunt Sally as I do, it is clear to me that she would want Option Y." When no surrogate has that level of personal familiarity, that's when the second paradigm kicks in. Rather than the *wishes* of the person, now it is the *good* of the person that matters. And good is assumed to be what most reasonable people would choose as good, given the norms of the relevant community. That's quite an assumption, true; for everyone realizes that *this person* is not *most people*. But even so, the **BIS** does provide a responsible way of moving forward when vital, person-specific information is unavailable.

Suicide: see **Parasuicide**

Supererogatory: going above and beyond what is obligatory. One might call it the moral equivalent of "extra credit." This category has been important in traditional Roman Catholicism, which has held that in addition to what is morally required of every good person, there are additional, praiseworthy "counsels of perfection." They represent a higher, saint-level order of moral achievement.

Superimposed: one condition arising out of, or developing on top of, another condition. Examples include: **delirium** superimposed on **dementia**; and Major Depressive Disorder superimposed on low-grade Persistent Depressive Disorder (AKA "dysthymia"). The latter is called "double depression."

Super-Spreader: an epidemiological shopterm meaning a person, place, or event responsible for transmitting a highly contagious disease to a large number of individuals. See **Typhoid Mary** and **80/20 Rule** (in **Numbers**)

Supported Decision-Making: an alternative to guardianship, potentially appropriate for, for example, a patient whose decision-making capacity fluctuates. According to this model, the person in question chooses trusted allies to comprise a team which will help with his or her decisions—explaining procedures, on the one hand; and on the other, interpreting words and behavior as indications of patient preferences.

Surrogate Decision-Maker: (AKA health care proxy or agent) for a patient who lacks decision-making capacity, the **SDM** is an advocate, someone who can make healthcare choices on his or her behalf. See **Surrogate Hierarchy**

Surrogate Hierarchy: the prioritization of who shall be the **surrogate decision-maker** for a patient lacking in **decision-making capacity**. In the United States, this is determined at the state level. A few states make legal provision in general but stop short of establishing a surrogacy ladder. "In the 35 states that [do] establish a surrogate hierarchy, the highest-priority classes always include spouse, child, and parent, though 8 states also insert partner or 'chosen adult' on or immediately below the first ladder rung."[12] On the other hand, there are six states that have no surrogate consent laws. They are: Massachusetts, Minnesota, Missouri, Nebraska, Rhode Island, and Vermont.

Sustainable Development: the ideal of societies advancing, expanding, and exploring ways of meeting the needs of their current citizenry without harming the environment, depleting its resources, or otherwise limiting the ability of earth's future inhabitants to do the same. Arising in the 1980s, **SD** melded the previously often-opposed ideas of progress and conservation into a single unified concept, one that furnished a basis for calls for changing the nature of how societies change. See **Precautionary Principle**

Sutton's Law: a directive to start with the obvious diagnostic test. This physician's principle was named after Willie Sutton, the famous holdup-meister. Legend has it that when he was asked why he robbed banks, his answer was, "Because that's where the money is." Dr. William Dock came up with Sutton's Law as his way of saying: don't waste time and money on a routine battery of conventional procedures if the evidence calls for something else—do the obvious! See **Shotgunning**

Symmetry Arguments: construed generally, these can be applied to ethical questions about any twosome or contrast. For instance, "if a doctor has a duty to be truthful to a patient, does the same apply to the patient's

12. DeMartino et al., "Who Decides?," para. 14.

statements to a doctor?"[13] However, the usual association is with Epicurean philosophy and Lucretius's Symmetry Argument, which is: since we had nothing to fear or to be concerned about prior to birth; and since our nonexistence after we die will be the same as our nonexistence before we were born, that means that death should not frighten or concern us now. See **Asymmetry Argument**

Symptom Management: in **palliative care**, an emphasis on treating patients' symptoms and side effects, and improving their quality of life, as opposed to addressing and attempting to cure their underlying medical problems. (AKA comfort care and supportive care.)

13. Higgs, "Asymmetry/Symmetry Arguments," 16.

Letter T

Tarasoff Rule: from the first of two rulings by the California Supreme Court in *Tarasoff v. Regents of the University of California* (1974), the rule was that mental health professionals have an obligation to warn authorities or potential victims about threats posed by patients in their care; and that this duty supersedes provider-client confidentiality requirements. The facts of the case are convoluted, but the essentials are: a troubled young man told his psychotherapist that he planned to kill a female acquaintance. The therapist told law enforcement that the client should be hospitalized; but he did not warn the woman herself. The young man carried out his deadly plan and the victim's family sued the therapist. His defense was that he had no duty to warn her because she was not his client. The court rejected this and found that when a patient in a professional's care poses a serious threat of violence to a third party, the therapist has a "duty to warn" the intended victim. This ruling was widely criticized on such grounds as that patient-therapist confidentiality should be more sacrosanct than that, and that predicting dangerousness is seldom so simple. ▪ **Tarasoff II:** the case was reheard in 1976, and the "duty to warn" was replaced by a "duty to protect" by various means. Next, other court cases around the country began producing what were possibly too-broad applications of the case, those applications going as far as to create duties regarding even accidental harm to random victims. "As a result, some case law shifted to require that the threat be clearly made, and that the duty extended only to reasonably foreseeable victims—not to the general public. Many states subsequently adopted statutes known as 'Tarasoff-limiting statutes,' which gave specific criteria (i.e., a credible threat made against an identifiable victim)."[1] See **Duty to Warn / Duty to Protect**

Teratogenic Drugs: meds and other substances that are capable of negatively impacting the development of an embryo or fetus, resulting, for example,

---

1. Knoll, "Psychiatric Practice Grand Rounds," para. 8.

in birth defects, or even in the stopping of the pregnancy altogether. The list of **TDs** is lengthy. ▪ **Teratogens:** a broader category. In addition to drugs, it includes radiation, chemicals, and infections—anything that can cause an embryo or fetus to develop abnormally.

Terminal Extubation: withdrawing the endotracheal tube and thus ending the use of mechanical ventilation with a patient who is expected not to be able to live without it.

Terminal Weaning: though the endotracheal tube remains in place, mechanical support (ventilator rate, pressure, and/or oxygen level) is slowly reduced with a patient who is expected to not be able to live without it. The decrease can take minutes, hours, or days.

Tertiary Care Center: a highly specialized hospital offering dedicated intensive care units, advanced diagnostic services, and highly trained personnel. It is usually the "last stop" for referrals from neighboring, smaller hospitals. However, see **Quaternary Care Center**

Test-Tube Baby: a newborn conceived by artificial means, through **in vitro fertilization**. An egg is fertilized in a laboratory dish and then implanted in the mother-to-be's uterus. Louise Brown, the first such infant to be conceived in this way, was born in 1978. See **Designer Baby**

Texas Sharpshooter Fallacy: a research shopterm built around the idea of a farmer who wanted to be thought of as an expert marksman. He shot up the side of his barn—and then afterward drew targets around the tighter clusters of bullet holes. Instant sharpshooter! This term frequently comes up in discussions of post hoc hypotheses being treated as a priori, and especially of random agglomerations of data being hailed as a pattern. Such finaglings are among the questionable research practices credited with spawning the present-day **replication crisis** that vexes psychology and other disciplines. See **A Priori vs. A Posteriori**

Text Recycling: (AKA **Self-Plagiarism**) using and receiving credit for one's own textual material multiple times without referencing it as such. Opinions vary; but there is broad agreement that the practice can raise serious ethical issues, depending on the context. See **Self-Plagiarism** (listed under **Plagiarism**) and compare with **Fabrication**; **Falsification**; **Plagiarism**; and **Salami Slicing**

Therapeutic Illusion (θεραπεία = medical treatment; healing): an unwarranted confidence—on the part of either physicians or patients—in the possible pluses, and an unwise disregard for the possible minuses, of various interventions. In short, an overly optimistic belief in what human beings can control and in what medicine can accomplish. See **Evidence-Based Medicine (EBM)**

Thrombus: a blood clot attached inside an artery or an organ, impeding the flow of blood. If one breaks off, it becomes an **embolus** and thus may be said to have "embolized." ▪ **Thrombosis:** blood clot formation, which is good during hemorrhage, but life-threatening otherwise. See: **Coronary Thrombosis**

Time-Limited Trial (TLT) (of treatment): a course of therapy for a set period of time. The physician and the patient or surrogate agree to an intervention for a set time frame. This option provides "a way to experience a treatment's impact over a specified period and then allow patient, families, and clinicians to re-evaluate if it is achieving the patient's goals."[2] Often favored for end-of-life care.

Titration: seeking the optimum dosage of a medication—balancing beneficial effectiveness with burdensome side effects—by making a number of small adjustments in the amount taken. Informally, "titrating off" of a drug means carefully tapering off as opposed to quitting cold turkey.

Total Parenteral Nutrition (TPN): a means of feeding without involving the gastrointestinal tract. When someone's digestive system won't allow or can't handle food eaten normally, liquid nourishment is sent into a vein through a thin, flexible tube.

Tox Screen: a blood, urine, or saliva test used to determine what drugs are in a person's system. The most common of such drug and alcohol tests is the Urine Drug Screen (UDS). (It is common to hear, "Did we get a UDS?")

Trace Evidence vs. Touch DNA Evidence: two terms from forensic science. The first refers to pieces of physical evidence left behind after a crime. Often but not always miniscule, these can include hair, fibers, soot, soil, flecks of paint, and gunshot residue. They can also be important sources of our second kind of evidence. There the focus is on everything "touched" by a perpetrator at the scene of a crime. Fingerprints are a prime example: forensic scientists seek to connect persons under investigation with crime scenes by analyzing the DNA from skin cells and amino acids found above all in fingerprints.

2. Siropaides and Arnold, "Time-Limited Trials," para. 1.

"Trake" (written "trach") **(Tracheostomy):** tracheotomy and tracheostomy are overlapping terms. The former is technically the procedure by which an opening is cut through a patient's neck and into the trachea; the latter is the actual opening itself; however, the two terms can be used interchangeably. Thus "trach" can indicate the performance of the surgical procedure; or it can refer to the breathing tube inserted through the tracheostomy in order to secure an open airway. A very common combo is the "PEG and trach" for patients who need a protected airway and are to be fed directly into their stomach. See **PEG Tube**

Transhumanism: a social-ethics orientation that favors altering human life in partnership with developments in science and bioengineering. The aim is to improve the human condition, if not to reinvent the human person altogether, by directing and applying technological advances for human benefit. The idea is for lifespans to be lengthened; disease, distress, and suffering to be brought under control; and the human race's physical, intellectual, and emotional limitations to be turned into things of the past.

Transplant Rejection: when the immune system of the recipient of a transplant recognizes a transplanted organ or tissue as foreign and attacks it. It can be immediate, within a few months, or, with "chronic rejection," may happen over a period of years.

Triage: "a process of screening patients on the basis of their immediate medical needs and the likelihood of medical success in treating those needs. . . . The process of triage was first developed and refined in military medicine and was later extended to disaster and emergency medicine."[3] The wounded are assigned to a category. These are fairly uniform and can be summarized as: (1) life-saving medical attention is required immediately; (2) significant therapeutic attention is required, but not immediately; (3) observation is advised with medical treatment to be provided when possible, if necessary; (4) little or no medical care is called for; and (5) the patient's injuries are life-endangering and cannot be successfully remedied with the time and resources available. Some recent lists add: (6) treatment for bodily harm is not indicated, but traumatic stress issues may have to be addressed.

Trisomy: in humans, this is the most common type of chromosomal anomaly. Specifically, a cell has three instances of a particular chromosome instead of two. And although only four of the trisomies are listed below, triplicity can be found in any of the twenty-three chromosomes. To indicate which

3. Winslow, "Triage," 3108.

chromosome is involved, the appropriate number is suffixed. ▪ **Trisomy 13:** (Patau's Syndrome) a genetic disorder causing pronounced developmental problems: both physical defects and intellectual disabilities. And while there can be exceptions, clinical experience shows that 90 percent of such babies die within the first year; and many after only a few days or weeks. ▪ **Trisomy 16:** of all the trisomies, this one is the most common; and it has the unhappy distinction of causing the most miscarriages. The miscarriages are due to the fact that in its usual form—when the extra chromosome is found in all of the cells—trisomy 16 is incompatible with life. ▪ **Trisomy 18:** (Edwards Syndrome) another genetic disorder causing combinations of serious birth defects. These include physical abnormalities and severe cognitive impairment. Few infants with this condition (5 to 10 percent) live past their first year. ▪ **Trisomy 21:** (Down Syndrome) among human babies surviving to birth, this is the most prevalent chromosomal irregularity, affecting about 1 in every 700 newborns. It is no doubt the most easily recognized by the general populace because of the distinct facial features and familiar cognitive delay—and because they survive long enough to make it into public. Yet it is under-researched. "In the U.S., Down syndrome is the least funded major genetic condition by our National Institutes of Health despite being the most frequent chromosomal disorder."[4] See **Aneuploidy**.

True Believer: Eric Hoffer's term for the person who—needing to escape from feelings of powerlessness, worthlessness, and hopelessness—becomes fanatically devoted to, and gets lost in, a religious or political movement. "A mass movement attracts and holds a following not because it can satisfy the desire for self-advancement, but because it can satisfy the passion for self-renunciation."[5]

Tumor: one type of swelling or lump. It is caused by the abnormal growth of new tissue, either benign (not cancerous), premalignant (precancerous), or malignant (cancerous). See **Cancer**

Tuskegee Syphilis Study: a long-term experiment, "Tuskegee Study of Untreated Syphilis in the Negro Male," conducted by the United States Public Health Service from 1932 to 1972. The name came from the Tuskegee Institute (now Tuskegee University) in Alabama, which assisted with its administration. The study followed the natural course of syphilis in African American men in Macon County, Georgia. Candidates were deceptively recruited, told that they would receive free treatment for "bad blood," not that

4. Global Down Syndrome Foundation, "Facts and FAQ," para. 1.

5. Hoffer, *True Believer*, 21.

they would be guinea pigs for venereal disease research. Moreover, when the disease became treatable with penicillin in the mid-1940s, they were neither provided with it, informed about it, nor told that they needed it. The study was stopped in 1972 after a government employee leaked details to the press. The news created a public uproar, and major reforms followed. Regret about the egregious ethical violations proved to be a major factor in the launch of the bioethics movement as we know it today.

Twinkie Defense: in 1979, Dan White was tried in San Francisco for murdering Mayor George Moscone and Supervisor Harvey Milk. He was found guilty, but only of voluntary manslaughter. For many observers, that was too light a sentence—including many of the reporters covering the trial. They went to print with what then became an urban legend: that the defense attorney's argument had been that "The Twinkies made him do it!" That is, that White was mentally impaired because he had eaten too many Twinkies (a cream-filled snack cake commonly regarded as unhealthy.) The truth is that, although Twinkies had come up in court testimony, it was in a different light: an expert witness testified that the defendant's consumption of sugary junk food was a symptom of his clinical depression (not that it had caused his cognitive impairment or contributed to the crime). The term lives on today to designate any flimsy-to-absurd legal defense strategy. See **Insanity Defense**

Two-Doctor or Two-Physician Rule, The: a highly problematic notion. For a basic introduction, see Cassandra Rivais's blogpost, "A Reflection on Two-Physician Consent," in *Bioethics Today*.[6] When consent or authorization for patient treatment is in view, whether the sign-off of a second physician adds heft or not depends on the state. In New York, for individuals who lack decision-making capacity and lack a surrogate, the Family Health Care Decisions Act stipulates the following: "For major medical treatment, a physician may act only upon the concurrence of another physician that such major medical treatment is necessary." And "a physician may withhold or withdraw life-sustaining treatment for individuals without a surrogate only upon the independent concurrence of another physician that life-sustaining treatment offers no medical benefit to the patient because the patient will die imminently and the provision of life-sustaining treatment would violate accepted medical standards."[7] However, in the state of California, the rules are different. "A common misconception related to consent law is that if

6. Rivais, "Reflection on Two-Physician Consent."

7. New York State Senate, "Senate Passes Family Health Care Decisions Act," paras. 28, 29.

two doctors agree that a patient would benefit from a particular procedure or treatment, the two doctors may consent on behalf of the patient. This is a myth. There is no provision in California or federal law that permits two doctors to consent on behalf of a patient."[8] To complicate matters, other states have other definitions. In Illinois, for example, "the two-doctor rule" usually refers to worker's compensation cases and whether an injured party can have recourse to a second physician of choice.

8. California Hospital Association, *Consent*, 59.

Letter U

Unbefriended Patient: see **Unrepresented Patient**

Uniform Anatomical Gift Act: one of the various exemplar codes designed for, and adopted into law by, the American states, with an eye to standardizing the way particular issues are regulated. This one addresses the donation of human organs, tissues, and other body parts for transplantation. "U.S. citizens are probably most familiar with the part of the [act] that created a process for choosing to become an organ donor by completing a short form on a driver's license or state identity card."[1]

Uniform Determination of Death Act: another of the model codes intended to serve as a guide for state lawmakers' efforts at bringing nationwide order and uniformity to the regulation of a specific area. The intent here is to provide a way of determining death that is both medically responsible and legally sound, and that can be applied in all cases. The **UDDA**'s answer: a person is dead either: (a) when all circulatory and respiratory functions have ceased irreversibly; or (b) when all functions of the entire brain, including the brain stem, have ceased irreversibly. Beyond this, the act stipulates that these determinations have to be made in line with recognized medical standards. See **Brain Death; Circulatory-Respiratory Death;** and **Dead Donor Rule**

Unit 731: see **Japanese Medical War Crimes**

Universalism, Moral: ethical theories that unite in claiming, contra **relativism**, that particular acts can be right or wrong despite opinions, customs, and historical developments suggesting otherwise. For instance: to say, "Even though slavery was once widely practiced in the United States, it was wrong then, it's wrong now, and it will always be wrong," is to make

1. Tubbs, *Handbook of Bioethics Terms*, 175.

a universalist claim. Some portrayals equate this with moral objectivism; others set universalism and objectivism apart. Here they are taken to be two sides of the same coin: universal norms apply extensively; objective norms apply independently. Compare with **Absolutism, Moral; Emotivism; Fallibilism, Moral; Subjectivism** and **Universalizability**.

Universalizability: referring to the precept "right or wrong for one must be right or wrong for all." Generally associated with the **categorical imperative** in the ethics of **Kant**, in recent times this principle has been a bone of contention between liberal and **communitarian** ethicists, the latter maintaining that moral norms, being specific to a community and shaped by its history, need not be omniapplicable.

Unrepresented Patient: (AKA Unbefriended Patient) a person in need of medical attention who has none of the following: **decision-making capacity**; an **advance directive** or **POLST** form; or a **surrogate decision-maker**. "Unrepresented individuals include older individuals who have outlived family members . . . those with mental or behavioral health impairments; homeless individuals; and those for whom potential decision-makers are remote and do not wish to be involved in medical decision-making."[2]

Urosepsis: severe bacterial infection that complicates a urinary tract infection. If left untreated, urosepsis can progress to septic shock. See **Sepsis**

US Health Service STD Research in Guatemala: see **Guatemala Syphilis Experiments**

Utilitarianism: see **Act-Utilitarianism; Consequentialism; Rule-Utilitarianism;** and **Bentham, Jeremy,** and **Mill, John Stuart** (in **Part 2**)

---

2. Healthcare Ethics Blog, "'Unrepresented Patients' and Vulnerability," para 3.

Letter V

Vaccination: the introduction of a biological agent to prompt the body to oppose and repel a disease. The agent is commonly made from an inactive or less virulent form of a pathogen, be it a virus (measles and mumps) or bacteria (typhoid and tuberculosis). The body's immune system recognizes the foreign substance and works up a resistance to it, developing a protection against the actual disease. Note: in common parlance, the terms "immunization" and "inoculation" are used interchangeably with "vaccination"; and even among specialists, keeping them clearly distinguished is not a uniform priority. That said, vaccination (nowadays) means simply the administration of a vaccine. Immunization can be a broader category: the administration plus the response of the body's immune system. And inoculation can be a wider category in yet another way: the use of an immunity-producing agent, whether a vaccine or some other product. See **Vaccination, Opposition to;** and **Anti-Vaxxers; Jenner, Edward;** and **Wakefield, Andrew** (in **Part 2**)

Vaccination, Opposition to: ranging from merely skeptical to actively hostile—and including "slow-vax" proponents of paced-out or customized vaccine schedules—inoculation opt-outers can be characterized as sharing certain related convictions: concerns about whether public-health immunizations pose risks that outweigh their benefits; convictions that they aren't necessary; suspicions about Big Pharma, Big Government, doctors, science (and their thought-of-as-sinister financial interdependence)—these are some common notions. Regarding departing from the traditional medical approach, one ringleader is Robert W. Sears, AKA "Dr. Bob." His book *The Vaccine Book: Making the Right Decision for your Child* (2007) commends delaying and/or skipping certain shots.[1] Such views, and vaccine non-compliance generally, are opposed by medical-science and public-health experts. Yet widespread disinclination and/or delay advocacy continue. As a

---

1. Sears, *Vaccine Book.*

result, vaccine-preventable diseases, which in recent years had all but disappeared, have now begun to make a comeback. Measles is the prime example. Around the turn of the millennium, public health researchers regarded it as officially eradicated. But that changed. In 2019, there were 1,289 confirmed cases in the United States alone. For this and other reasons, WHO (the World Health Organization) includes "vaccine hesitancy" as one of its top threats to global health. See **Vaccination;** and **Anti-Vaxxers; Jenner, Edward;** and **Wakefield, Andrew** (in **Part 2**)

Valetudinarian: a person who: (a) is chronically weak and vulnerable to health problems; or more usually, (b) is prone to imagine him- or herself to be that way, being unwarrantedly anxious about personal health matters. See **Illness Anxiety Disorder**

Variation in Care / Practice Variability: not always viewed in a negative light, but when it is, differences in treatment from patient to patient or from region to region are pairable with descriptives like "unwarranted" and "inappropriate." One concern is that variability signals that standard-of-care medicine is not being consistently adhered to. In hospital settings, shift-to-shift differences would raise the same concern, the worry being that patients are receiving inconsistent and therefore suboptimal care. See **Evidence-Based Medicine (EBM)**

Vasopressors: medicines that increase blood pressure by constricting (narrowing) blood vessels. They are used to treat extremely low blood pressure, especially in critically ill patients. Someone with septic shock would be a prime example. See **Pressors;** also **Septic Shock,** under **Sepsis**

Vector vs. Vehicle: the epidemiologists' names for two different categories of transmitters of a disease. Definitions of the first term differ considerably.[2] One typical version is: a vector is a living organism that either: (a) accommodates the growth or development of its disease pathogen before transferring it to a new host ("biological transmission"); or (b) does not do so, but simply carries and passes it on ("mechanical transmission"). Examples include mosquitos and ticks, which may be biological vectors, and fleas and house flies, which can be mechanical vectors. The second category is vehicle. These are inanimate objects (such as food, water, air, and fluids of the body) which are capable of introducing a disease-causing agent to a new host. ▪ **Vector-Borne Diseases:** those that are transmitted via a **vector.**

---

2. See, for example, Wilson et al., "What Is a Vector?"

Examples are dengue fever, Lyme disease, malaria, Tularemia, West Nile Virus, and Zika virus.

Vegetative State: see **Persistent Vegetative State**

Ventilator, Inventor of: see **Bird, Forrest M.** (in **Part 2**)

Ventilatory Support: use of a ventilator to maintain the breathing of a patient who is unable to breathe or who is breathing insufficiently.

Ventricular Support: (AKA mechanical circulatory support or a ventricular assist device) usually a medical apparatus implanted in a patient whose heart needs help pumping blood. Use can be temporary or long-term. See **ECMO** and **Weaning**

Ventricular Tachycardia (VT or V-tach) and Ventricular Fibrillation (VF or V-fib): these are abnormalities in the way the heart beats (that is, **arrhythmias**). For both, problems begin in the lower parts of the heart, the ventricles; and for both, use of a defibrillator "is the single most important intervention a rescuer can take."[3] With the former, a too-fast heart rhythm means that the heart is not able to pump blood adequately. With the latter, the situation is even more serious; heartbeats are so fast and irregular that the pumping of blood effectively stops altogether. **VF** is a leading cause of sudden cardiac death. See **Defibrillation**

Viability, Fetal: the capacity of a fetus to continue life, growth, and development outside its mother's womb. It is sometimes said that this means the ability to live independently, but "independent newborn," unless amply qualified, seems problematic. Laurence McCullough succeeds in avoiding this difficulty when he states that the concept of viability "has both a biological and a biomedical component. In obstetrics, viability means the ability of a fetus to survive *ex utero* albeit with the full technological support of neonatal critical care."[4] See **Periviability vs. Previability**

Viral Load (AKA viral burden, titre, or titer): the measure of the particles of a virus in an infected person's blood once the virus has had the opportunity to replicate. As a general rule, the higher the **VL**, the greater the severity of the infection.

Virtue (Ἀρετή): positive habits that make for good moral character or personal excellence. The ethics of virtue is one of the three central alternatives

3. Venes, *Tabor's Cyclopedic Medical Dictionary*, 631.
4. Pinching, "Viability," 268.

in ethical philosophy and in subdisciplines such as bioethics. The other two are **deontology** (right and wrong acts) and **consequentialism** (beneficial and harmful outcomes). In contrast to those two, virtue ethics concentrates on who one pervasively is, that is, on the content of one's character. So for example, it recommends being a conscientious and honorable person rather than a selfish and unscrupulous one. **Aristotle** (in **Part 2**) is generally thought of as the prime mover for this approach. In his view, what matters is making the moderate response, which will be located at an optimum point between two extremes. His treatment of twelve virtues include: courage, temperance, liberality, magnificence, and more.[5] And although during the modern era the ethics of virtue lost much of its cachet, that changed during the second half of the twentieth century. Tom Beauchamp and James Childress, offering what arguably counts as the mainstream, contemporary bioethics perspective, situate its relevance in this way: "What matters most in the moral life is not adherence to moral rules, but having a reliable character, a good moral sense, and an appropriate emotional responsiveness . . . [for] morality would be a cold and uninspiring practice without appropriate sympathy, emotional responsiveness, excellence of character, and heartfelt ideals that reach beyond principles and rules."[6]

Virtue-Signaling: self-serving moral posturing in which a person conspicuously advocates a popular cause, or expresses a moralistic opinion—but does so for appearances' sake. Usually an attempt is being made either to showcase one's membership in an in-group or to attempt to gain acceptance into one, but one-upmanship **VS** is also possible.

Vitalism: an extreme extension of the **sanctity-of-life** position with or without any religious overtones. The view holds that the continued physical existence of a person is a nonnegotiable value; it overrides all other considerations; unfavorable circumstances or consequences do not matter. In its practical application, the view often boils down to: (a) the doctors must always "do everything"; and (b) advice about withholding or withdrawing treatment will be resisted and probably resented. See **Quality of Life**

Volume Expanders: solutions used to increase blood pressure.

---

5. Aristotle, *Nicomachean Ethics*, 39–115.
6. Beauchamp and Childress, *Principles*, 30.

Letter W

War: see **Just War Theory**

Warm Handoff: medicalese for an approach to patient referral that places a premium on personal investment and communication, both between clinicians and with the patient. It is face-to-face whenever possible, or if not, then on the phone. For one thing, **WH** is a way to maintain **continuity of care** within a multidisciplinary team and/or integrated healthcare system. And for another, it is intended to facilitate patient buy-in and to prevent feelings of being passed along from one silo to the next. Contrast with **Collusion of Anonymity**.

Weaning: gradually transitioning from dependence to full independence. Two common examples are tapering off of a medication, and gradually decreasing (or intermittently discontinuing) **ventricular support**.

"Who Gets the Kidney?": a question that has passed into common parlance as shorthand for a dire dilemma associated with the allocation of scarce resources. (Example: in a discussion of any sort of budget restraint or organizational limit, someone can ask, "So, how far away are we from, 'Who gets the kidney?'")

Withholding and Withdrawing Life-Prolonging Treatment: a distinction between refraining from beginning an intervention, on the one hand, and discontinuing it after it's been started, on the other. The AMA *Code of Medical Ethics* maintains that there is no moral difference between withdrawing and withholding life-sustaining treatment.[1] The majority opinion among bioethicists would seem to agree. To wit, they point out that, on balance, allowing for a moral separation between these two treatment decisions has too much going against it. Starting with: (a) it cannot be rationally defended;

1. AMA Council on Ethical and Judicial Affairs, "Opinion 2.20," para. 2.

and (b) it leads to confused and often inhumane consequences. Yet, their discussions nevertheless concede that at the bedside, many clinicians persist in regarding the two differently, as if a choice to end a life-sustaining form of care is ethically weightier and bears on the doctor-patient relationship differently than a decision not to initiate it. And we could add that surrogates' feelings about the matter generally align with and support the clinicians' intuitions. See **Acts and Omissions Doctrine** and **LOT (Limitation of Treatment)**

Witnessed vs. Unwitnessed: a **cardiac arrest** can be categorized as either. One issue is how quickly care could be provided. As in: "Patients who are witnessed and/or monitored at the time of cardiac arrest demonstrate a significantly higher rate of survival to hospital discharge compared to those patients who are neither monitored nor witnessed."[2] Further differentiations are possible: "bystander-witnessed," "out-of-hospital," etc.

Workup: an orderly and thorough examination of a patient—medical history, physical exam, lab tests, imaging procedures, etc.—for diagnostic and therapeutic decision-making purposes.

Wounded Healer: a concept advanced by Henri Nouwen that has been highly influential with clergy, but also among clinicians, therapists, and other helping professionals. Nouwen's basic point: "The great illusion of leadership is to think that man can be led out of the desert by someone who has never been there."[3] Struggles and scars do not disqualify a person from a place among the healing professions, the best of whom will always be fellow sufferers.

Wrongful Conception vs. Wrongful Birth vs. Wrongful Life: these are medical malpractice claims that raise vexing ethical issues. In the first of the three, a healthcare provider is faulted for the birth of an unwanted child, healthy or not, because of a failed sterilization or abortion procedure, or something similar. With **WB**, a clinician is charged with failing to provide adequate genetic counseling regarding a future child's birth defects, or with neglecting to share the diagnosis of actual defects once they became evident. **WL** claims are typically made on behalf of a child born with severe genetic anomalies. A medical professional is charged with being responsible for them, or more properly for the child's life because of them. The implication is that the infant's health is so devastatingly compromised that it is, and will

2. Brady et al., "In-Hospital Cardiac Arrest," para. 7.
3. Nouwen, *Wounded Healer*, 72.

continue to be, worse than no life at all. As noted, the ethical implications
are far reaching and profound.

Letter X

Xenograft: (AKA xenotransplant) the grafted tissue or transplanted organ or transferred cells from a donor, the member of one species, to a recipient, the member of another species. One sometimes finds this term used to refer to the procedure, that is, as a synonym for **xenotransplantation** (ξένος = foreign or strange). See **Baby Fae** (in **Part 2**)

Xenotransplantation: the process of removing a **xenograft** (tissue, organ, or cells) from a donating individual which is the member of one species, for transplantation in another individual who is a member of a different species. See **Baby Fae** (in **Part 2**)

Letter Y

Yuck Factor: a term coined by bioethicist Arthur Caplan and taken up by Leon Kass. It indicates a visceral reaction of disgust, especially accompanying ethical misgivings about yucky new developments in the biosciences, as the following illustrates: "At a recent public lecture given at Rutgers University by the controversial Professor Peter Singer, almost all of those who opposed his very liberal and consequentialist ethical views about cloning cited 'the yuck factor' to bolster their objections."[1] It would seem, however, that the neologism can be used in reference to any negative-feeling-based objection, whether ethics and biotechnology are involved or not.

1. Fethe, "Yuck Factor," para. 5.

Letter Z

Zebra: shorthand for the diagnostic rule of thumb, "When you hear hoof-beats, think of horses, not zebras." A "zebra" is an unexpected and unlikely condition—or by extension, a patient with such a condition. The aphorism, from Dr. Theodore E. Woodward in the 1940s, was his advice to medical interns: start with the commonly seen diagnostic alternatives before turning to the rarely seen ones. Similar to **Sutton's Law**. See **Fascinoma**

Zero-Sum Game vs. Win-Win Situation: the former is a competition, like the World Series, where every win for one team is a loss for the other team. The "sum" is called "zero" because with each game (+1) + (-1) = 0. The latter, by contrast, is an interaction where there are no losers because everyone benefits. For example, "Jack Sprat could eat no fat. His wife could eat no lean. And so betwixt the two of them, they licked the platter clean." They both won.

Zoonosis (ζῷον = animal; νόσος = sickness), (either zō-ON-uh-sis or zō-uh-NŌ-sis): diseases that can be transmitted from nonhuman animals to humans (and possibly vice versa). (Some sources also include insect-to-human transmission.) COVID-19 is a zoonotic disease, as are rabies, anthrax, and tularemia. ▪ **Zooanthroponosis** (ἄνθρωπος = a human being), (ZŌ-ō-AN-thrō-pō-NŌ-sis): a disease such as tuberculosis that can be passed from humans to nonhuman animals.

Zygote (ζυγωτός): a cell formed by the union of a sperm and an egg; so, a fertilized ovum. It has a complete set of all the genetic information required for the growth of a new individual.

Numbers

80/20 Rule: (AKA the Pareto Principle) among epidemiologists, the possibility that during an epidemic, 20 percent of the infected individuals could be responsible for 80 percent of the transmissions. Interestingly, early evidence for the coronavirus pandemic suggests that transmissions do indeed show an 80/20 split. "For Covid-19, this means that 80% of new transmissions are caused by fewer than 20% of the carriers—the vast majority of people infect few others or none at all, and it's a select minority of individuals who are aggressively spreading the virus."[1] But note: it should not be assumed that every disease is so tidy. In most cases, the "rule" may be little more than a helpful illustration, a rough guesstimate. See **Super-Spreader**

404 Moment: British hospital slang for the point in time when a patient's records cannot be found. It comes from the internet error message: "404 Page Not Found."

1799 Medical Hold: named after State of California Health and Safety Code § 1799, this is a twenty-four-hour hold ordered by an ER physician. It is intended for situations involving a patient with a behavioral disorder. Detention in the ER for up to twenty-four hours is to allow a psychiatric evaluation to determine if, because of a mental illness, the patient poses a danger to self or others, or is gravely disabled. And note: if a seventy-two-hour hold is subsequently imposed, it can't be added on to the twenty-four; instead, up to twenty-four hours of the 1799 period has to be counted as time already served, as it were.

5150 Psychiatric Hold: named after State of California Welfare and Institutions Code § 5150, this allows for someone with a behavioral disorder to be involuntarily confined in a psych ward for up to seventy-two hours,

---

1. Patel, "What's a Coronavirus Superspreader?," para. 3.

provided there is probable cause. Rationales include posing a danger to self or to others, or being gravely disabled. The hold can be initiated by a police officer or by certain mental health professionals. See **Lanterman-Petris-Short Act**

5250 Psychiatric Hold: named after State of California WIC § 5250, following the seventy-two hours of a 5150, this provides for involuntary confinement for an additional fourteen days. However, a court hearing is required. See **Lanterman-Petris-Short Act**

5260 Psychiatric Hold: named after State of California WIC § 5260, this authorizes a second fourteen-day period of psychiatric treatment, after the fourteen-day hold of 5250. It is specifically for a person suffering from a mental illness or from impairment because of chronic alcohol abuse, and who is judged to be imminently suicidal. A doctor's request for this additional period is called "recertification." See **Lanterman-Petris-Short Act**

5270 Psychiatric Hold: named after State of California WIC § 5270, this is like 5260 in that it allows for continued detention after the initial fourteen-day hold of 5250. However, it is for an additional thirty days, and it applies to a person with a grave disability due to a mental disorder. See **Lanterman-Petris-Short Act**

5300 Psychiatric Hold: named after State of California WIC § 5300, this is yet another authorization for confinement continuing beyond the initial fourteen-day hold of 5250. But here again, there are differences. This one allows for a 180-day hold for a person with a mental illness who poses a serious threat of harm to another party. See **Lanterman-Petris-Short Act**

5585 Psychiatric Hold: named after State of California Welfare and Institutions Code § 5585, it is like 5150 but applying to minors. It allows for a minor with a behavioral disorder to be involuntarily confined in a psych ward for up to seventy-two hours. Reasons for doing so include that he or she poses a danger to self or to others, or is gravely disabled. And as with 5150, this hold can be initiated by a police officer or by certain mental health professionals. See **Lanterman-Petris-Short Act**

PART 2

Historical Figures

People every bioethicist should know from the histories
of medicine, science, philosophy, religion, public health,
mental health, and other related fields

Abulcasis/Al-Zahrawi (936–1013): an Arab physician-pharmacist who lived in Spain, he is credited with being the father of operative surgery, having a famous collection of over two hundred surgical instruments, many of which he invented himself. Synthesizing the medicine and pharmacology of the Islamic Golden Age with the medical knowledge of ancient Greece and Rome, he wrote many influential texts, including a thirty-volume encyclopedia on medical procedures. Its section on surgery, translated into Latin, became Europe's standard reference work on the subject for the next five centuries, up through the Renaissance period.

Addams, Jane (1860–1935): regarded as the mother of social work, she was a leading reformer during the Progressive Era, championing women's suffrage, children's interests, public health, and world peace. "In her essay 'Utilization of Women in City Government,' [she] noted the connection between the workings of government and the household, stating that many departments of government, such as sanitation and the schooling of children, could be traced back to traditional women's roles in the private sphere. Thus, these were matters of which women would have more knowledge than men, so women needed the vote to best voice their opinions."[1] She was the first American woman to win the Nobel Peace Prize (1931).

Al-Aslamia, Rufaida (born c. 640): she is Islam's first woman nurse and as such, "the founder of nursing in the Muslim world."[2] Her father practiced medicine in Medina, Saudi Arabia, and she learned her clinical skills from him. Obtaining the Prophet Muhammad's permission to provide medical services to support his military exploits, she brought with her a team of women whom she had trained, and her tent became a battlefield care center—something of an early MASH unit, if you will. There is a building at the Aga Khan University School of Nursing that is named in her honor, as is an annual prize in nursing at the University of Bahrain.

Al-Razi: see **Rhazes**

Al-Ruhawi, Ishaq ibn 'Ali (9th century): author of the earliest, or at least the oldest surviving, Arab-language text on medical ethics. The *Adab al-Tabib* (*Morals of the Physician*) quotes and synthesizes the thoughts of a number of ancient authorities, **Galen** most especially.

Al-Zahrawi: see **Abulcasis**

---

1. Best MSW Programs, "50 Notable Social Workers in US History," para. 2.
2. Yahya, "Rufaida Al-Aslamia," para. 16.

Anti-Vaxxers: located at the far end of the "vaccine hesitancy" continuum, these recusants oppose public-health inoculations on a number of grounds. The chief fear in recent years has been that the MMR (measles, mumps, and rubella) vaccine causes autism. Credit for that mistaken notion rests with British ex-physician **Andrew Wakefield**. However, media figure Jenny McCarthy has publicized the cause, and other celebrities, plus a few doctors, have as well. Setting the stage, in 1982, NBC aired an investigatory program, "DPT: Vaccine Roulette." Although physicians' organizations criticized it as alarmist and misinformative, anti-vaccination groups were formed anyway. See **Jenner, Edward;** and **Vaccination; Vaccination, Opposition to** (in **Part 1**)

Apgar, Virginia (1909–74): an American obstetric anesthesiologist, she developed the **Apgar Score System** (in **Part 1**) in 1952. A simple assessment, it's relied on around the world. The backstory, possibly apocryphal, is that a med student raised a question with her in the hospital cafeteria: "You keep telling us to look at the baby—but what are we looking for?" The doctor is said to have jotted down five points on a napkin, creating the system on the spot.

Aquinas, Thomas (1225–74): Roman Catholicism's most influential theologian, he is also a major figure in the history of philosophy. In a recent poll of over 1,100 philosophers, he was voted ninth among "the most important Western philosophers of all time."[3] A "both/and" thinker, his system took up various streams of thought but especially the philosophy of **Aristotle** (whose writings had recently been rediscovered in the West) and synthesized them with the sacred doctrines of the church. In his teaching on ethics, he borrowed the Aristotelean idea that human activity always serves an ultimate goal: happiness. But he distinguished between imperfect happiness (felicitas), which is available in this life, and its perfect counterpart (beatitude), which is not. This was in service of the Christian insistence that the soul's true goal is the knowledge and love of the highest good: God. Aquinas's union of Christian and Aristotelean perspectives informs his discussions of **virtue** and **natural law**.

Aristotle (Ἀριστοτέλης) (384–322 BCE): conceivably the most broadly influential thinker who has ever lived, he and his teacher **Plato** can be classed as the twin fountainheads of Western philosophy. Aristotle's father was a physician, and the son's writings cover many topics related to medical science (anatomy, biology, physics, and zoology) medical humanities (aesthetics, literature, music, and theatre), and bioethics (ethics, government,

3. Leiter, "Most Important Western Philosophers."

politics, psychology, and theology). Though many of his conclusions about the natural world have been superseded in recent centuries, his fundamentally empirical methodology remains a permanently useful contribution to the human quest for knowledge. For whereas Plato taught that the physical world is a reflection of a more essential realm of ideals, reached only by thought, Aristotle held that truths about the physical world are found through experience—through systematic observation and careful comparison. For this, he can be regarded as "the godfather of **evidence-based medicine**."[4]

Asclepius (Ἀσκληπιός): the ancient Greek hero or demigod of medicine and healing. ▪ **The Rod of Asclepius** (Ράβδος του Ασκληπιού), a snake coiled around a pole, remains the recognized symbol of medical practice to this day, except when a different symbol—a winged staff with two snakes—is used. But that is the Caduceus. Historically associated with the god Hermes, the Caduceus has always symbolized commerce. It was only in the United States, in the latter half of the 1800s, that the one symbol began to replace the other. Historians tend to view this as a mistake. But then again, with the increasing commercialization of healthcare, perhaps the switch was appropriate.

Augustine (354–430): there is no theologian of equal stature in the period reaching from the Apostle Paul in the first century to **Thomas Aquinas** in the thirteenth. One option for presenting his ethics is to begin with the Bible verse he quotes most frequently.[5] That is, "and this hope is not deceptive because the love of God has been poured into our hearts by the Holy Spirit which has been given us" (Rom 5:5 JB). Although Paul is speaking of God's love for us (so it is generally held), Augustine fatefully understands him to be speaking about our love for God. As has been observed many times since Anders Nygren pointed it out, the Augustinian *caritas*, which is Latin for "love," is a synthesis of biblical *agape* (ἀγάπη) and Platonic *eros* (ἔρως). Poured into our hearts, *caritas* redirects us from the world of the senses to the higher realm, the City of God. In fact, so important is *caritas* in his thought that **A** could sum up the moral life with, "Thus a short and simple precept is given you once for all: Love, and do what you will."[6] See **Agape** and **Love** (in **Part 1**)

4. Sallam, "Aristotle," para. 1.
5. Burns, "Grace," 393.
6. Augustine, "Homilies on I John," 316.

Avenzoar / Ibn Zuhr (c. 1094–c. 1162): an Arab physician who lived in Spain, he was hailed in his day as the greatest clinician since **Galen**. The father of experimental medicine, he pioneered the use of surgical procedures on animals before attempting them on humans; for example, his first tracheotomy was performed on a goat. Asked by his friend **Averroes** to pen a manual on the particulars of treating patients, he wrote *al-Taisir* (*The Specifics of Medicine*). Paired with Averroes's *General Medicine*, the two were designed to serve as a single, thorough textbook of medical practice. Also significant: Avenzoar ushered his daughter and granddaughter into medicine as obstetricians, setting the stage for the broad acceptance of female doctors throughout the Muslim world.

Averroes / Ibn Rushd (1126–98): hailed as "The Prince of Science," he is regarded by some as the single most influential figure of the Islamic Golden Age. A polymath, he made original contributions to many fields, synthesizing ancient Greek and Islamic perspectives with his own personal observations. Translations of his commentaries on Aristotle awakened an interest in ancient Greek thought among the scholars of the West; in fact, there he was simply "The Commentator." But he also authored twenty books on medicine and served as the royal physician for the caliphate in Marrakesh. Preeminent among his medical works was *Katib al Kulliyat* (*General Medicine*), an encyclopedia comprised of seven treatises devoted to anatomy, physiology, pathology, symptomatology, pharmacology, hygiene, and therapeutics. He intended it as an overview and as a counterpart to another one—which he had his friend **Avenzoar** write—on the specifics of treating patients. The two works were designed to serve as a complete textbook of medical practice, and Latin translations printed them that way, as a single book.

Avicenna / Ibn Sina (980–1037): **Sir William Osler** called him "the author of the most famous medical textbook ever written." That work, *The Canon of Medicine*, was an elegant, systematic, and encyclopedic presentation of medicine from Greco-Roman and other sources, synthesized with the science and natural philosophy of Aristotle. In its Latin translation, it became the primary text in the medical schools of Europe on into the early modern period. A Persian scholar, Avicenna was born in present-day Uzbekistan and died in Iran. Many historians regard him as the most important medical scientist of the Islamic Golden Age. He was an early advocate of what today is called **evidence-based medicine (EBM)**: reliance on remedies which experience has shown to be repeatedly effective. And his contributions to the field of philosophy are equally great. There, as the chief exemplar of the Greco-Arabic tradition, he has a status that, to some, cannot be overstated.

"In his influence on the intellectual history of the world in the West (of India), he is second only to Aristotle."[7]

Ayer, A. J.: see **Logical Positivism** (in **Part 1**)

Baby Fae (October 14, 1984–November 15, 1984): the first infant recipient of the heart of a baboon in a cross-species or **xenotransplantation** procedure that shocked the world. Stephanie Fae Beauclair was born with hypoplastic left heart syndrome, an always-fatal birth anomaly that almost certainly meant that she would die within her first two weeks of life. Dr. Leonard Bailey, a pediatric cardiac surgeon at Loma Linda University Medical Center in Loma Linda, California, had been deeply involved in researching this area and he convinced the baby's mother to greenlight the unprecedented operation. The little child's new lease on life was tragically cut short twenty-one days later. But even so, she became world famous: she was both the first infant to undergo a cross-species transplant of any kind, and also the first infant to undergo a heart transplant procedure. See **Xenograft**

Baker, Sara Josephine (1873–1945): a pioneering figure in public health. As a young physician working part-time for New York City's Department of Health, she blazed new trails in what is now known as "preventive medicine." Her major concern was the health of the children of immigrants in the city's poorest neighborhoods. When a Division of Child Hygiene was created in 1908, she was given the directorship. (Later a Bureau, it was the first agency of its kind anywhere in the world.) "Dr. Jo" brought milk to children, taught mothers how to keep their babies healthy, established a widely imitated school health program, and represented child welfare concerns at the League of Nations. She may be more famous, however, for taking **Typhoid Mary** into custody. Mary Mallon was uncooperative, so two attempts were required: a frustrated foray with three police officers, and then a second, more determined effort with five.

Barber-Surgeons: in the Middle Ages, barbers played an important role in Europe's monasteries. Members of religious orders needed the official monk hair cut, shaved on top. So, barbers were in demand. Within that same time frame, surgery was outside the scope of practice of many physicians. As a consequence, when a surgical procedure was called for, the job fell to the tradesmen who had razors and were skilled in their use. Moreover, as monasteries came to serve as hospitals, barber-surgeons were on hand for bloodletting, teeth extraction, etc. Then there was the military; these

7. Gutas, "Ibn Sina [Avicenna]," para. 1.

paramedics, to borrow a term, were the ones providing medical care for the soldiers. In time, one of their number, **Ambroise Paré**, rose to become the father of modern surgery. (But consider this status in relation to **Abulcasis**.)

Barton, Clara (1821–1912): founder of the American Red Cross. She was a nurse during the American Civil War. Initially this was away from the front lines. But before long she was bringing supplies and providing care in combat zones; for this she was given the nickname "Angel of the Battlefield." Once the war was over, she traveled to Geneva, Switzerland, and was impressed by the work of the Red Cross, the international relief organization that had its headquarters there. Returning to the United States, she campaigned for, and in 1881 oversaw, the creation of the American counterpart. She served as the organization's first president, relinquishing the office in 1904 at the age of eighty-three.

Bayes, Rev. Thomas (1701–61): a British mathematician, theologian, and Presbyterian minister. Toward the end of his life, he wrote a paper on probability which went unpublished and unnoticed. A year after his death, a friend sponsored a public reading of it. The paper advanced what is now known as **Bayes's Theorem**. Providing a place for an investigator's prior knowledge in assessing a new piece of evidence, this theorem is important in many fields, including forensic science. It has been described as "to the theory of probability what the Pythagorean theorem is to geometry."[8] See **Bayesian** (in **Part 1**)

Bentham, Jeremy (1748–1832): the first of the two preeminent proponents of the utilitarian approach to ethics, the other being **John Stuart Mill** (1806–73). His magnum opus, *Introduction to the Principles of Morals and Legislation*, begins with the lines, "Nature has placed mankind under the governance of two sovereign masters, *pain* and *pleasure*. It is for them alone to point out what we ought to do, as well as determine what we shall do."[9] The philosophy built on that foundation was born of a passionate disapproval of the English legal system of the day, a system Bentham regarded as confused and unfair. What was called for, he believed, was a rigorous and thorough-going legislative reform guided by a rational criterion, the principle of utility. Utility means "useful," and for Bentham it meant useful in promoting the greatest amount of happiness—and, yes, happiness is quantifiable. Mill's subsequent utilitarianism is generally regarded as being less coherent that Bentham's, but as an engaging improvement, nevertheless.

8. Harold Jeffreys, quoted in Tietz, "Important Theorem of Thomas Bayes," para. 7.
9. Bentham, *Introduction to the Principles of Morals*, 1.

Bird, Forrest M. (1921–2015): an American aviator and biomedical engineer, he invented the first reliable, portable, medical-purpose mechanical ventilator. A pilot during WWII, he discovered an oxygen regulator in a downed German bomber. By making various improvements, he solved a problem the US military had at the time: newer aircraft were capable of flying to heights too high for humans to breathe. After the war, he turned his attention to medicine. In 1958, the Bird Universal Medical Respirator, or Bird Mark 7, became available.[10] He continued inventing and in 1970 introduced the Baby Bird for infants and children. See **Ventilatory Support** (in **Part** 1)

Blackwell, Elizabeth (1821–1910): the first woman to receive an American medical degree, she was also the first to be registered to practice medicine in the UK. Born in England and raised in the United States, she developed an interest in becoming a doctor and applied to med schools. Nearly thirty rejected her. Then in 1847, acceptance came from Geneva Medical College. But there is irony here. Confronted with her application, the Genevan faculty decided to pass the decision along to their (male) students—adding the deal-breaker that if even one student objected, she would be turned down. But the thought of a woman applying to med school struck the students as a joke; so just for laughs, they all voted yes. Her admission granted, Blackwell began her studies, excelled, and graduated at the top of her class. She opened a small practice in New York City and in time founded what became a medical college for women. Later she relocated to England, and in 1875, as professor of gynecology, she joined the newly built London School of Medicine for Women.

Bovet, Daniel (1907–92): a Swiss-born, Italian pharmacologist, he won the Nobel Prize for Physiology or Medicine in 1957. He conducted important research in therapeutic chemistry, first at the Pasteur Institute in Paris, and then at the Superior Institute of Health in Rome. Several major breakthroughs came along the way: antihistamines, sulfa drugs, and muscle relaxants. Of less enduring significance: in 1965, he and his research team published their finding that smoking tobacco cigarettes increases intelligence.

Calvin, John (1509–64): it was almost twenty years after **Martin Luther** set off the Protestant Reformation that this new kid on the block began systematizing its doctrines. He was a Frenchman living in Geneva. His theology was similar to Luther's. Yet differences are unmistakable; and in general they have to do with the subjectivity of the older reformer versus the objectivity

---

10. 1958 is the commonly cited year, but some sources disagree.

of the younger. Calvin had been trained as a lawyer: the single most important tenet of his ethics is his rendering of the three uses of the law. (This is doubly important because it would end up being a bone of contention between Calvinists and Lutherans later on). For the Genevan, the law of God has three purposes. First, it shows us the righteousness of God and our failure to comply with his requirements. Second, it blocks unrepentant troublemakers from wreaking the havoc that they would otherwise cause. And third, it incentivizes believers, stimulating them ("like a whip to an idle and balky ass") to do the works that please God.[11]

Carson, Rachel (1907–64): her book, *Silent Spring*, kickstarted the mid-twentieth-century environmental movement by raising alarms about the effects that DDT and other pesticides and herbicides have on nature's ecosystems. A successful writer, she was principally a marine biologist with the US Bureau of Fisheries. Then in 1962, her blockbuster appeared, forcefully advancing the thesis that slow-decaying synthetic chemicals are building up in our soil and water, creating a toxic environment. How bad is it? Civilization, she argued, is destroying itself. Countercriticism arose, much of it from, or forwarded by, commercial interests. Even so, rarely has one book inspired such dramatic changes in public policy. "Within a decade, almost all of the chemicals Carson had targeted, DDT notably among them, were either banned or severely restricted in the United States, Europe and much of the rest of the world."[12]

Chadwick, Sir Edwin (1800–90): in his day, this British reformer was the best-known advocate of sweeping governmental solutions to chronic social problems. He updated the country's Poor Laws (something the poor did not appreciate), worked for greater bureaucratic oversight of poverty relief efforts, and pushed for improvements in urban sanitation. Regarding the latter, he penned the highly consequential *Report on the Sanitary Condition of the Labouring Population of Great Britain* (1842). The first such document of its kind, it focused on the plight of those disadvantaged and harmed by Industrial Age progress; and it argued that miserable and unclean living conditions were responsible for disease, certainly, but also for crime and various social iniquities: "Correlating poorly planned environments with bad health and/or people's immoral behavior, Chadwick presented an argument that was difficult for critics to dismantle by making at the core of his case the ability of drains and clean water to improve morality. Sanitation, he proclaimed, would defuse rowdiness and decadence and make once

11. Calvin, *Institutes*, II. vii. 12.
12. Mann, "'Silent Spring and Other Writings' Review," para. 11.

'dangerous classes' compliant."[13] He played a major role in setting the stage for the UK's modern administrative state.

Charcot, Jean-Martin (1825–93): a French neurologist and professor of anatomical pathology. He excelled at associating clinical observations with disease pathologies, and was the first to identify many neurological disorders, including multiple sclerosis, **ALS (amyotrophic lateral sclerosis)** (known as Lou Gehrig's disease), and Parkinson's disease. In 1882, he set up Europe's first neurological clinic at Salpêtrière Hospital in Paris. He is also remembered for his use of hypnosis in connection with his work on hysteria. Many of his students went on to make significant contributions of their own, **Sigmund Freud** being the best known.

Crick, Francis (1916–2004): a British researcher with expertise in multiple scientific disciplines, he discovered, in partnership with James Watson, the spiral ladder, "double helix" structure of DNA, reporting it in the journal *Nature* in 1953. In 1962, he was a co-recipient of the Nobel Prize in Physiology or Medicine for "discoveries concerning the molecular structure of nucleic acids and its significance for information transfer in living material."[14]

Crumpler, Rebecca Lee (1831–95): the first female African American physician in the United States. After serving as a nurse, she entered the New England Female Medical College, graduating and becoming a "Doctress of Medicine" in 1864. She specialized in caring for women and children, and had a startup practice in Boston. When the Civil War ended, she moved to Richmond, Virginia to provide medical services to recently freed slaves. A few years later, she returned to and resumed practicing in Boston. In 1883, she wrote *A Book of Medical Discourses*. Possibly the first medical text penned by an African American, it was also the first by a female physician.

Curie, Marie (1867–1934): the Polish-born scientist who coined the term "radioactivity," she was the world's "first female celebrity scientist."[15] For starters, she and her husband, Pierre, discovered the radioactive elements polonium and radium. When they were jointly awarded the Nobel Prize in Physics in 1903, she became its first woman laureate. When he was killed in a street accident in 1906, she stepped into his teaching position at the Sorbonne, becoming the school's first female professor. And yet another first: winning the Nobel Prize in Chemistry in 1911 made her the first person to

---

13. Morley, "City Chaos, Contagion, Chadwick, and Social Justice," para. 24.

14. "Nobel Prize in Physiology or Medicine 1962," para. 1.

15. Krulwich, "Ghost of Madame Curie," para. 4.

be awarded twice. Others have matched that feat since, but not in two different fields of science. Her theorizing inaugurated the field of atomic physics; and her discoveries led to advances in medicine: diagnostic (improvement in newly emergent X-ray photography) and therapeutic (radiation in the treatment of cancer). During World War I, she came up with the idea of outfitting a fleet of ambulances to bring mobile X-ray capability to frontline field hospitals. The vehicles were called "Petite Curies." She didn't know how to drive, but once she learned, she became her own chauffeur (and auto mechanic!), helping to bring the latest in medicine to where the action was.

Diocles of Carystus (Διοκλῆς ὁ Καρύστιος) (c. 375–c. 295 BCE): a major Greek physician, in ancient times he was esteemed as second only to **Hippocrates**. Dental historians cite him as the first to commend rubbing one's gums and teeth to promote oral health.

Dioscorides (Διοσκουρίδης) (c. 40–c. 90 CE): the father of the field of pharmacy. He was a Greek physician in the Roman army at the time of Emperor Nero, presumably serving in the Mediterranean East. The plants covered in his *De Materia Medica* are mostly limited to that region. A five-volume pharmacopeia, it became the go-to reference work on medical herbs and pharmacology, with an influence that remained unparalleled for 1,500 years.

Dix, Dorothea (1802–87): an American reformer, she campaigned for improvements in the treatment of people with mental illnesses. It all began when she was invited to teach Sunday school at a nearby prison and was deeply disturbed by what she saw. So she began visiting other facilities and ascertained that inhumane treatment and miserable living conditions were widespread. It was not uncommon for someone with a mental illness to be chained to a wall and/or flogged—or to be left unclothed, unclean, and neglected in unheated darkness. She contacted state politicians and agitated for change, first in Massachusetts, and then in Rhode Island, New York, and beyond. In the next forty years, her persistent advocacy prompted fifteen states and Canada to build the first generation of state asylums. Her influence extended to Europe as well.

Drew, Charles Richard (1904–50): known as the father of blood banking for his work during WWII. He received the Doctor of Medical Science degree from Columbia University in 1940. Because his dissertation opened up new possibilities in blood preservation and transfusion, he was asked to pilot the Blood for Britain Project (this was before America entered the war), and soon thereafter began directing the American Red Cross's first blood bank. An innovative administrator, he set up decentralized donation stations and specially equipped vans, forerunners of today's bloodmobiles. But there was a problem. "Ironically, the Red Cross excluded African Americans from donating blood, making Drew himself ineligible to participate in the very program he established."[16] The military got involved, ruling that, yes, African Americans could give blood, but that all blood donations would have to be segregated along racial lines. So in protest, Drew resigned from the Red Cross in 1942. He returned to his former teaching post at Howard University and became Head of the Department of Surgery at what is now Howard University Hospital. He "broke barriers in a racially divided America to become one of the most important scientists of the 20th century."[17]

Durham (or Derham), James (1762–c. 1802): the first African American with a publicly recognized medical practice. He grew up in slavery and was passed along from owner to owner. Each of these was a physician who gave him medical training. The last of their number made him an assistant in his New Orleans office—and then in 1783, gave him his freedom and sponsored the opening of his own independent medical practice. (Alternately, Durham is said to have purchased his freedom.) His new venture was quite successful, especially in treating diphtheria. On a trip to Philadelphia, he met with and impressed the famed Benjamin Rush. In fact, Rush presented Durham's paper on diphtheria to the city's College of Physicians. Later, back in New Orleans, Durham brought many patients through a yellow fever epidemic, losing fewer patients than anyone else in the region. In 1801, city authorities took steps against those who were practicing without a medical degree. Durham's services were curtailed; and what happened next is unclear. Since he had already corresponded with Dr. Rush about relocating to Philadelphia, such a move seems entirely plausible. But whether he did, along with when and how he died, is unknown.

Empedocles (Ἐμπεδοκλῆς) (c. 490–c. 430 BCE): the pre-Socratic philosopher responsible for the idea that fire (πῦρ), earth (γῆ), air (ἀήρ), and water (ὕδωρ) are the roots (ῥιζώματα) of all things. This schema of four elements (στοιχεῖα, the label later attached by Plato) guided Western medicine for centuries until the Renaissance. E further proposed that all phenomena result from those four basics being acted upon by a creative principle, love (φιλία), and a destructive principle, strife (νεῖκος), drawn into combinations by the former, and split apart by the latter. Born in present-day Sicily, he was a physician and was considered by **Galen** to be the founder of Italian medicine.

16. ACS, "Charles Richard Drew," para. 14.
17. ACS, "Charles Richard Drew," para. 1.

Erasistratus (Ἐρασίστρατος) (c. 304–c. 250 BCE): a protégé of **Herophilos** in Alexandria, he and his mentor excelled at dissecting cadavers and at drawing medically relevant lessons. As the senior physician is hailed as the father of anatomy, Erasistratus is regarded as the founder of physiology. In time, he became the royal physician for Seleucus Nicator, king of Syria, where he famously diagnosed the king's lovesick son, or so legend has it. He stood out in his day for rejecting **Hippocrates's** theory of **humors**, for opposing bloodletting and purgative interventions, and for preferring treatments emphasizing diet, exercise, hygiene, and bathing. (See **Herophilos** for allegations that the two physicians' dissections were performed on live prisoners.)

Eustachi, Bartolomeo (c. 1510–74): historians of dentistry consider his *Libellus de dentibus* (*A Little Treatise on the Teeth*) to be a breakthrough text in the development of dental science, the first adequate exposition of the structure and function of the teeth. An Italian Renaissance teacher of anatomy, his studies of the human body rivaled, and at points surpassed, those of his better-known contemporary, **Andreas Vesalius**.

Fae, Baby: see **Baby Fae**

Fauchard, Pierre (1678–1761): a French physician, he is regarded as the father of modern dentistry and as the inventor of a new branch of medicine.[18] He earned this status by authoring *The Surgeon Dentist*. A massive, two-volume treatise, it was the Western world's first scientifically comprehensive book on dentistry, "the definitive dental reference for 100 years."[19] Taking his field seriously, Fauchard took steps to warn about the dangers of the charlatan and wannabe dentists of his time.

Fleming, Sir Alexander (1881–1955): a Scottish bacteriologist, he discovered penicillin in 1928. And it was serendipitous. Returning from vacation one day, he set about cleaning the petri dishes he had been using for experiments with bacteria. Near an open window, one exposed dish was clearly contaminated with mold; and where the mold was, there were no bacteria. Isolating the active substance, he gave it the name penicillin. Its mass production by American pharmaceutical companies marks the beginning of the age of antibiotics.

Freud, Sigmund (1856–1939): few doctors have had as broad an impact on as many areas of life as this founder of psychoanalysis. After studying with

18. Deltombe, "Pierre Fauchard," 6.
19. Deltombe, "Pierre Fauchard," 5.

Jean-Martin Charcot in Paris, he returned to Vienna, and in 1886, opened a private practice to treat nervous and brain disorders. Having adopted "the talking cure" with which psychoanalysis would become associated, he began formulating his famous emphases: the unconscious mind, the importance of childhood trauma, the role of sex, the dynamics of transference, and the nature of dreams. And of course there are his signature theories: that the human psyche is comprised of an ego, an id, and a superego; and that neuroses and psychoses arise because of conflicts between them at a level the troubled individual is unaware of. These new ideas transformed psychiatry and psychology, for they challenged the reigning paradigm (as per **Emil Kraepelin**) that the way to treat behavioral disorders is to look for physiological causes. Compare with **Pinel, Philippe;** and **Skinner, B. F.**

Galen (Γαληνός) (c. 129–c. 216 CE): a Greek systematizer in a Roman context, his forwarding of the ancient Greek medical tradition ended up dominating Western medicine for the next 1,400 years. Galen got his start providing life-saving care to gladiators in Pergamum, his hometown. Relocating to Rome, in less than a decade he was the emperor's court physician. His theories drew heavily on those of **Hippocrates**. For instance, he agreed that health depends on a balance between the four **humors**. He made improvements, however, whenever his own findings called for them. The result was a medical methodology with remarkable staying power. It wasn't until the sixteenth and seventeenth centuries that advances in bioscience began to reveal errors in what had long been trusted as the final answers to medicine's questions. See **Vesalius, Andreas**

God Committee, The: the nickname attached to the "Admissions and Policies Committee of the Seattle Artificial Kidney Center at Swedish Hospital." In 1961 or 1962 (sources disagree), seven individuals were recruited to determine how to allocate the world's first-ever, ongoing hemodialysis treatments. Patients were to be connected to a life-saving artificial kidney. But the hospital's capacity was limited; so a panel of seven was created to make the patient selections. There were two physician-advisors, but the actual members of the committee were chosen to represent a cross-section of American society: a surgeon, a lawyer, a pastor, a banker, a housewife, a state government official, and a labor leader. Early on this group agreed on the criteria they would use to guide their choice-making: age, sex, marital status and number of dependents, income, net worth, emotional stability, educational background, occupation, past performance and future potential, and references. When the committee's work hit the press, ethical questions were raised. Yet the program was successful, and once more artificial kidneys became available, the panel was dissolved. Unfairly, more recent references to **death panels** have these early decision-makers as a prototype. See **Health Care Rationing** and **"Who Gets the Kidney?"** (in **Part 1**)

Goodall, Jane (born 1934): a British ethologist known for her prolonged, up-close studies of chimpanzees in their natural habitat. Coming to the Gombe Stream Reserve in Tanzania, Africa, in 1960, she began her ground-breaking investigations into the primates' behavior, concluding that their social life is not as different from humans' as scientists had traditionally assumed. She observed chimpanzees making tools, for example. Reports of her findings were faulted for lacking the critical distance necessary for scientific objectivity. For many, however, she and her frequently mentioned "Trimates," Dian Fossey (who began studying gorillas in 1966) and Biruté Galdikas (orangutans in 1971), represented a new, improved primatology. In time, each segued into advocacy for animal welfare and global conservation.

Gregory, John (1724–73): a professor of medicine at the University of Edinburgh during the Scottish Enlightenment, he is credited with being the English-language "inventor" of the discipline of medical ethics, and a role model for that other medical ethicist, **Thomas Percival** (1740–1804). His influences were Francis Bacon and David Hume. He stressed as obligations: prioritizing the interests of the patient over those of the practitioner; and making improvements in the practice of medicine for the physicians of generations to come. Medicine is a profession, he taught; it is a public trust and therefore should not be ruled by the commercial interests of the merchant-class. Plus he seems to have been quite a charismatic figure. When he passed away, Elizabeth Montagu, the leading benefactress of the day, observed, "One loved Dr. Gregory for the sake of virtue and virtue (one might almost say) for the sake of Dr. Gregory."[20]

Herophilos/Herophilus (Ἡρόφιλος) (c. 335–c. 280 BCE): the first physician to undertake systematic dissections of human cadavers, in public no less, he is regarded as the father of anatomy (ἀνατομή = cutting up). Born in Chalcedon, his home base was Alexandria; and although scalpelling corpses was forbidden generally, for a run of decades in Alexandria it was not. Herophilos and his protégé, **Erasistratus**, were thus able to make several anatomically significant discoveries. There may be a morally repugnant twist to this story, however. It is alleged that these weren't just dissections, but vivisections (*vivus* = alive). For during the reigns of Ptolemy I and II, grisly punishments for condemned criminals could include being cut open while

20. McCullough, *John Gregory*, 172.

still conscious. Ancient sources allege that some six hundred prisoners were vivisected by the two experimenters. However, this vivisection angle is disputed by some modern scholars.

Hesy-Re (or Hesyre or Hesy-Ra) (the years around 2,650 BCE): the world's earliest known dentist, he was a prominent religious and court official during the reign of Djoser, Pharaoh during the Third Dynasty of ancient Egypt. Of his many recorded titles, one is "The Greatest of Those Who Deal with Teeth and of Physicians."

Hildegard of Bingen (1098–1179): a Benedictine Mother Superior, she was a saint, a mystic, and a leader in a number of other endeavors, medicine being just one. Overseeing her monastery's infirmary and herb garden, she developed a distinctive perspective on health and healthcare. That perspective, recorded in her manual of medical practice, *Causae et curae*, finds parallels between the "green" growth of herbs and plants and the holistic health of men and women. The same principle of *viriditas* ("greenness") is at work in both, she maintained, so that insights regarding the former can be applied to tending the latter. Medical historian Victoria Sweet puts this in the form of a question. "If the healing power in the body is a kind of 'greening power,' then is not medicine a kind of gardening?"[21]

Hilleman, Maurice (1905–2005): an American microbiologist, he is responsible for a majority of today's best-known and most commonly used vaccines. These include the vaccines for measles, mumps, rubella, hepatitis B, and chickenpox. Developing over forty in his long and productive career makes Hilleman the most successful vaccinologist in medical history.

Hippocrates (Ἱπποκράτης) (c. 460–c. 370 BCE): down through the millennia, he has been revered as the father of Western medicine. However, it is doubted that he authored the **Hippocratic Oath**, nor the full corpus of the roughly seventy books gathered under his name. How to distinguish Hippocrates's teachings from those of his followers is a matter best left to the historians. That said, he can safely be credited with incorporating the four **humors** into medicine—reconceived as the basic body fluids of blood (αἷμα), yellow bile (ξανθὴ χολή), black bile (μέλαινα χολή), and phlegm (φλέγμα)—and then adding that health is a matter of their properly balanced mixture in sync with the seasons. But his truly revolutionary achievement lies elsewhere. Hippocrates disengaged medicine from the superstitious beliefs and magical practices that it had been compacted with

---

21. Sweet, "Hildegard of Bingen," 401.

from time immemorial. The actual causes of diseases are natural, he argued, and their remedies need to be natural as well. He may not have been the first ancient physician to make such a "natural turn." A traditional view holds that **Imhotep** deserves this honor, though this has been disputed. But be that as it may, with Hippocrates a medical subculture developed. Interference from the gods no longer a concern, medicine could be systematized; physicians could be trained; and ethical standards could be articulated. Thus medicine as a professional discipline was made possible by Hippocrates. See **Empedocles** and **Galen**

Holmes, Oliver Wendell, Sr. (1809–94): his day job was as a physician and professor of anatomy and physiology. And in that role, he was the first to warn fellow doctors that puerperal (childbirth) fever could be contagious, transferrable from one maternal patient to the next. Credit for this often goes to **Ignaz Semmelweis**; but Holmes was earlier, making the claim in a medical paper presented in Boston in 1843, "The Contagiousness of Puerperal Fever." The paper was also memorable in another way. In addition to "thorough ablution," he recommended a twenty-four-hour waiting period between patients. However, he is better remembered for his contributions to nineteenth-century American literature; he authored some of the poetic gems that generations of American schoolchildren memorized. (And just so there's no confusion, this isn't the famous Supreme Court Justice. That's his son, Oliver Wendell Holmes Jr.)

Hume, David (1711–76): a philosopher of the Scottish Enlightenment, he challenged the confidence his contemporaries placed in human reason, both as a window on reality and as a foundation for morality. He also posed what is now known as "The Is-Ought Problem." The issue, as Hume saw it, is that thinkers are forever making unwarranted shifts from observation ("is" statements) to obligation ("ought" statements)—when actually the two are quite different. Bioethicists are familiar with the tension between knowing "What *can* be done for this patient?" on the one hand, and deciding "What *should* be done?" on the other. That is, knowing about "can" does not provide certainty about "should"—and that's Hume's basic point. It's sometimes called "Hume's Guillotine," and the point is often related to the **naturalistic fallacy** (in **Part 1**) of **G. E. Moore** (in **Part 2**)

Ibn al-Baitar or **Ibn al-Bayṭār** (1197–1248): an Arab botanist and pharmacist, he is an important figure in the history of pharmacy. Born in Spain, he traveled across North Africa, lived in Egypt, and died in Damascus. This geographically expansive research-area shows in that his *Compendium on*

Simple Medicaments and Foods introduces 200 plants which had previously been unknown. It takes information about the medicinal uses of foods, plants, and drugs inherited from antiquity—roughly 1,000 entries—and presents it alphabetically, integrating 300 to 400 more from scholars of more recent centuries, plus his own findings. His sources include twenty Greek scientists and 150 Arabic scholars.

Ibn al-Nafis (c. 1213–88): an Arab physician from Damascus who practiced medicine in Cairo, he was the first to accurately describe, long before William Harvey, how blood circulates. Departing from the traditional view of his day, one that traces back to **Galen**, he hypothesized that blood moves from the right ventricle to the lungs to "be mingled there with air," and then back to the left ventricle. This achievement was credited to Harvey until the twentieth century.

Ibn Rushd: see **Averroes**

Ibn Sina: see **Avicenna**

Ibn Zuhr: see **Avenzoar**

Imhotep (c. 2667–c. 2600 BCE): some 2,200 years before **Hippocrates**, this Egyptian priest, vizier, and architect of the step pyramid at Saqqārah was also a medical pioneer—or not. Scholars disagree. The traditional view is that he wrote one of the world's earliest medical texts, explaining treatments for forty-eight different conditions and using close to 100 anatomical terms in the process. While magical spells and incantations are not avoided, the document's descriptions of trauma and surgery are decidedly natural and practical. However, a contemporary view notes that this text is from a full thousand years later; that tracing it back to Imhotep is a matter of sheer speculation; and that we have no direct evidence that this talented man ever practiced medicine. Either way, in the centuries after he died his status was elevated from pharaoh's chancellor to patron saint, and then ultimately to the Egyptian god of healing, adopted as such by the Greeks, who equated him with **Asclepius**.

Imlach, Francis Brodie (1819–81): a Scottish dentist, he led dentistry in its transition from a less socially significant trade into a full-fledged medical profession. In 1879, he was elected President of the Royal College of Surgeons (Edinburgh), the first dentist ever to be so honored. His election signaled that dentistry now had a place alongside clinical surgery. He was also the first to use chloroform on a dental patient during a tooth extraction.

Jaspers, Karl (1883–1969): though better known as an existentialist philosopher, he was first a psychiatrist (1908–15) and he had a lasting impact on its practice. He "brought the methods of phenomenology—the direct investigation and description of phenomena as consciously experienced—into the field of clinical psychiatry. This so-called descriptive psychopathology created a scientific basis for the practice of psychiatry, and emphasized that symptoms of mental disorder should be diagnosed according to their form rather than to their content."[22] The form of a hallucination, for example, is seeing something that isn't there; and that's sufficient for a clinical diagnosis. The particulars, what the person sees, can be important, but not for classification purposes. He also introduced the biographical method which places an emphasis on a patient's personal history and subjective understanding of his or her condition. These contributions endure.

Jenner, Edward (1749–1823): an English physician, he is the father of immunology. In his day, rumor had it that milkmaids who contracted cowpox were protected from smallpox. Putting it to the test, Jenner transferred matter from a milkmaid's cowpox lesion to a cut on a young boy's arm. The lad became sick and then recovered; after he did, the doctor inoculated him with smallpox, the more serious disease. It didn't take; so the procedure was a success. The scientific breakthrough was this: the demonstration that the vaccinatee was now immune. Since the Latin terms for "cow" and "cowpox" are *vacca* and *vaccinia*, Jenner named his new treatment **vaccination**. See **Anti-Vaxxers**; **Wakefield, Andrew**; and **Vaccination, Opposition to** (in **Part 1**)

Kant, Immanuel (1724–1804): one of philosophy's watershed figures, he started out as a German rationalist until the skeptical thought of **David Hume** woke him from his "dogmatic slumbers." His subsequent philosophy provides places for empirical knowledge, religious faith, and ethical obligation. Regarding the latter, he insists that ethics cannot rest on the unfree promptings of individual desire, but only on the autonomous determination of universal reason. This Kant calls "the categorical imperative." It is sometimes explained as doing one's duty for the sake of doing one's duty. Yet as that stands, it is misleading. Duty for Kant does not consist of obedience to dictates imposed from without; rather duty is the moral necessity that reason assigns to itself, independent of individual desires, interests, and circumstances. Often this is equated with **deontology**. See **Categorical Imperative** and **Universalizability** (in **Part 1**)

22. Burton, "Brief History of Psychiatry," para. 13.

Kraepelin, Emil (1856–1926): a German psychiatrist, he dominated the field between the asylum era of **Philippe Pinel** and the psychoanalytic era of **Sigmund Freud**. Kraepelin is famous for his watershed classification of mental disorders. Against the prevailing view of the time (that the various symptoms were manifestations of a single mental disturbance), he separated out schizophrenia, which he labeled "dementia praecox," from manic-depressive psychosis. Moreover, he advanced the notion that particular symptoms could appear in any disorder, so that what matters is not symptoms but patterns of symptoms. Especially influential in the early twentieth century, his categories laid the foundation for present-day classification systems such as the **DSM (Diagnostic and Statistical Manual of Mental Disorders)**, and the International Classification of Diseases (ICD). But there's also this: he had a Social Darwinist side. "Kraepelin was an ardent proponent of eugenics and of 'degeneration theory,' which propagated that the Aryan race was degenerating into higher rates of mental illness and other conditions due to various undesirables in its midst."[23]

Lacks, Henrietta (1920–51): her cell line is the subject of the book, *The Immortal Life of Henrietta Lacks*.[24] And her case raises a number of questions about research with human subjects. An African American with cervical cancer, she passed away in 1951. However, before she died and without her knowledge, as part of a diagnostic procedure, a tissue sample was removed from her cervix. At the time, taking such a sample for study without the patient's informed consent was not unusual; but her cells turned out to be highly unusual. They were "immortal" in vitro in the sense that they reproduced very quickly and kept on reproducing. These were the first lab-growable human cells ever, and, for many years they were the only ones. They would soon become crucial in many significant experiments; in fact in 2013, a tally put the number of experiments at more than 74,000. And as one would expect, profits generated along the way have been astronomical. Yet, for many years, Ms. Lacks's family members were left in the dark. Only belatedly have they been recognized as stakeholders with certain rights, although a right to compensation does not seem to be one of them.

Lister, Joseph (1827–1912): the British surgeon who transformed medicine by introducing antiseptics to surgery. Taking inspiration from the work of **Louis Pasteur,** especially his thought about preventing infection with chemicals, Lister began applying dressings soaked in carbolic acid to wounds to great effect. Next, he added the washing of hands and the

23. Strous et al., "Reflections on 'Emil Kraepelin,'" 300.
24. Skloot, *Immortal Life of Henrietta Lacks.*

sterilizing of instruments. At one point, before these innovations, the death rate for his amputee-patients ranged between 45 and 50 percent; afterward, it fell to 15 percent. His new disinfectant approach soon gained widespread acceptance in several countries. Many surgeons in London and the United States were late-joiners, but by 1890, his Antiseptic System had changed medicine forever. See **Holmes, Oliver Wendell, Sr.,** and **Semmelweis, Ignaz;** and **Sepsis** (in **Part 1**)

Luther, Martin (1483–1546): in 1517, this German monk tacked up a detailed account of church practices that he thought needed correcting. He had no plan to split Western Christianity in two, but that's what the Reformation, the movement he launched, did. In shepherding its progress, he forged a revolutionary understanding of Christian theology. And ethics. Against the Medieval Church's idea of "works righteousness," he taught that salvation is by faith alone. Against its elaborate clericalism, he taught the priesthood of all believers. And against the claim that its hierarchal authority structure rested on an evolving ecclesiastical tradition, he argued that: (a) the pope was the Antichrist; and (b) believers have only one authority, Scripture. In April 1521, at a fateful meeting before Emperor Charles V, Luther was asked to officially repudiate such heresies. His reply was, "Unless I am convinced by Scripture and plain reason—I do not accept the authority of popes and councils, for they have contradicted each other—my conscience is captive to the Word of God, I cannot and I will not recant anything, for to go against conscience is neither right nor safe. God help me. Amen."[25] Roland Bainton observes, "Here we have the epitome and the extent of Protestant individualism."[26]

Lynch, Virginia (born 1941): she is known as the "Mother of **Forensic Nursing**." The idea of a new medical specialty came to her because of her ER nurse experience. She had learned that for cases of abuse, rape, and even murder, the chances of perpetrators being brought to justice were lessened by the fact that preserving evidence was not on the radar screen of most medical personnel. But nurses could be trained to do otherwise, Lynch thought. So in 1986, she proposed and helped to design the first graduate program in forensic nursing. She went on to serve on the faculty of the program in Forensic Nursing and Forensic Health Science at the University of Colorado. And she is the editor of *Forensic Nursing* (2006), the first medico-legal textbook written specifically for nurses.

---

25. The traditional, additional wording, "Here I stand. I cannot do otherwise," is not found in the official transcripts of the Diet of Worms and is doubted by scholars.

26. Bainton, *Reformation*, 61.

Mahoney, Mary Eliza (1845–1926): the fact that she graduated in 1879 from the school for nurses at the New England Hospital for Women and Children—the first hospital in the United States to offer such nurse-training—makes Ms. Mahoney the first formally trained African American nurse. Most of her subsequent professional employment was as a private care nurse. She was one of the first African American nurses to join the organization that would evolve into the American Nurses Association. And she was a determined champion of women's rights. And when she was seventy-five, she was among the first women in Boston to register to vote subsequent to the ratification of 19th Amendment, on August 26, 1920.

Maimonides / Moses ben Maimon (1138–1204): the best-known Jewish scholar of the Middle Ages, he was a rabbi, a philosopher, and a physician, **Sir William Osler** calling him "the Prince of Physicians." His birthplace was Córdoba (Spain) but his family had to relocate to Morocco and then to Egypt because of religious persecution. In time, he achieved a reputation for being the greatest physician of his generation, and as a result he was appointed the family doctor for the sultan, Saladin the Great, and his family. He interpreted the practice of medicine as a duty fulfilling the Hebrew scriptural command to return lost items to their rightful owners, for a healer restores health to the person who is sick.

Mill, John Stuart (1806–73): the chief advocate, along with his predecessor, **Jeremy Bentham**, of utilitarianism. Mill made alterations to Bentham's program; and they are generally regarded as allowing for a stronger and more defensible—but also less consistent—ethical theory. Both men construed ethics in terms of the greatest happiness principle. Mill introduced a distinction between higher pleasures and lower, so as to emphasize *quality* of happiness over *quantity*. He argued, "It is better to be a human being dissatisfied than a pig satisfied; better to be Socrates dissatisfied than a fool satisfied. And if the fool, or the pig, is of a different opinion, it is because they only know their own side of the question. The other party to the comparison knows both sides."[27] His arguments in *On Liberty* appear to be inconsistent with, or at least unrelated to, his utilitarianism, even though he claims the opposite. Be that as it may, *On Liberty* is highly regarded for identifying the tyranny of the majority as a potential problem in political democracies.[28]

Miller, Willoughby (1853–1907): a notable figure in the history of dentistry, Miller was an American dentist who served as Professor of Operative

27. Mill, *Utilitarianism*, 10.
28. Mill, *On Liberty*.

Dentistry at the University of Berlin. He conducted groundbreaking re-search into oral microbiology. One result was his book, *Micro-Organisms of the Human Mouth*, which called attention to the crucial role that these organisms play in promoting tooth decay. An oral hygiene revolution, with an emphasis on brushing and flossing, was a direct result.

Moore, G. E.: see **Naturalistic Fallacy** (in **Part 1**)

Mother Teresa (1910–97): famous for working with the destitute in Calcut-ta (now Kolkata), India. Born in Macedonia, her name was Agnes Gonxha Bojaxhiu. She was given the name Sister Mary Teresa when she became a Sisters of Loreto nun at age eighteen. After just six weeks with the Sisters, she was sent to India to teach at a Roman Catholic school for girls. Then one day, she heard "a call within a call." God told her to move out beyond the confines of her school and into the slums of the city, for her ministry was now to be one of caring for the poorest of the poor. Before long, she received papal authorization to start her own order, The Missionaries of Charity. Widely honored for her life of sacrifice, she received the Nobel Peace Prize in 1979.

Nightingale, Florence (1820–1910): she was "The Lady with the Lamp," during the Crimean War, a nickname she earned by continuing to make her rounds—after dark, after the medical officers had finished for the day—with a lamp in her hand. She had been sent to the military hospital in Scutari to oversee the care of Britain's wounded soldiers. What she found was horrific: the diseases fostered by poor care and unsanitary conditions were caus-ing far more fatalities than the wounds of war were. Soon she had things cleaned up and turned around, and many lives were spared. But there is more. Because she was not just a nurse and an organizer but also a deter-mined record-keeper and a highly original statistician, she was able to keep track of, and then to visually depict, the hospital's mortality rate problem and its solution, making it easy to understand. To do so, she invented a new kind of graph (today it is called a Polar-Area Diagram or Coxcomb). It made it clear that the military's number one threat was not the enemy wounding the soldiers, but rather the diseases killing the wounded. Her ef-forts convinced many and led directly to the transformation of how patients were—and are—cared for in both military and civilian hospitals alike. So while her name is easy to find on the "Most Famous Nurses" lists, it's also there among the "Most Influential Women Mathematicians," as well.

Osler, Sir William (1849–1919): a Canadian who is often credited as "the Father of Modern Medicine," he contributed much to the science and practice of medicine and to the training of new physicians. He co-founded the Johns Hopkins School of Medicine, broke new ground in bringing students out of the lecture hall to receive instruction at the bedside—and he created the residency system used in teaching hospitals today. Plus he is the originator of the quote, "The person who takes medicine must recover twice. Once from the disease and once from the medicine."

Paré, Ambroise (1510–90): a member of the Parisian **Barber-Surgeons** guild, he was the official surgeon for four French kings. His skill and prominence had an elevating effect on the social status of his profession; and he is regarded as the father of modern surgery. (But note the "modern" and compare this honorific title to that of **Abulcasis**, centuries earlier.) Moreover, Paré is often cited in histories of dentistry, for he wrote on a number of dentistry topics. And he originated the famous aphorism "I bandaged him; God healed him." Although a Catholic in public, he may have been a Huguenot (French Calvinist). As such, his life would have been in jeopardy on the occasion of the St. Bartholomew's Day Massacre, August 24, 1572, when the mass slaughter of Huguenots began. A story has it that he was at the bedside of Admiral de Coligny, a leading Calvinist and the most obvious target for assassination. The admiral was indeed set upon and killed. But Paré's life was spared, for although King Charles IX had ordered the extrajudicial executions, perhaps reluctantly, he saw to it that his personal surgeon was hidden away, locked inside a clothes closet.

Pasteur, Louis (1822–95): a French research chemist and microbiologist, he transformed several scientific disciplines, created the fields of microbiology and immunology, and revolutionized the practice of medicine. Starting out studying crystals, he soon turned to fermentation, developing the pasteurization process for which he is most widely known. In time, he successfully demonstrated that microorganisms cause not just fermentation but also disease. Later in life, he developed vaccines for chicken cholera, anthrax, and rabies. It is said, "Edward Jenner invented vaccination, Louis Pasteur invented vaccines."[29]

Percival, Thomas (1740–1804): he gave us the phrase "medical ethics." And his seminal text by that name had an immense influence on the American Medical Association's Code of Ethics (1847), an influence that persisted through a number of code revisions. The backstory is this: Manchester, England's Infirmary had been the scene of a protracted and raucous turf war. Dr. Percival, one of the city's most respected physicians, was asked to

29. Institut Pasteur, "Final Years," para. 1.

draw up a set of professional behavioral standards to help the physicians, surgeons, and apothecaries get along. He did; his guidance was accepted into the operational rules of the hospital; he disseminated them in pamphlet form, and then made them publicly available as *Medical Ethics* (1803). "Percival created an ethics for a new medical milieu, the eighteenth-century hospital, in which multiple practitioners shared the care of patients who were generally needy and of a social class distinctly below that of their patrons and physicians."[30] It is now acknowledged that Percival's contribution follows the trailblazing work of **John Gregory** (1724–73), the two men being regarded as the twin pioneers of modern medical ethics.

Piaget, Jean (1896–1980): the Swiss psychologist responsible for a highly influential account of the cognitive development of children—an account that Albert Einstein described as so simple that only a genius could have thought of it. Early on, Piaget had become intrigued by the answers children gave on intelligence tests; so he followed through. "I engaged my subjects in conversations patterned after psychiatric questioning, with the aim of discovering something about the reasoning process underlying their right, but especially their wrong answers."[31] He came up with a theory: that human knowing takes place in developmental stages. In this, he was breaking new ground. He was the first person to investigate cognitive development systematically—and the first to do so on the basis of empirical observation. He called his approach genetic epistemology, for it sought to understand the nature of knowledge by charting how it is constructed in the growing individual.

Picotte, Susan La Flesche (1865–1915): the first Native American to earn a medical degree, she graduated in 1889 at the top of her class from the Women's Medical College of Pennsylvania. She came back home to serve as a Presbyterian medical missionary on the Omaha Reservation. Reform-minded, she was a public health advocate, the leader of reservation temperance initiatives, and the guiding force behind a successful drive to build the area's first hospital.

Pinel, Philippe (1745–1826): a French physician, he founded the discipline of psychiatry while at the Bicêtre and Salpêtrière asylums in Paris. Bicêtre was a prison, a hospital, and an asylum for 4,000 men. Two hundred of these were mental patients; and some, chained to walls, were featured in freakshows for paying customers. It should be noted that at Bicêtre "the

30. Jonsen, *Short History*, 59.
31. Jean Piaget, in Evans, *Dialogue with Jean Piaget*, 119.

unchaining of the insane," for which Pinel is often credited, took place before he arrived in 1793. But that he continued the humanization process,
there is no doubt, for he broke new ground in giving mental patients individualized, psychiatric attention: daily visits, personal interviews, and the
recording of their case histories. Two years later he moved to Salpêtrière, an
institution for 7,000 women, and there he famously ordered the removal of
the chains from eighty residents. His approach, which he called *traitement
moral*, was widely imitated. See **Moral Treatment** (in **Part 1**)

Plato (Πλάτων) (c. 427–c. 347 BCE): prior to the modern era, he was un-
questionably the West's most influential philosopher, a status now sometimes reassigned to **Aristotle**. Although his multifaceted thought evolved, it
is customary to describe its signature argument as follows. In the world that
we think we know, there are no perfect or fixed examples, only imperfect
and changing ones, so how is trustworthy knowledge possible? The answer
is that we can understand all the deficient objects of human experience by
discerning what they are examples of, forms or ideas (εἴδη), which more
than a few commentators have compared to ontological blueprints. It is
these that provide the basis for the world's rational intelligibility. And of all
these, so Plato explains in *The Republic*, the uppermost is the form of the
good, the ethical centerpiece of his thought. It is analogous to the sun, for
its radiance lights up all the other ideas, and thereby, the empirical world
as well.

Popper, Karl: see **Falsification, Popper's Principle of** (in **Part 1**)

Rhazes/Al-Razi: (c. 854–c. 925) a Persian physician who practiced in Bagh-
dad, his writings were influential during the Islamic Golden Age and later in
the West. Among other noteworthy contributions, they provided medicine's
first accurate descriptions of, and distinctions between, smallpox and measles. Generally following the teachings of **Hippocrates** and **Galen**, he went
his own way when his clinical observations differed from their orthodoxies.
Thus he was an independent thinker, something that held true in matters of
religion as well: trusting in human reason, he rejected the Qur'an and didn't
buy the claim that Mohammed was a divinely inspired prophet.

Rogers, Carl (1902–87): "What I hear you saying is—" there was a time
when those words were not the commonest of all counseling office clichés;
but that was before American psychologist Carl Rogers revolutionized psychotherapy. And if they sound trite now, it's because of how pervasive his
influence has been. At a time when psychology was dominated by the dark
hues of the Freudian and Skinnerian orientations, humanistic psychology

arrived on the scene as a sunnier "third force," a viable, therapy-friendly alternative to the other two. Humanistic psychology was an extended family of overlapping methodologies; it included gestalt and existential therapies and transactional analysis (*I'm Okay, You're Okay*.)[32] But at the head of the family was the nondirective, client-centered, "Rogerian" approach, in which the therapist's role was recast as a "coparticipant in the process of self-actualization" which meant first and foremost being an accepting and empathetic listener.[33] See **Directive vs. Nondirective Counseling** (in **Part 1**)

Salk, Jonas Edward (1914–95): an American physician and leading research virologist, he developed the first widely used, safe, and effective polio vaccine. Prior to that time, polio had been a frightful contagion. After all, President Franklin Delano Roosevelt's paralysis was attributed to poliomyelitis. (Medical science now leans toward Guillain-Barre Syndrome instead.) As per a 2009 PBS documentary, "Apart from the atomic bomb, America's greatest fear was polio."[34] Working at the University of Pittsburgh School of Medicine, Dr. Salk led a team in a seven-year search for a vaccine. On April 12, 1955, when it was announced that they had one, he was widely esteemed as a miracle worker. Asked who owned the vaccine's patent, he answered, "There is no patent."

Scheele, Carl Wilhelm (1742–86): a German-Swedish pharmaceutical chemist who, though he lived off the beaten path and operated without elaborate equipment, nevertheless advanced pharmacy in a number of ways. "He began in a corner of the stock room of Unicorn Apothecary in Gothenburg. With rare genius, he made thousands of experiments, discovered oxygen, chlorine, prussic acid, tartaric acid, tungsten, molybdenum, glycerin, nitroglycerin, and countless other organic compounds that enter into today's daily life, industry, health, and comfort."[35] For example, Sweden would emerge as a leading exporter of matches because Scheele uncovered the secret of mass producing phosphorus. Yet sadly, credit for some of his achievements went to others. We know, for example, that he discovered oxygen in 1771; but Joseph Priestley got published first. He died at age forty-three; the fact that he liked to taste and smell the chemicals he was working with may have had something to do with it.

32. Harris, *I'm Okay—You're Okay*.

33. Jones and Butman, *Modern Psychotherapies*, 256.

34. PBS's American Experience, as quoted in Patel, "Polio Eradication in India," para. 1.

35. Bender, "Scheele," 21.

Schweitzer, Albert (1875–1965): a German physician whose life and views had a significant impact on many areas of life, too many to recount. He won the Nobel Peace Prize in 1952 for advancing a philosophy of "Reverence for Life." A Lutheran pastor, his work *The Quest of the Historical Jesus* reoriented the liberal "higher criticism" of his day.[36] An influential scholar of music, he was internationally famous as a concert organist. Pivotally, at the age of thirty, he discerned a call to the mission field; accordingly, he enrolled in med school so that he could serve as a medical missionary. In 1913, he opened the Schweitzer Hospital in Lambaréné, in French Equatorial Africa (now Gabon), and he raised funds for its operation by giving benefit concerts and lectures back in Europe. This was the mission locale where he spent most of the rest of his life. "At Lambaréné, Schweitzer was doctor and surgeon in the hospital, pastor of a congregation, administrator of a village, superintendent of buildings and grounds, writer of scholarly books, commentator on contemporary history, musician, [and] host to countless visitors."[37]

Seacole, Mary (1805–81): she is famous for her freelance nursing during the Crimean War. Her mother was African-Jamaican; her father was a Scottish officer in the British army; she self-identified as Creole. And while she had no formal training, she knew about herbal and folk remedies from her mother, and she had cared for victims of cholera and yellow fever. So when the British army needed nurses, she applied multiple times, only to be rejected each time. Buoyantly undeterred, she went to Crimea anyway as a "sutler" (a provisioner; a civilian who sells supplies in proximity to a military campaign). Together with her business partner, Thomas Day, she set up the British Hotel—although that name may be misleading. "While Seacole's original intention had been to open 'a mess table and comfortable quarters for sick and convalescent officers,' in fact she established a hut which served as an all-in-one store-restaurant for officers, with a 'canteen' for ordinary soldiers."[38] From that base of operations, she was able to care for the sick and wounded both in and out of the combat zone—and to provide catering services to battlefield spectators. Deeply appreciated by the soldiers, her popularity matched that of **Florence Nightingale**.

Semmelweis, Ignaz (1818–65): a Hungarian physician, he discovered the cause of puerperal (childbirth) fever and brought antiseptic protections into the delivery room. While at Vienna General Hospital's First Obstetrical Clinic he observed that mothers in the wards where med students were

---

36. Schweitzer, *Quest of the Historical Jesus*.
37. "Albert Schweitzer," para. 6.
38. National Geographic Education Staff, "Mary Seacole," para. 21.

being educated fared much worse than those where midwives were trained. The mortality rate from puerperal fever in the former could be two to three times the rate in the latter. And one thing that med students did that midwifes did not do was perform autopsies on fever victims. Dr. Semmelweis theorized that the student-doctors brought "cadaverous particles" from the one assignment to the next. So he began requiring them to wash their hands in a chlorinated lime solution prior to each maternal examination. The clinic's tragic loss-of-life problem decreased dramatically. Antiseptic protocols were embraced in Semmelweis's native Hungary; elsewhere not so much. In fact, most medical professionals found the idea that their hands were unclean to be insulting and ridiculous. The good doctor did not take this well; his mental health deteriorated; he died miserably in an asylum. It would not be until **Louis Pasteur's** germ theory and **Joseph Lister's** clinical procedures took hold that he would receive the recognition he deserved. See **Holmes, Oliver Wendell, Sr.**

Sertürner, Friedrich (1783–1841): at the time he discovered morphine, he was "an obscure, uneducated, 21-year-old pharmacist's assistant with little equipment but loads of curiosity."[39] In a major scientific breakthrough, he isolated and extracted morphine from opium. And he named his new find "morphium," after Morpheus, the Greek god of dreams. For dosage experiments, he began with stray dogs and a mouse picked up off the floor. He also ran tests on himself and three friends. Since all this involved the first isolation of any alkaloid from a plant source, it marks the beginning of the field of alkaloid chemistry. Some scholars go so far as to claim that Sertürner single-handedly "transformed pharmaceutical chemistry from a state of alchemy to an acknowledged branch of science."[40]

Skinner, B. F. (1904–90): Professor of Psychology at Harvard University from 1958 to 1974. On lists of influential psychologists, he often comes in at number one. His specific contributions are, first, to behaviorism. He held that in dealing with living beings, humans included, observable behavior is where the action is; unobservable mental operations are not—which means that science can ignore them. And second, he advanced his radical behaviorism as a political philosophy. As he puts it in *Beyond Freedom and Dignity*,

> We have moved forward by dispossessing autonomous man.
> . . . In the traditional view, a person is free. He is autonomous

---

39. University of Chicago Medicine, "As Morphine Turns 200," para. 6.
40. Krishnamurti and Rao, "Isolation of Morphine," para. 2.

in the sense that his behavior is uncaused. He can, therefore, be held responsible for what he does and justly punished if he offends. That view, together with its associated practices, must be re-examined when a scientific analysis reveals unsuspected controlling relations between behavior and environment.[41]

For Skinner, human beings do not actually possess the dignity or the free will traditionally ascribed to them; and since they don't, there is no reason why a scientific elite, once put in charge of society, shouldn't start to work, modifying human behavior scientifically, and thus making the world a happier and more productive place.

Smith, James McCune (1813–65): the first African American to earn a degree in medicine; to operate a pharmacy; and to write articles published in American medical journals. Born in New York City when slavery was being phased out, he wasn't free until the broad emancipation of July 4, 1827. An excellent student, he hoped to become a doctor, but American schools disallowed his entrance because of race. So he attended Glasgow University in Scotland instead, graduating with a medical degree in 1837—at the top of his class. Returning to America, he began what soon became a very successful medical practice. But he was most influential as a thoughtful and learned abolitionist. He wrote the intro to one of Frederick Douglass's autobiographies; and Douglass credited him with being the single most important influence on his life.

Snow, John (1813–58): in a poll of British physicians he was voted the "greatest doctor of all time," surpassing even Hippocrates![42] Not everyone puts him in first place; but many agree that he is a major figure, listing him as the father of public health and/or epidemiology. His initial claim to fame was in a different field, however: anesthesiology. He improved the administration first of ether and then of chloroform; his expertise and reputation were such that he was asked to anesthetize Queen Victoria for the birth of her eighth and ninth children. Then in 1854, cholera, which had been a perennial threat, struck an area of London called Soho. Dr. Snow charted the cholera deaths on a map. Guided by his theory that the disease was waterborne (not the accepted idea at the time), he looked for a water source. He determined that it had to be a specific water pump on Broad Street. So he prevailed upon the Board of Guardians, skeptics all, to have the pump

41. Skinner, *Beyond Freedom and Dignity*, 19–20.

42. UCLA Department of Epidemiology, Fielding School of Public Health, "Dr. John Snow," para. 1.

handle removed. It was, and the outbreak subsided. The citizenry—learning that a public water source was responsible for a killer disease, probably because it was contaminated with sewage—demanded and got a complete overhaul of the city's water system.

Summerlin, William (born 1938): a notorious figure in the annals of research fraud, his subterfuge was both over-the-top and the first of several to come to light during the 1970s. Dr. Summerlin was a dermatologist investigating transplantation immunology in mice at the Memorial Sloan-Kettering Cancer Center in New York in 1974. He claimed that he had succeeded in transplanting patches of skin from black mice onto white mice. But lab assistants soon discovered that his scientific breakthrough involved a secret instrument: a black marking pen. **Painting the mice** became a shopterm for cheating in a scientific experiment.

Typhoid Mary (1869–1938): the famous **super-spreader** responsible for between thirty-three and fifty-one cases of typhoid fever (if not more) and for three deaths. Mary Mallon was an Irish-born cook in turn-of-the-twentieth-century New York, employed serially by wealthy families. She herself was asymptomatic, but members of households would become ill shortly after she signed on—and soon thereafter she would leave without anyone suspecting. Finally, the Health Department caught up with her and she was taken into custody. She tested positive, becoming the first person in the United States proven to be an asymptomatic typhoid **carrier**. Placed in involuntary isolation, after three years she was released on the condition that she no longer hire herself out as a cook. But she did. Under the leadership of **Sara Josephine Baker**, she was apprehended a second time and was taken back to Riverside Hospital (a facility for patients with quarantinable diseases, located on an island in New York's East River). There she was confined for the rest of her life, 1915 to 1938. For her part, Ms. Mallon never accepted the idea that she posed a threat, for how could she make anyone else sick if she wasn't sick herself? See **Subclinical** (in **Part 1**)

Vesalius, Andreas (1514–64): the father of modern anatomy, he was a Renaissance physician born in Brussels. After receiving his medical degree from the University of Padua in 1537, he was appointed lecturer in surgery and anatomy. Customarily lectures were theory-heavy and involved much quoting from ancient sources, particularly **Galen**; and any actual demonstration-dissecting was delegated to the déclassé **barber-surgeons**. But Vesalius pioneered a more hands-on teaching style, performing his own dissections, which put him a position to realize that Galen could be wrong at points—wrong enough that he must not ever have worked on human cadavers. Vesalius came to realize that Galen's theories rested on animal anatomy plus inference. For some historians, the 1543 publication of his *De Humani Corporis Fabrica Libri Septem* (Latin = *On the Fabric of the Human Body in Seven Books*) signals the beginning of modern medicine. See **Eustachi, Bartolomeo**

Wakefield, Andrew (born 1957): the British ex-gastroenterologist who ignited present-day opposition to public-health immunizations. In 1998, he and twelve fellow-researchers published a report implying a connection between the measles, mumps, and rubella vaccine (MMR) and autism. Soon it became clear that their claim could not be supported, and ten of the twelve coauthors issued a retraction. In time, Wakefield's continued effort was exposed as faulty and marred by conflicts of interest—and indeed as an "elaborate fraud."[43] Found guilty of dishonesty and irresponsibility by the UK's General Medical Council, he was **struck off** the medical register, losing his ability to practice medicine. Undeterred, he has continued to make his case, a case that has been roundly repudiated by the medical science and public health communities. See **Anti-Vaxxers** and **Jenner, Edward; Vaccination** and **Vaccination, Opposition to** (in **Part 1**)

Wald, Lillian (1867–1940): a nurse, social worker, public health official, and key mover and shaker during the Progressive Era. She founded Henry Street Settlement during the apex of Settlement House Movement (the latter an initiative introduced in the United States by **Jane Addams**). The settlement house concept involved members of society's better-off choosing to "settle" in impoverished urban neighborhoods in cities like New York, to be a leaven-like positive influence. From her Henry Street base of operations, Wald spearheaded causes such as public school nursing and at-home care. It was she who coined the term "public health nursing." By 1913, her organization of nurses and support staff had grown to ninety-two; soon it would evolve into the Visiting Nurse Service of New York, the world's first public health nursing operation. She was also active in the humanitarian causes of her day: world peace, labor unions, racial equality, and women's suffrage. In 1922, the *New York Times* recognized her as one of the twelve greatest living women.

Zhang Xi-chun (1860–1933): the Chinese scholar-physician remembered for his overtures in **integrative medicine**. In 1918, after a stint as a military physician, he was appointed Dean of the Li Da Chinese Medical Hospital.

43. BMJ, "BMJ Declares MMR Study 'An Elaborate Fraud,'" para. 1.

There he championed partnering the medicines of East and West. This was a time of mostly mutual antagonism between the two systems. But Zhang believed that the drugs favored by the West were better for alleviating symptoms; that the herbs of traditional Chinese medicine were superior for effecting a cure; and that a both/and approach was best for patients. So, for example, for treating febrile arthritis, he paired aspirin with gypsum fibrosum (one of the go-to "herbs that drain fire" in Chinese proprietary medicine). At the height of his success, he founded the highly influential Tianjin Institute for Integrated Chinese and Western Medicine in 1928. After his death, a posthumous, thirty-volume collection of his writings was published, its title showcasing his life's motto, *Medical Essays Esteeming the East and Respecting the West.*

Bibliography

Abramsky, Sasha. "The Coronavirus Could Be the Black Swan of 2020." *The Nation*, February 25, 2020. https://www.thenation.com/article/society/coronavirus-economy-trump-election/.

ACS. "Charles Richard Drew." https://www.acs.org/content/acs/en/education/whatischemistry/african-americans-in-sciences/charles-richard-drew.html.

"Albert Schweitzer—Biographical." https://www.nobelprize.org/prizes/peace/1952/schweitzer/biographical/.

AMA Council on Ethical and Judicial Affairs. "Opinion 2.20—Withholding or Withdrawing Life-Sustaining Medical Treatment." *Virtual Mentor* 13.12 (2013) 1038–40. Doi: 10.1001/virtualmentor.2013.15.12.coet1–1312.

American Heart Association. "Understanding Blood Pressure Readings." https://www.heart.org/en/health-topics/high-blood-pressure/understanding-blood-pressure-readings.

American Medical Association. "About." https://www.ama-assn.org/about.

American Medication Association. "Anesthesiology Programs with the Most Residency Positions." https://www.ama-assn.org/residents-students/residency/anesthesiology-programs-most-residency-positions.

———. "Physician-Assisted Suicide." https://www.ama-assn.org/delivering-care/ethics/physician-assisted-suicide.

APHL (Association of Public Health Laboratories). "Commercially Available Zika Virus Diagnostic Assays: Considerations for Use." https://www.aphl.org/programs/preparedness/Documents/Considerations-for-Use-of-Commercial-Zika-Assays_062916.pdf.

Appiah, Kwame Anthony. *Cosmopolitanism: Ethics in a World of Strangers*. New York: Norton, 2006.

Aquinas, Thomas. "Consequences of Charity." In *Summa Theologiæ* 35, edited by Thomas Gilby, 81–85. 61 vols. London: Blackfriars, 1972.

———. "Law and Political Theory." In *Summa Theologiæ* 28, edited by Thomas Gilby, 5–8. 61 vols. London: Blackfriars, 1966.

Aristotle. *Nicomachean Ethics*. New York: Barnes & Noble, 2004.

Augustine. "Homilies on I John." In *Augustine: Later Works*, edited by John Burnaby, 259–348. Library of Christian Classics: Ichthus Edition. Philadelphia: Westminster, 1955.

———. "The Spirit and the Letter." In *Augustine: Later Works*, edited by John Burnaby, 195–250. Library of Christian Classics, Ichthus Edition. Philadelphia: Westminster, 1955.

Bainton, Roland. *The Reformation of the Sixteenth Century*. Boston: Beacon, 1952.

Beauchamp Tom L., and James F. Childress. *Principles of Biomedical Ethics*. 7th ed. New York: Oxford University Press, 2013.

Behnke, Stephen. "Multiple Relationships and APA's New Ethics Code: Values and Applications." *Monitor on Psychology* 35.1 (January 2004) 66. https://www.apa.org/monitor/jan04/ethics.

Bender, George A. "Scheele—Greatest of the Pharmacists-Chemists." *A History of Pharmacy in Pictures*, 1–41. https://docplayer.net/21757104-A-history-of-pharmacy-in-pictures.html.

Bentham, Jeremy. *Introduction to the Principles of Morals and Legislation*. Buffalo, NY: Prometheus, 1988.

Bernstein, Maurice. "Medical Slang Leading to Logical Fallacy: A Practice to Be Avoided." http://www.bioethics.net/2013/05/medical-slang-leading-to-logical-fallacy-a-practice-to-be-avoided/.

Best MSW Programs. "50 Notable Social Workers in US History." https://www.bestmswprograms.com/great-american-social-workers/.

BMJ. "BMJ Declares MMR Study 'An Elaborate Fraud'—Autism Claims Likened to 'Piltdown Man' Hoax." https://www.bmj.com/press-releases/2012/06/26/bmj-declares-mmr-study-%E2%80%9C-elaborate-fraud%E2%80%9D-autism-claims-likened-%E2%80%9Cpiltdown-.

Boyd, Kenneth M. "Ad hominem or ad personam." In *The New Dictionary of Medical Ethics*, edited by Kenneth M. Boyd et al., 5. London: BMJ, 1997.

———. "A priori / a posteriori." In *The New Dictionary of Medical Ethics*, edited by Kenneth M. Boyd et al., 15. London: BMJ, 1997.

Brady, William, et al. "In-Hospital Cardiac Arrest: Impact of Monitoring and Witnessed Event on Patient Survival and Neurologic Status at Hospital Discharge." *Resuscitation* 82.7 (July 2011) 845–52. doi: 10.1016/j.resuscitation.2011.02.028.

Buber, Martin. *I and Thou*. Translated by Walter Kaufmann. New York: Scribner, 1970.

Burns, J. Patout. "Grace." In *Augustine through the Ages: An Encyclopedia*, edited by Allan Fitzgerald et al., 391–98. Grand Rapids: Eerdmans, 1999.

Burton, Neel. "A Brief History of Psychiatry." *Psychology Today*, June 2, 2012. https://www.psychologytoday.com/us/blog/hide-and-seek/201206/brief-history-psychiatry.

California Hospital Association. *Consent: California Hospital Consent Manual*. 46th ed. Sacramento: California Hospital Association, 2019. https://www.sierra-view.com/documents/consent2019_enterprisenew.pdf.

Calvin, John. *Institutes of the Christian Religion*. Edited by John T. McNeill. Library of Christian Classics 20. Philadelphia: Westminster, 1960.

CASA: Court-Appointed Special Advocates—Child Intervention Services. "Job Description." https://casacis.org/wp-content/uploads/2013/07/Advocate-Job-Description-1.pdf.

The Catholic Church. "Catechism of the Catholic Church." 2nd ed. http://www.scborromeo.org/ccc/p3s1c1a4.htm.

CDC: Centers for Disease Control and Prevention. "Case Investigation and Contact Tracing: Part of a Multipronged Approach to Fight the COVID-19 Pandemic."

https://www.cdc.gov/coronavirus/2019-ncov/php/principles-contact-tracing.
html.

⸻. "National Notifiable Diseases Surveillance System (NNDSS)." https://wwwn.
cdc.gov/nndss/data-collection.html.

⸻. "Quarantine and Isolation." https://www.cdc.gov/quarantine/
quarantineisolation.html.

Clark, Kyle, and Andrew George. "A Court Corrects a Medical Injustice." *Wall Street
Journal*, March 7–8, 2020, A13.

Dabis, Márta. "Introduction to Relational Bioethics via House MD (TV series)." Course
description for a Yale University Sherwin B. Nuland Summer Institute in Bioethics
summer seminar, June 2016, 1–39. https://bioethics.yale.edu/sites/default/files/
files/Seminar%20Outlines%2020161.pdf.

Deltombe, Xavier. "Pierre Fauchard, His Life and His Work." *Journal of Dentofacial
Anomalies and Orthodontics* 14.1 (March 2011) 1–6. doi: 10.1051/odfen/2011102.

DeMartino, Erin S., et al. "Who Decides When a Patient Can't? Statutes on Alternate
Decision Makers." *New England Journal of Medicine* 376.15 (April 2017) 1478–82.
https://www.ncbi.nlm.nih.gov/pmc/articles/PMC5527273/.

Dewey, John. *Human Nature and Conduct: An Introduction to Social Psychology*. New
York: Holt, 1922.

Duignan, Brian. "What Is the Difference between Criminal Law and Civil Law?"
https://www.britannica.com/story/what-is-the-difference-between-criminal-law-
and-civil-law.

"Durham Rule." *Law Library—American Law and Legal Information*. https://law.jrank.
org/pages/6321/Durham-Rule.html.

Dyer, Clare. "Doctor Who Was Struck Off for Misconduct Is Restored to the Register
after Changing His Ways." *BMJ News* (February 24, 2020) 368. doi: https://doi.
org/10.1136/bmj.m723.

Emba, Christine. "Opinion: Is It Time to Revise Our Federal Drug Laws?" *Washington
Post*, April 25, 2016. https://www.washingtonpost.com/news/in-theory/
wp/2016/04/25/is-it-time-to-revise-our-federal-drug-laws/.

Evans, Richard I. *Dialogue with Jean Piaget*. New York: Dutton, 1973.

Farrell, Barbara, and Dee Mangin. "Deprescribing Is an Essential Part of Good
Prescribing." *American Family Physician* 99.1 (January 2019) 7–9. https://www.
aafp.org/afp/2019/0101/p7.html.

Fethe, Charles. "The Yuck Factor." *Philosophy Now* 29 (2000). https://philosophynow.
org/issues/29/The_Yuck_Factor.

Filabi, Azish. "Bad Apples, Bad Barrels or Bad Barrel Makers" *Ethical Systems* (blog),
September 29, 2015. https://www.ethicalsystems.org/bad-apples-bad-barrels-or-
bad-barrel-makers/.

Fischhoff, Baruch. "The Realities of Risk-Cost-Benefit Analysis." *Science* 350.6260
(October 30, 2015). http://science.sciencemag.org/content/350/6260/aaa6516.

Fletcher, Joseph. *Situation Ethics—The New Morality*. Philadelphia: Westminster, 1966.

Frankena, William K. "The Naturalistic Fallacy." *Mind* 48.192 (October 1939) 464–77.
https://www.jstor.org/stable/2250706?seq=1.

Freedman, Benjamin. "Equipoise and the Ethics of Clinical Research." *New England
Journal of Medicine* 317 (July 1987) 141–45. doi: 10.1056/NEJM198707163170304.

Fromm, Erich. *The Art of Loving*. New York: Bantam, 1970.

Gandhi, Mohandas K. *An Autobiography: The Story of My Experiments with Truth.* Boston: Beacon, 1972.

George, Andrew T., et al. "Stent Cases and the Criminalization of Medical Judgment." *Circulation* 140 (December 2019) 2051–53. https://doi.org/10.1161/CIRCULATIONAHA.119.042879.

Getz, Lindsey. "A Closer Look at Family First—The Pros and Cons of Recent Foster Care Legislation." *Social Work Today* (2021). https://www.socialworktoday.com/archive/exc_0319.shtml.

Gill, N. S. "Is 'First Do No Harm' Part of the Hippocratic Oath?" *ThoughtCo.*, October 20, 2019. https://www.thoughtco.com/first-do-no-harm-hippocratic-oath-118780.

Gilligan, Carol. *In a Different Voice: Psychological Theory and Women's Development.* Cambridge, MA: Harvard University Press, 2016.

Gillon, Raanan. "Persons and Personhood." In *The New Dictionary of Medical Ethics*, edited by Kenneth M. Boyd et al., 186. London: BMJ, 1997.

Global Down Syndrome Foundation. "Facts and FAQ about Down Syndrome." https://www.globaldownsyndrome.org/about-down-syndrome/facts-about-down-syndrome/.

Government of Canada. "Medical Assistance in Dying." https://www.canada.ca/en/health-canada/services/medical-assistance-dying.html.

Gray, Kurt, and Daniel M. Wegner. "Moral Typecasting: Divergent Perceptions of Moral Agents and Moral Patients." *Journal of Personality and Social Psychology* 96.3 (March 2009) 505–20. doi: 10.1037/a0013748.

Grenz, Stanley J., and John R. Franke. *Beyond Foundationalism: Shaping Theology in a Postmodern Context.* Louisville: Westminster John Knox, 2001.

Gura, Melanie. "Differentiating between Nursing Scope of Practice and Standards of Care." *EP Lab Digest*, October 5, 2010. https://www.eplabdigest.com/blog/The-Importance-Nursing-Scope-Practice-and-Standards-Care.

Gutas, Dimitri. "Ibn Sina [Avicenna]." *Stanford Encyclopedia of Philosophy* (2016). https://plato.stanford.edu/entries/ibn-sina/.

Hammett, Emma. "All about Defibrillators—What They Are and How to Use Them." *First Aid for Life*, March 23, 2021. https://firstaidforlife.org.uk/all-about-defibrillators-aeds-what-they-are-and-how-to-use-them/.

Harris, Thomas A. *I'm Okay—You're Okay.* New York: Avon, 1967.

The Healthcare Ethics Blog. "'Unrepresented Patients' and Vulnerability: Patients without Decision Makers." https://www.healthethicsblog.com/single-post/2017/11/01/-unrepresented-patients-and-vulnerability-patients-without-decision-makers.

Healthwise Staff. "Autogenic Training." *HealthLinkBC* (2016). https://www.healthlinkbc.ca/health-topics/ta7045spec.

Higgs, Roger. "Asymmetry/Symmetry Arguments." In *The New Dictionary of Medical Ethics*, edited by Kenneth M. Boyd et al., 16. London: BMJ, 1997.

———. "Closure, moral." In *The New Dictionary of Medical Ethics*, edited by Kenneth M. Boyd et al., 44. London: BMJ, 1997.

Hoffer, Eric. *The True Believer: Thoughts on the Nature of Mass Movements.* New York: Harper and Row, 1966.

Hollenbach, David, SJ. *The Common Good and Christian Ethics.* Cambridge: Cambridge University Press, 2002.

HSMA. "About." https://www.harleystreetmedicalarea.com/about.

Institut Pasteur. "The Final Years: 1877–1887." *History*. https://www.pasteur.fr/en/institut-pasteur/history/troisieme-epoque-1877-1887.

Ioannidis, John P. A. "Why Most Published Research Findings Are False." *PLoS Medicine* 2.8 (August 2005), 0696–0701. https://upload.wikimedia.org/wikipedia/commons/8/8e/Ioannidis_%282005%29_Why_Most_Published_Research_Findings_Are_False.pdf.

Iowa State University. "Standard Operating Procedures—SOPs." https://www.ehs.iastate.edu/research/laboratory/SOPs.

Jennings, Bruce. "Index." In *Bioethics*, edited by Bruce Jennings, 6:3347–3535. 4th ed. 6 vols. Farmington Hills, MI: Gale, Centage Learning, 2014.

Johnson, R. Skip. "Codependency and Codependent Relationships." https://bpdfamily.com/content/codependency-codependent-relationships.

Jones, James W., and Laurence B. McCullough. "Extending Life or Prolonging Death: When Is Enough Actually Too Much?" *Journal of Vascular Surgery* 60 (2014) 521–22.

Jones, Stanton L., and Richard Butman. *Modern Psychotherapies*. Downers Grove: InterVarsity, 1991.

Jonsen, Albert R. *A Short History of Medical Ethics*. New York: Oxford University Press, 2000.

Jonsen, Albert R., et al. *Clinical Ethics: A Practical Approach to Ethical Decisions in Clinical Medicine*. 8th ed. New York: McGraw Hill, 2015.

Kant, Immanuel. *Foundations of the Metaphysics of Morals*. Translated by Lewis White Beck. Indianapolis: Bobbs-Merrill Educational, 1959.

Kennedy, Donald. "The Old File-Drawer Problem." *Science* 305.5683 (July 2004) 451. doi: 10.1126/science.305.5683.451.

King, Martin Luther, Jr. "A Proper Sense of Priorities." *Speeches and Sounds: Martin Luther King* (1968). http://www.aavw.org/special_features/speeches_speech_king04.html.

Klerman, Gerald L. "Psychotropic Hedonism vs. Pharmacological Calvinism." *Hastings Center Report* 2.4 (September 1972) 1–3. doi: 10.2307/3561398.

Knoll, James L. "Psychiatric Practice Grand Rounds: The Tarasoff Dilemma." *Psychiatric Times*, September 26, 2019. https://www.psychiatrictimes.com/view/psychiatric-malpractice-grand-rounds-tarasoff-dilemma.

Kondziella, Daniel, and Peter Koehler. "Disorders of Consciousness." *Neurology Medlink*, October 4, 1993. https://www.medlink.com/article/disorders_of_consciousness.

Kramer, Peter. *Listening to Prozac*. New York City: Viking, 1993.

Krishnamurti, Chandrasekhar, and SSC Chakra Rao. "The Isolation of Morphine by Sertürner." *Indian Journal of Anaesthesia* 60.11 (November 2016) 861–62. doi: 10.4103/0019-5049.193696.

Krulwich, Robert. "The Ghost of Madame Curie Protests . . ." *National Public Radio*, May 18, 2011. https://www.npr.org/sections/krulwich/2011/05/18/136400018/the-ghost-of-madame-curie-protests.

Kuhn, Thomas S. *The Structure of Scientific Revolutions*. 2nd ed. Chicago: University of Chicago Press, 1970.

Lamkin, Matt, and Carl Elliott. "Avoiding Exploitation in Phase I Clinical Trials: More than (Un)Just Compensation." *Journal of Law, Medicine, and Ethics* 46.1 (Spring 2018) 52–63. https://doi.org/10.1177/1073110518766008.

Leiter, Brian. "The Most Important Western Philosophers of All Time." *Leiter Reports* (blog), April 24, 2017. https://leiterreports.typepad.com/blog/2017/04/the-most-important-western-philosophers-of-all-time.html.

Le Page, Michael. "What Is CRISPR? A Technology That Can Be Used to Edit Genes." https://www.newscientist.com/term/what-is-crispr/.

Lischer, Richard. *The Preacher King.* New York: Oxford University Press, 1997.

Lorenz, Hendrik. "Ancient Theories of Soul." *Stanford Encyclopedia of Philosophy*, October 23, 2003. https://plato.stanford.edu/entries/ancient-soul/#4.

Macdonald, Anne. "When Does Moral Distress Become Moral Injury?" *ResearchGate*, July 15, 2019. https://www.researchgate.net/post/When-does-moral-distress-become-moral-injury.

MacIntyre, Alasdair. *Whose Justice? Which Rationality?* Notre Dame: University of Notre Dame Press, 1988.

Mann, Charles C. "'Silent Spring and Other Writings' Review: The Right and Wrong of Rachel Carson." *Wall Street Journal*, April 26, 2018. https://www.wsj.com/articles/silent-spring-other-writings-review-the-right-and-wrong-of-rachel-carson-1524777762.

Martin, Paul M. V., and Estelle Martin-Granel. "2,500-year Evolution of the Term Epidemic." *Emerging Infectious Diseases* 12.6 (June 2006) 976–80. doi: 10.3201/eid1206.051263.

Maxwell, Robert J. "Queuing." In *The New Dictionary of Medical Ethics*, edited by Kenneth M. Boyd, et al., 209. London: BMJ, 1997.

McCarthy, Joan. "Principlism or Narrative Ethics: Must We Choose between Them?" *Journal of Medical Ethics* 29 (2003) 65–71.

McCullough, Laurence B. *Historical Dictionary of Medical Ethics.* Lanham, MD: Rowman & Littlefield, 2018.

———. *John Gregory and the Invention of Professional Medical Ethics and the Profession of Medicine.* Philosophy and Medicine 56. Dordrecht, Netherlands: Kluwer, 1998. https://epdf.pub/john-gregory-and-the-invention-of-professional-medical-ethics-and-the-profession.html.

Military Health System. "Medical Surveillance Monthly Report." https://health.mil/Military-Health-Topics/Combat-Support/Armed-Forces-Health-Surveillance-Branch/Reports-and-Publications/Medical-Surveillance-Monthly-Report.

Mill, John Stuart. *On Liberty.* Cambridge, MA: Hackett, 1978.

———. *Utilitarianism.* New York: Barnes & Noble, 2005.

Morley, Ian. "City Chaos, Contagion, Chadwick, and Social Justice." *Yale Journal of Biology and Medicine* 80.2 (June 2007) 61–72. https://www.ncbi.nlm.nih.gov/pmc/articles/PMC2140185/.

Nair-Collins, Michael, et al. "Abandoning the Dead Donor Rule? A National Survey of Public Views on Death and Organ Donation." *Journal of Medical Ethics* 41.4 (2015) 297–302. https://jme.bmj.com/content/41/4/297.

National Geographic Education Staff. "Mary Seacole." *National Geographic Resource Library*, November 27, 2013. https://www.nationalgeographic.org/article/mary-seacole/.

National Institute for Permanent Family Connectedness. "What Is Family Finding and Permanency?" http://www.familyfinding.org/.

New York State Senate. "Senate Passes Family Health Care Decisions Act." Press release, February 24, 2010. https://www.nysenate.gov/newsroom/press-releases/senate-passes-family-health-care-decisions-act.

Niebuhr, Reinhold. *The Children of Light and the Children of Darkness*. New York: Scribner, 1944.

———. *The Irony of American History*. New York: Scribner, 1952.

NMDOH: New Mexico Department of Health. "MFW Families." https://www.nmhealth.org/about/ddsd/pgsv/mfw/family.

"The Nobel Prize in Physiology or Medicine 1962." https://www.nobelprize.org/prizes/medicine/1962/summary/.

Noddings, Nel. *Caring: A Feminine Approach to Ethics and Moral Education*. Berkeley: University of California Press, 1982.

Nouwen, Henri. *The Wounded Healer: Ministry in Contemporary Society*. New York: Image, 1979.

Office of Research Integrity. "Definition of Research Misconduct." U.S. Department of Health & Human Services. https://ori.hhs.gov/definition-misconduct.

Orr, Robert D. "Incorporating Spirituality into Patient Care." *AMA Journal of Ethics* 17.5 (2015) 409–15. doi: 10.1001/journalofethics.2015.17.5.spec1–1505.

Palin, Sarah. "Obama and the Bureaucratization of Health Care." *Wall Street Journal*, September 8, 2009. https://www.wsj.com/articles/SB10001424052970203440104574400581157986024.

PA Media. "Hospital Waiting List Numbers in England Triple Since Last Year." *Guardian*, September 10, 2020. https://www.theguardian.com/society/2020/sep/10/hospital-waiting-list-numbers-in-england-triple-since-last.

Patel, Neel V. "What's a Coronavirus Superspreader?" *MIT Technology Review*, June 15, 2020. https://www.technologyreview.com/2020/06/15/1003576/whats-a-coronavirus-superspreader/.

Patel, Ravi. "Polio Eradication in India: Lessons for Pakistan?" *Stanford Journal of Public Health* (2013). https://web.stanford.edu/group/sjph/cgi-bin/sjphsite/polio-eradication-in-india-lessons-for-pakistan/.

Pickover, Ella. "Treating A&E Patients in Hospital Corridors Becoming 'Norm,' Nurses Warn." *Independent.co.uk*, February 26, 2020. https://www.independent.co.uk/news/health/emergency-treatment-corridors-normal-royal-college-nursing-a9359466.html.

Pimentel, Roger, and Jon Muller. "The Containment Approach to Managing Defendants Charged with Sex Offenses." *Federal Probation* 74.2. https://www.uscourts.gov/sites/default/files/74_2_6_0.pdf.

Pinching, Anthony J. "Evidence-Based Medicine." In *The New Dictionary of Medical Ethics*, edited by Kenneth M. Boyd, et al., 91. London: BMJ, 1997.

———. "Viability." In *The New Dictionary of Medical Ethics*, edited by Kenneth M. Boyd, et al., 268. London: BMJ, 1997.

Plantinga, Alvin. *Warrant: The Current Debate*. New York: Oxford University Press, 1993.

Pope, Thaddeus. "Top 10 North American Death Panels." *Bioethics.net*, December 2013. http://www.bioethics.net/2013/12/top-10-north-american-death-panels/.

Public Health Department. "Emergency Care: Definition." https://publichealth.gwu.edu/departments/healthpolicy/CHPR/nnhs4/GSA/Subheads/gsa116.html.

Rawls, John. *Political Liberalism*. New York: Columbia University Press, 1993.

Richardson, Henry S. "John Rawls (1921–2002)." *Internet Encyclopedia of Philosophy.* Edited by James Fieser and Bradley Dowden. https://iep.utm.edu/rawls/#SH2f.

Rivais, Cassandra. "A Reflection on Two-Physician Consent." *Bioethics Today* (blog), January 26, 2018. https://www.amc.edu/bioethicsblog/post.cfm/a-reflection-on-two-physician-consent.

Roland, Denise. "Obscure Model Puts Price on Healthy Year of Life." *Wall Street Journal,* November 5, 2019, A1.

Rushton, Cynda. "Moral Distress and Building Resilience." *Johns Hopkins Nursing,* February 8, 2017. https://magazine.nursing.jhu.edu/2017/02/moral-distress-and-building-resilience/.

Sallam, H. N. "Aristotle, Godfather of Evidence-Based Medicine." *Facts, Views & Vision in ObGyn* 2.1 (2010) 11–19. https://www.ncbi.nlm.nih.gov/pmc/articles/PMC4154333/.

Schweitzer, Albert. *The Quest of the Historical Jesus.* New York: Simon & Schuster, 1968.

Scott, Sarah. "Martin Buber (1878–1965)." *Internet Encyclopedia of Philosophy.* Edited by James Fieser and Bradley Dowden. https://iep.utm.edu/buber/.

Sears, Robert. *The Vaccine Book: Making the Right Decision for your Child.* Boston: Little, Brown, 2007.

Shojania, Kaveh G., and Mary Dixon-Woods. "'Bad Apples': Time to Redefine as a Systems Problem." *BMJ Quality & Safety* (June 2013) 1–4. doi: 10.1136/bmjqs-2013–002138.

Singer, Peter. "The Challenge of Brain Death for the Sanctity of Life Ethic." *Ethics and Bioethics in Central Europe* 8.3–4 (2018) 153–65. doi:10.2478/ebce-2018–0012.

———. "Famine, Affluence, and Morality." *Philosophy and Public Affairs* 1.3 (Spring 1972) 229–43. https://www.jstor.org/stable/2265052.

Siropaides, Caitlin Holt, and Robert Arnold. "Time-Limited Trials for Serious Illness." *Palliative Care Network of Wisconsin* (2020). https://www.mypcnow.org/fast-fact/time-limited-trials-for-serious-illness/.

Skinner, B. F. *Beyond Freedom and Dignity.* New York: Knopf, 1971.

Skloot, Rebecca. *The Immortal Life of Henrietta Lacks.* New York: Crown, 2010.

Spector-Bagdady, Kayte, and Paul A. Lombardo. "U.S. Public Health Service STD Experiments in Guatemala (1946–1948) and Their Aftermath." *Ethics & Human Research* (March 2019) 29–34. https://doi.org/10.1002/eahr.500010.

Sperry, Len, and Harry Prosen. "Contemporary Ethical Dilemmas in Psychotherapy." *American Journal of Psychotherapy* (1998) 54–63.

Stein, Dan J. "Pharmacological Enhancement: A Conceptual Framework." *Philosophy, Ethics, and Humanities in Medicine* (2012) 1–12.

Steinberg, David. "Altruism in Medicine: Its Definition, Nature, and Dilemmas." *Cambridge Quarterly of Healthcare Ethics* 19 (2010) 249–57.

Strous, Rael D., et al. "Reflections on 'Emil Kraepelin: Icon and Reality." *American Journal of Psychiatry* 173 (2016) 300–301. https://ajp.psychiatryonline.org/doi/pdfplus/10.1176/appi.ajp.2016.15111414.

Stryker, Rachael, and Roberto González. *Up, Down, and Sideways: Anthropologists Trace the Pathways of Power.* New York: Berghahn, 2014.

Sulmasy, Daniel P. "A Biopsychosocial-Spiritual Model for the Care of Patients at the End of Life." *Gerontologist* 42 (October 2002) 24–33. https://doi.org/10.1093/geront/42.suppl_3.24.

Sweet, Victoria. "Hildegard of Bingen and the Greening of Medieval Medicine." *Bulletin of the History of Medicine* 73.3 (Fall 1999) 381–403. https://www.jstor.org/stable/44445287?read-now=1& refreqid=excelsior%3A5364fa1e4c036aa74fd4f2c 1cfac387e&seq=21#page_scan_tab_contents.

Systems Innovation. "Newtonian Paradigm." https://www.systemsinnovation.io/post/newtonian-paradigm.

Taleb, Nassim Nicholas. *The Black Swan: The Impact of the Highly Improbable*. New York: Random House, 2007.

Temple, William. *Studies in the Spirit and Truth of Christianity*. London: MacMillan, 1914.

Texas Association of Freestanding Emergency Centers. "What Constitutes a Medical Emergency?" https://www.tafec.org/assets/docs/TAFEC_PrudentLayperson.pdf.

Tietz, Tabea. "The Important Theorem of Thomas Bayes." *SciHi Blog*, April 17, 2018. http://scihi.org/theorem-thomas-bayes/.

Tillich, Paul. *Theology of Culture*. Oxford: Oxford University Press, 1959.

Torrey, E. Fuller. "Impaired Awareness of Illness: Anosognosia." https://mentalillnesspolicy.org/medical/anosognosia-studies.html.

Tubbs, James B., Jr. *A Handbook of Bioethics Terms*. Washington, DC: Georgetown University Press, 2009.

UCLA Department of Epidemiology, Fielding School of Public Health. "Dr. John Snow Voted the Greatest Doctor." https://www.ph.ucla.edu/epi/snow/snowgreatestdoc.html.

University of Chicago Medicine. "As Morphine Turns 200, Drug That Blocks Its Side Effects Reveals New Secrets." May 18, 2005. https://www.uchicagomedicine.org/forefront/news/as-morphine-turns-200-drug-that-blocks-its-side-effects-reveals-new-secrets.

Venes, Donald, ed. *Tabor's Cyclopedic Medical Dictionary*. 22nd ed. Philadelphia: Davis, 2013.

Wachter, Robert, and Lee Goldman. "The Emerging Role of 'Hospitalists' in the American Health Care System." *New England Journal of Medicine* 335 (August 1996) 514–17. doi: 10.1056/NEJM199608153350713.

Whitlock, Jennifer. "Doctors, Residents, and Attendings: What's the Difference?" *Very Well Health* (2020). https://www.verywellhealth.com/types-of-doctors-residents-interns-and-fellows-3157293.

Wijdicks, Eelco F. M. "How Harvard Defined Irreversible Coma." *Neurological Care* 29.1 (August 2018) 136–41. doi: 10.1007/s12028-018-0579-8.

Wilson, Anthony James, et al. "What Is a Vector?" *Philosophical Transactions of the Royal Society B: Biological Sciences* (March 2017). doi: 10.1098/rstb.2016.0085.

Winslow, Gerald R. "Triage." In *Bioethics*, edited by Bruce Jennings, 3108–12. 4th ed. Farmington Hills, MI: Gale, Centage Learning, 2014.

World Health Organization. "Burden of Disease: What Is It and Why Is It Important for Safer Food?" https://www.who.int/foodsafety/foodborne_disease/Q%26A.pdf.

Yahya, Samar. "Rufaida Al-Aslamia: The First Muslim Nurse." *Saudi Gazette*, March 31, 2017. http://saudigazette.com.sa/article/175811/Rufaida-Al-Aslamia-the-first-Muslim-nurse.

Youngner, Stuart J. "Medical Futility." In *Bioethics*, edited by Bruce Jennings, 4:1951–56. 4th ed. 6 vols. Farmington Hills, MI: Gale, Centage Learning, 2014.